Y0-AGC-532

Transdermal Delivery of Drugs

Volume II

Editors

Agis F. Kydonieus, Ph.D.
President
Hercon Laboratories Corporation
Subsidiary of Health-Chem Corporation
South Plainfield, New Jersey

Bret Berner, Ph.D.
Manager
Pharmaceutical Division
Ciba-Geigy Corporation
Ardsley, New York

CRC Press, Inc.
Boca Raton, Florida

Library of Congress Cataloging-in-Publication Data

Transdermal delivery of drugs.

Includes bibliographies and index.
1. Ointments. 2. Skin absorption. 3. Drugs--
Controlled release. I. Kydonieus, Agis F., 1938-
II. Berner, Bret. [DNLM: 1. Administration, Topical.
2. Delayed-Action Preparations. 3. Drugs--administra-
tion & dosage. 4. Skin Absorption. WB 340 T7723]
RS201.03T7255 1987 615′.67 86-2585
ISBN 0-8493-6483-3 (set)
ISBN 0-8493-6484-1 (v. 1)
ISBN 0-8493-6485-X (v. 2)
ISBN 0-8493-6486-8 (v. 3)

Direct all inquiries to CRC Press, Inc., 2000 Corporate Blvd., N.W., Boca Raton, Florida, 33431.

International Standard Book Number 0-8493-6483-3 (set)
International Standard Book Number 0-8493-6484-1 (v. 1)
International Standard Book Number 0-8493-6485-X (v. 2)
International Standard Book Number 0-8493-6486-8 (v. 3)

Library of Congress Card Number 86-2585
Printed in the United States

PREFACE

The introduction of the first transdermal patch containing scopolamine brought about a tremendous interest in the usage of intact skin as a portal of entry of drugs into the systemic circulation of the body. Several transdermal products followed into the marketplace, in particular, devices containing nitroglycerin, clonidine, isosorbide dinitrate (Japan), and estradiol (Switzerland). Some two dozen drugs are now in different steps of transdermal product development. A plethora of transdermal development departments and companies have emerged. While the potential advantages of transdermal delivery such as (1) avoidance of hepatic "first-pass" metabolism, (2) maintenance of steady-state plasma levels of drug, and (3) convenience of dosing were readily identified, the limitations of the barrier and immune properties of skin are only now being defined. Continued technological advances are requiring either circumventing these responses of the skin or adroit identification of conditions in search of controlled-release therapies. The goals of these volumes are to collect the current knowledge to further research in transdermal delivery and to serve as an introduction to the novice.

The series of volumes is divided into four main sections pertaining to Methodology, The Transdermal Device, The Skin, and The Drug. For the recent practitioner in the field, an overview section has been included to provide a background about the controlled release devices, the diffusion of drugs through polymers, and the anatomy and biochemistry of skin.

In the methodology section, the techniques used to determine in vitro and in vivo skin permeation are presented. The special considerations concerning animal and human experimentation are described including in vivo methodology, skin condition, and individual variations.

A section on transdermal devices concludes the first volume. Here we asked scientists from six companies to discuss briefly their transdermal technology and product development areas.

The volume on skin contains chapters on the parameters affecting skin penetration, including a chapter on aging, pharmacokinetics of transdermal delivery, models for predicting the permeability of drugs through skin from the physicochemical parameters of the drug, the correlations among human skin, reconstituted skin, artificial membranes, and the potential of increasing skin permeability by the use of chemical enhancers or vehicles. Finally, a chapter on the crucial area of cutaneous toxicology describes contact dermatitis and microorganism growth and infections.

In the third volume, the drug parameters important to transdermal delivery are discussed. The thermodynamics governing transdermal delivery and models and typical approaches for prodrugs are also presented. Finally, a literature review of the permeability of drugs through the skin is presented. This compilation of existing skin permeation data should serve as a useful reference tool.

Obviously, in this rapidly expanding field, several important omissions must have occurred despite our effort to include significant developments known by 1984, when most of the manuscripts were collected. Nevertheless, we hope this effort will prove to be of value to scientists and product development engineers seeking up-to-date information in this area.

We are indebted to the authors for their cooperation in adhering to manuscript specifications and to Mrs. Robin Tyminski for her efforts in typing and assisting in the editorial endeavors. Finally, we would like to thank the management of Health-Chem Corporation, the parent of Hercon Laboratories, who have been strong advocates of controlled release for many years and have given the editors all the support required to complete this undertaking.

Agis F. Kydonieus
Bret Berner

THE EDITORS

Agis F. Kydonieus, Ph.D., is President of Hercon Laboratories Corporation, a subsidiary of Health-Chem Corporation, New York. Dr. Kydonieus graduated from the University of Florida in 1959 with a B.S. degree in Chemical Engineering (summa cum laude) and received his Ph.D. from the same school in 1964.

Dr. Kydonieus is a founder of the Controlled Release Society and has served as a member of the Board of Governors, Program Chairman, Vice President, and President. He is presently a trustee of the Society. He is also founder of Krikos, an international Hellenic association of scientists, and has served a treasurer and a member of its Board of Directors. He is also a member of the editorial board of the *Journal of Controlled Release,* and a member of many societies including the American Association of Pharmaceutical Scientists, American Institute of Chemical Engineers, and the Society of Plastics Engineers.

Dr. Kydonieus is the author of over 125 patents, publications, and presentations in the field of controlled release and biomedical devices. He is the Editor of *Controlled Release Technologies* and *Insect Suppression with Controlled Release Pheromone Systems,* both published with CRC Press.

Bret Berner, Ph.D., is Manager of Basic Pharmaceutics Research for CIBA-GEIGY, Inc. Dr. Berner received his B.A. degree from the University of Rochester in 1973 and his Ph.D. from the University of California at Los Angeles in 1978. Before joining CIBA-GEIGY in 1985, he was Director of Research, Hercon Division of Health-Chem Corporation. Dr. Berner also held the position of staff scientist with Proctor & Gamble, Co. following his graduation from UCLA.

Dr. Berner's current research directs novel drug delivery research groups including transdermal, gastrointestinal, and other delivery routes, polymer systems, pharmacokinetics, pharmacodynamics, and analytical chemistry.

CONTRIBUTORS

Joseph J. Anisko, Ph.D.
Director of Information and Communications
Nelson Research and Development
Irvine, California

Charanjit R. Behl
Pharmaceutical Research and Development
Hoffmann-La Roche, Inc.
Nutley, New Jersey

Nancy H. Bellantone
Pharmaceutical Research
Pfizer, Inc.
Groton, Connecticut

Bret Berner, Ph.D.
Manager
Pharmaceutical Division
Ciba-Geigy Corp.
Ardsley, New York

S. Kumar Chandrasekaran
Vice President, Technical Affairs
Sola-Syntex Ophthalmics
Phoenix, Arizona

Eugene R. Cooper, Ph.D.
Alcon Labs, Inc.
Fort Worth, Texas

Gordon L. Flynn, Ph.D.
Professor
Department of Pharmaceuticals
College of Pharmacy
University of Michigan
Ann Arbor, Michigan

Sharad K. Govil
Research and Development
Key Pharmaceuticals, Inc.
Pembroke Pines, Florida

Gary Lee Grove, Ph.D.
Director
Skin Study Center
Philadelphia, Pennsylvania

Richard H. Guy, Ph.D.
Assistant Professor of Pharmacy and Pharmaceutical Chemistry
Departments of Pharmacy and Pharmaceutical Chemistry
University of California
San Francisco, California

Jonathan Hadgraft, D.phil.
Professor of Pharmaceutical Chemistry
The Welsh School of Pharmacy
University of Wales Institute of Science and Technology
Cardiff, Wales, U.K.

Timothy A. Hagan
College of Pharmacy
University of Michigan
Ann Arbor, Michigan

W.I. Higuchi, Ph.D.
Distinguished Professor and Chairman
Department of Pharmaceutics
College of Pharmacy
University of Utah
Salt Lake City, Utah

Sui Yuen E. Hou
College of Pharmacy
University of Michigan
Ann Arbor, Michigan

Bernard Idson, Ph.D.
Senior Research Fellow
Department of Pharmacy Research and Development
Hoffmann-La Roche, Inc.
Nutley, New Jersey

Benjamin K. Kim
Director, Drug Delivery Systems
Nelson Research
Irvine, California

Tamie Kurihara-Bergstrom
Ciba-Geigy Corp.
Ardsley, New York

Agis F. Kydonieus, Ph.D.
Executive Vice President
Hercon Division
Health-Chem Corp.
South Plainfield, New Jersey

James J. Leyden, M.D.
Professor of Dermatology
Department of Dermatology
University of Pennsylvania
Philadelphia, Pennsylvania

Edward E. Linn
Formulations Research
Lederle Labs
American Cyanamid
Pearl River, New York

Vithal Rajadhyaksha
Sr. Vice President Research and Development
Nelson Research Centerpointe
Irvine, California

Pramod P. Sarpotdar, Ph.D.
Senior Research Scientist
Research Laboratories
Eastman Kodak Co.
Rochester, New York

Ward M. Smith
College of Pharmacy
University of Michigan
Ann Arbor, Michigan

Rajaram Vaidyanathan, Ph.D.
Director
Product Development
Nelson Research
Irvine, California

David Yeung, M.S.
Senior Research Investigator
Dermatological Research
Richardson-Vicks Incorporated
Shelton, Connecticut

Cheng-Der Yu
Manager
Pharmaceutical Development
Cooper Laboratories, Inc.
Mountain View, California

Joel L. Zatz. Ph.D.
Professor of Pharmaceutics
College of Pharmacy
Rutgers College of Pharmacy
Piscataway, New Jersey

TABLE OF CONTENTS

Volume II

SKIN

Volume III

DRUG

Skin

Chapter 1

PARAMETERS OF SKIN CONDITION AND FUNCTION

Gordon L. Flynn, Edward E. Linn,
Tamie Kurihara-Bergstrom, Shard K. Govil,
and Sui Yuen E. Hou

TABLE OF CONTENTS

I. INTRODUCTION

While it has been known for many decades that the skin is a significant permeation barrier, the topical avenue as a route of drug administration has only recently been appreciated. We consider some basic questions about the skin and some skin permeability parameters which are important to the development of topical dosage forms. A deeper understanding of the barrier properties of the skin in health and disease and after trauma is needed in order to answer many of these questions. In particular, the barrier properties of skin are important for:

1. The delivery of drugs into skin for local effects
2. The delivery of drugs through the skin for their systemic effects
3. The choice of the best drugs for topical therapy from an existing family of drugs
4. The development of drugs whose chemical properties are specifically tailored for percutaneous absorption
5. The design of therapeutic strategies and systems for administration of drugs when the skin is impaired by disease or trauma
6. The development of enhancers to promote the absorption of drugs with low skin permeability
7. The management of severe water loss and the resulting thermal energy drain in patients with dysfunctional skin, such as seen in extensive burns and preterm infants
8. The diagnosis of cutaneous diseases and trauma
9. The assessment of the cutaneous toxicity of drugs and adjuvants

Critical to all these aspects of skin permeation delivery is a knowledge of the general condition of the skin and how this relates to its barrier function. Parameters of skin condition important for these applications are numerous and include both environmental influences and many patient-related factors. Examples of the more important parameters are outlined in Table 1. In this review chapter, we treat these factors and the probable manner in which they affect the microstructure of the skin and thus impact on the permeability of the skin.

The detailed anatomical structure of the skin and the chemical compositions of its distinguishable phases are the keys to understanding effects on skin permeability. Briefly, the three layers of the skin, which act as a series of diffusional resistances, are the stratum corneum, the living cellular epidermis, and a region of the dermis which lies above the locally active vasculature. Entrance of diffusing molecules into the bloodstream within the dermis is the usual endpoint of the percutaneous absorption process. Topically applied chemicals may also access the general system by diffusing through skin appendages. Though numerous, eccrine glands have extremely small openings and are either empty or profusely active and are therefore discounted as an important absorption route. Hair follicles, which represent about 0.1% of the body surface, may be a possible shunt through the stratum corneum. Diffusion through hair follicles occurs through sebum, a soft, concentrated lipid, to deeper living layers of the skin where entry into the general system is by way of the follicular vasculature. In nonsteady-state penetration, the first molecules probably reach living cells by this pathway. For most drugs, transepidermal passage is the singularly most important route of entry. It follows that the influence of the parameters listed in Table 1 on skin barrier function is through alterations of the tissues of the transepidermal route. Alteration of the horny layer is central to the altered barrier function.

Permeation via the transepidermal route begins with a solution-diffusion process in the stratum corneum. There appear to be two distinguishable conduit regimes. The first is formed directly from the acutely flattened cellular building blocks of the horny layer. The cell units are 30 to 40 μm in diameter and $^1/_4$- to 1-μm thick; they are filled with a semicrystalline,

Table 1
PARAMETERS OF SKIN CONDITION AND RELATED BARRIER FUNCTION

- Environmental factors
  - Temperature
  - Humidity
- General subject factors
  - Race
  - Age
  - Gender
  - Anatomical site
  - General health of subject
  - Disease and trauma
- Factors associated with skin conditioning
  - Bathing/cosmetic habits
  - Use of skin penetration enhancers
  - Occlusion/hydration

polar biopolymer (keratin). A considerable portion of the keratin is found as tightly compacted bundles of fibrils. The individual fiber strands are believed to have a slight helical twist. An amorphous fraction of keratin is interspersed through these highly organized bundles of α-keratin fibers.[2] Presently, a debate exists as to whether lipids are intimately associated with the keratin bundles.[3] Moreover, the intracellular material of the fully differentiated corneocyte is so structurally dense and crystalline that only a tiny fraction of it appears to be available for diffusion. Intuitively, we picture this fraction to be hydrated portions of keratin, making it a substantially polar phase which in all likelihood is capable of supporting a limited flux of highly polar or ionic permeants.

The bulk of the lipid of the stratum corneum resides in seams which lie between and separate the cellular units and may act to cement the cell layers together.[1] This intercellular region constitutes the second permeation regime in the stratum corneum. This lipid region may account for 20% or more of the total dry weight of the horny layer (a conservative figure would be 5 to 10%). The bulk of this lipid is apparently synthesized by corneocytes in transit through the epidermis. It is first collected in intracellular vesicles (inclusion bodies) and these are expressed through the membrane wall and into the intercellular spaces as one of the final stages of cellular differentiation.[1] There are indications that the lipid may be organized in bilayers.[3] Thermoanalytical studies and other physical probes of isolated stratum corneum indicate both the lipid and protein domains have a degree of crystallinity.[4]

After traversing the stratum corneum, a permeant must diffuse across the living epidermis, a 100 μm or more avascular wedge of living cells. Few molecules have difficulty in passively negotiating this zone. Molecules too hydrophobic to dissolve in the watery cytosol of the cells may find this and the underlying dermal zone difficult to pass due to their limited solubility in the bulk of the tissue. Large and extremely polar molecules like vidarabine also have difficulty in crossing the living cellular region; such molecules have problems crossing individual cell membranes.[5] However, the living epidermal resistance encountered by solutes of extreme polarity is far less than the resistance of the intact stratum corneum. Therefore, for polar drugs, the resistance of the living epidermis only becomes important on denuded skin.

Diffusion across the layer of the dermis above the actively functioning vascular appears to be through the watery, gelatinous ground substance which fills the interstitial space between dermal collagen and elastin fibers. While diffusional resistance of the dermis will usually be nominal, the diffusional resistance could conceivably be significant if diffusive penetration to great depth was necessary to attain the circulation. The flowing blood can be as close to the epidermis as a few micrometers or it can be millimeters deep.

Table 2
ACTIVATION ENERGY FOR IN VITRO PERMEATION OF SKIN MEMBRANES

Compound	Ea (kcal/mol)	Type skin membrane	Ref.
Water	14.3	Human stratum corneum	6,7
	6.3	Delipidized human stratum corneum	6
Methanol	>15	Hairless mouse skin	8
Ethanol	16.4	Human epidermis	6,7
	>15	Hairless mouse skin	8
Propanol	16.5	Human epidermis	6,7
Butanol	16.7	Human epidermis	6,7
	>15	Hairless mouse skin	8
Pentanol	16.5	Human epidermis	6,7
Hexanol	10.9	Human epidermis	6,7
	>15	Hairless mouse skin	8
Heptanol	9.9	Human epidermis	6,7
Octanol	8.7	Human epidermis	6,7
	>15	Hairless mouse skin	8
Phenol	14.4	Human epidermis	9
	16.8	Hairless mouse skin	[a]
m-nitrophenol	13.3	Human epidermis	9
p-nitrophenol	17.6	Hairless mouse skin	[a]

[a] Unpublished results from the author's laboratory.

II. ENVIRONMENTAL PARAMETERS

A. Temperature

Temperature can have two effects on transdermal delivery; the first mediated through diffusional activation energies within the various tissues of the skin and the second as a result of the physiologic responses of the skin. Neither process is well studied as it relates to the clinical dimensions of topical drug usage.

The permeability of intact skin is a remarkably temperature sensitive process based on in vitro studies. Activation energies for permeation of homologous alcohols reportedly range between 9 and 17 kcal/mol for human epidermis[6,7] and, based on limited data, may be of somewhat greater magnitude in whole hairless mouse skin.[8] Values of this magnitude have also been reported for the permeation of human epidermis by phenol and *m*-nitrophenol, 14.4 and 13.3 kcal/mol, respectively.[9] Yet to be published data of our own indicates phenol and *p*-nitrophenol have activation energies of 16.8 and 17.6 kcal/mol, respectively, through hairless mouse skin. These large activation energies were clearly shown by Scheuplein and co-workers[6,7] to be due to diffusion across the stratum corneum of the human epidermal membranes. When the horny tissue is altered through extraction with a lipid solvent, the permeability coefficients of polar nonelectrolytes are known to markedly increase and, in the case of water, the diffusion activation energy was shown to drop to a value only slightly higher than for its self diffusion.[7] A collection of activation energy data are presented in Table 2. One can speculate that warming the stratum corneum reduces the degree of crystallinity and this leads to the large observed activation energies. Crystallinity changes upon warming to about 60°C appear totally reversible.

Typically, the stratum corneum assumes temperatures closer to is external surroundings than to body temperature. Conceivably in open, exposed areas, the horny layer can thus be 10°C, 20°C, or even more degrees cooler than 37°C. As a practical limit, it may be as much as 5°C hotter than 37°C depending on the environmental temperature. Using 15 kcal/mol as a representative activation energy for diffusive passage across the stratum corneum, one can expect permeation rates to vary by roughly a factor of two for each 10°C difference in the skin surface temperature in this temperature region. Therefore, except in the most extreme instances, the permeation rate of a drug should not vary by more than a factor of three or four as the result of diffusional activation energy effects. For example, the in vitro permeability of rabbit ear stratum corneum to tritiated water[10] decreases 2.7 times by lowering the temperature from 37 to 20°C. This corresponds to an activation energy of 10.5 kcal/mol.

Another effect of temperature may be subtly linked to percutaneous absorption in living subjects. The vascular plexus of the skin is highly anastomosed. As part of the homeostatic control of body temperature, blood is either coursed through the distal capillary field of the skin to facilitate heat removal or shunted through lower layers of the vasculature deep within or even beneath the dermis to conserve body heat. In exposed, chilled skin the vasculature near the surface of the skin is closed and one can assume the point of systemic access consequently retreats to deeper regions. This presumably could have a profound effect on the local clearance and systemic uptake of topically applied drugs. However, when the skin temperature of the abdomen of guinea pigs was lowered from 38 to 20°C only fivefold decreases in the permeabilities of salicylic acid and carbinoxamine were effected.[11] This corresponds to an activation energy for each of the compounds of 16.2 kcal/mol, a value hardly out of the range expected for a strictly physical kinetic effect. However, data on living animal subjects only exist for a few compounds as these and it might prove misleading to generalize the known results.

B. Humidity

It is well established that the horny layer of skin becomes dry and relatively inelastic at very low relative humidity. When the ambient humidity is high, the skin (the stratum corneum) becomes soft and supple. Protracted exposure to dry air as may occur during the cold winter months can produce a "dry skin condition" in which the skin surface is scaly and pruritic. At its worst, dry skin is crisscrossed with deep fissures. Skin in this fissured state is visibly damaged and inflamed and is evidently highly permeable to applied chemicals. Certain clinical tests for the severity of dry skin such as the lactic acid sting test are based on the increased permeability of the skin when it is excessively dry.[12] Apparently such test chemicals are able to diffuse directly through the microscopic cracks and crevices caused by the dryness.

The permeability of skin in lesser states of dryness is uncertain. Water is the principal plasticizer of the stratum corneum and drying of horny tissue stiffens its keratin fibers by removing moisture from between the strands, thereby increasing strand-to-strand interactions. This stiffening should cause a decrease in the permeability of any substance which preferentially courses through the intracellular keratin regime. Blank et al.[13] estimate there is a factor of two decrease in the diffusivity of water within the stratum corneum as the relative humidity drops from 93 to 46%. This is partially offset by a concurrent 50% decrease in the thickness of the horny layer over the same humidity range. Nevertheless, this work establishes directly the important principle that the surface moisture content of the skin has direct bearing on its barrier function. Occlusive techniques in topical therapy which involve the permeability of substances other than water have long been premised on the belief that moisture aids diffusion through the horny matrix. Clearly, one would like to know the clinical degree of dryness and its effect on the skin permeability of any given agent. Such data are virtually nonexistent.

Humidity has been directly related to skin permeability by way of its effect on insensible perspiration. Hammarlund et al.[14] studied transepidermal water loss in newborn infants as a function of relative humidity and the body site of the infant. Measurements performed on

19 infants placed in incubators indicated a linear relationship between the evaporation rate and humidity at constant ambient temperature. A 1.4-fold lower evaporation rate was observed at high relative humidity (60%) than at low relative humidity (20%). Similar studies[15] have verified that the driving force for passive diffusion of water through the skin is reduced in proportion to the degree of moisture in the ambient air. This principle is taken into account in providing an artificial environment for preterm infants.

III. GENERAL SUBJECT FACTORS

A. Race

Striking differences in skin coloration exist across the races of the family of man. These differences relate to the nature, numbers, geometries, and distribution of melanin pigment granules deposited in the epidermis by melanocytes. There is no particular reason to believe that the melanin content of skin has great bearing on the permeability of the skin. There does however seem to be a limited amount of information which suggests the skins of different races differ in other ways which do relate to permeability. For instance, whealing responses induced via the topical application of histamine to the forearms of caucasians and negroes proved caucasian skin to be the more reactive with statistical certainty.[16] One plausible explanation is differential permeability. Somewhat more convincing is the evidence that black skin is less permeable to ^{14}C-fluocinolone acetate than white skin.[17] However, the most intriguing evidence that there are racially derived permeability differences in the cutaneous barrier is provided by Weingand et al.[18] They found that caucasians reacted more strongly to irritants than negroes when the respective skins were intact. On stripped skin, however, the responses were equivalent. In searching for the cause of the different responses, they discovered that black skin required more strippings than white skin to denude it though there was no difference in thickness. Subsequently, it was discovered that Negro stratum corneum actually contains more layers (22 to 17 with $p < 0.01$) and is more dense. Furthermore, tritiated water diffused more slowly through black skin. In light of the above observations, it appears that black skin may be generally less permeable.

B. Age

The relationship between aging on the barrier qualities of human skin is also a poorly studied subject. A review of existing data may be found in the chapter on aging. There is substantial clinical evidence that the skin of premature infants is extremely permeable. The most convincing evidence comes from studies of transepidermal water loss. Hammarlund and Sedin,[19] for instance, studied transepidermal water loss in newborn infants relative to their gestational age. Evaporation rates were highest in the infants of lowest gestational age and susceptibility to changes in ambient relative humidity was also greatest. An exponential relation was found between the evaporation rate and the degree of prematurity.

Numerous poisonings of premature infants inadvertently contacted with phenolic disinfectants or diaper marking dyes have demonstrated both the increased permeability of such skin and the premature infants increased susceptibility to the toxicants.[20] Since, by outward appearance the skins of premature neonates seem normal, mystery surrounds the barrier deficiency of their skin. There appears to be fundamental insight yet to be unlocked here as to how the stratum corneum functions to impede the diffusion of organic chemicals and water. Microscopically observed differences in neonatal skin and adult skin suggest the organization of the tissues differ in significant ways.[21]

From birth to old age the skin continuously changes. During puberty and past the sixth decade of life the changes are rapid and dramatic. Yet, except for the preterm infant, there are little data to suggest that permeability differs all that much between old and young. This is not necessarily unexpected as regardless of age, skin must offer much the same essential protection from the dessicating influences of the land environment. Studies on the absorption of linoleic acid seem to show youthful skin is somewhat more permeable than adult skin to this particular substance.[22]

C. Gender

Though there are striking differences in the general appearance of skin and the distribution and prominency of hair between postadolescent males and females, there is no convincing evidence to suggest that the anatomical dissimilarities have much bearing on the barrier function of the tissue. The essential need for protection from water loss, which does not differ between the sexes, seems to impart qualities to the skin which determine its membrane function more than any other factor.

D. Anatomical Site

The influence of anatomical location on skin permeability is a reasonably well-researched subject. Site-related variation in irritancy of human skin has been reported.[23] Studies carried out in vivo and in vitro indicate human scrotal skin is more permeable than abdominal skin to several test substances.[24] Site-related variations in penetration rates or organic phosphates through cadaver skin membranes have been demonstrated.[25] Regional variations in the percutaneous absorption of hydrocortisone[26] and some pesticides[27] have also been noted in humans. High follicular densities have been linked to high permeability of some agents[26] but not others.[28]

The human transepidermal water loss rate has also been shown to vary with the anatomical regions for adult skin (Table 3) and for the skin of the newborn (Table 4). Based on the Scheuplein and Blank compilation,[7] the diffusion of water through adult skin increases in the order: back, abdomen, and forearm < back of the hand < forehead < palm, sole, and scrotum. It can be seen that in newborn infants higher evaporation rates are observed on the face and other peripheral parts of the body than are observed on the torso,[14] which is consistent with the data for adults.[7] Generally speaking, the rates appear slightly higher in the infants.

The permeation of scopolamine is one of the best documented instances of site-to-site variability. In readying this drug for transdermal delivery, it was discovered that it permeates cadaver epidermis removed from the rear of the ear lobe up to ten times more rapidly than it passes through epidermis taken from the thigh. For this drug, skin from the postauricular area was much more permeable than the back, chest, and stomach skin, which were comparably permeable. Skin from the torso was, in turn, more permeable than forearm skin with thigh skin being the least permeable of all the sites chosen for study. A transdermal patch was subsequently designed to be worn behind the ear. Similar studies involving the permeability of ^{14}C-hydrocortisone have indicated that scrotal skin and the skin of the jaw are ten times more permeable than forearm skin, which is, in turn, about seven times more permeable than skin taken from the plantar surface of the foot arch.

Another detailed study relating absorption to the site of application involved urinary recovery of hydrocortisone.[26,29] The data are shown in Table 5. Here it can be seen that callused surfaces were the least permeable. Consistent with water loss rates, the skin of the torso and the face is more permeable to hydrocortisone than skin at the extremities. Such data suggest that molecules of vastly different size and with different physicochemical attributes will permeate skin sites in different relative orders, making all predictions and extrapolations tenuous.

In examining the site dependencies of permeation of human skin, one finds a surprising lack of correlation between the differences in permeability and position-to-position differences in the thickness of the horny layer. A thick callus may be relatively impermeable to large organic molecules. At the same time, it allows relatively facile passage of water. Even

Table 3
SITE VARIATION IN WATER'S PERMEABILITY OF ADULT SKIN

Site	Steady-state flux[a] dM/dt (mg/cm²/hr)	Estimated stratum corneum thickness (μm)
Plantar surface of foot	3.90	600
Scrotum	1.70	5
Palm of hand	1.14	400
Forehead	0.85	13
Back of hand	0.56	50
Abdomen	0.34	15
Volar surface of forearm	0.31	16
Back	0.29	11

[a] Data taken from compilation of Schemplein and Blank.[7]

Table 4
SITE VARIATION IN WATER'S PERMEABILITY OF SKIN OF THE FULL TERM NEONATE

Site	Steady-state flux[a] dM/dt (mg/cm²/hr)
Palm of hand	1.9
Forehead	1.8
Check	1.25
Sole of foot	1.1
Buttocks	0.9
Volar surface of forearm	0.9
Back	0.8
Chest	0.5
Abdomen	0.35

[a] Data from Hammarlund et al.[14]

Table 5
REGIONAL VARIATIONS IN THE SYSTEMIC ABSORPTION OF HYDROCORTISONE MEASURED BY URINARY EXCRETION

Site	% of dose absorbed[a]
Scrotum	42
Jaw	13
Forehead	6
Scalp	3.5
Back	1.7
Forearm (ventral)	1.0
Palm of hand	0.83
Ankle	0.42
Foot arch (plantar)	0.14

[a] Data from Feldman and Maibach.[26]

in those instances where a callus is a profoundly effective barrier, it appears to be relatively permeable when permeability per unit thickness is considered. Similarly, there appears to be no simple relationship between permeability and hairiness of the skin. Since the stratum corneum provides the principal diffusion pathways even on hairy skin, the local horny layer structures themselves must be different in some fundamentally important way in instances where hairiness appears to be a factor. Whether there are (1) function-altering differences in percentages of lipid and protein making up the stratum corneum as suggested by Elias et al.,[1] (2) differences in physical integration of these barrier bearing phases, (3) actual differences in the chemical compositions of the phases, or (4) even differences in their physical states (such as degree of crystallinity) between hairy and nonhairy sites is not known. It seems likely that careful, systemic histologic and biophysical analysis of the skins of the various sites might reveal critical aspects of the tissue properties which relate to permeability.

E. General Health of Subject

Many general diseases have their skin manifestations and in some, the skin responses are pathognomic for the disease. Where the changes in the skin amount to discoloration or altered pigmentation with no physical breakup of the exterior structures of the skin, it is possible that the permeability condition of skin is little altered. Persons in a severe state of malnourishment or even suffering frank starvation seem to have skin which meets the minimal barrier function for conservation of body water and heat. In the famous controlled starvation experiment performed on conscientious objectors in Minnesota, it was observed that the epidermis of the volunteers thinned, that the pilosebaceous glands atrophied and disappeared, all acne cleared, and the fatty insulation of the hypodermis was reabsorbed.[30] Even at the end of the 32-week experiment and before rehabilitation, the stratum corneum was intact, but drier than normal, resembling the skin of the very elderly. Minimum function essential for survival was conserved.

F. Disease and Trauma

Kligman states that too little attention is paid to the statistics regarding prevalence of skin disease in the general population. In fact, skin disease runs as high or higher than 10%.[31] Areas of broken, weeping lesions on skin are easily recognized as representing a situation where the stratum corneum is incompetent and highly permeable. It is not yet fully appreciated but is at the same time axiomatic that whenever the stratum corneum is formed in haste (as it often is in skin disease and mild trauma) its construction is faulty and the level of barrier protection is reduced. Thus, the vast majority of persons with irritated or diseased skin are in a barrier-compromised state and are at higher risk of experiencing the systemic toxicities of topical drugs.

Ichthyosis is a congenital disease in which the horny layer is dry, scaly, and markedly thickened. These attributes of the horny structure suggest it should be less permeable than normal skin. Transepidermal water loss studies suggest, however, that the permeability of ichthyosiform skin[32] is as high or higher than normal skin (Table 6). Values for ichthyosiform skin in Table 6 actually fall into the high range of normal values for skin as revealed in Tables 3 and 4. However, it does not necessarily follow that the permeation of large organic drug molecules through ichthyosiform skin will be similar in rate to normal skin. This question does not appear to have been addressed experimentally.

There is no doubt that in psoriasis, the permeability of the skin is increased. The risk of systemic toxicity of corticosteroids has been shown on numerous occasions to be increased in psoriatic patients.[33] The tissue is also measurably more permeable to water.[34] In this disease, there is a generalized parakeratosis and the horny layer thickness is several times that of normal skin. The psoriatic horny layer exhibits chemical and marked structural differences with respect to normal skin.

Table 6
TRANSEPIDERMAL WATER LOSS IN ICHTHYOSIFORM DERMATOSES

Skin condition	Transepidermal flux of water[a] (g/m²/hr)
Normal	1.8 ± 0.04
Ichthyosis regaris	2.1 ± 0.01
X-linked ichthyosis	2.6 ± 0.02
Lamellon ichthyosis	2.3 ± 0.2
Epidermolytic hyperkeratosis	3.4 ± 0.09

[a] Data taken from Frost, Weinstein, Bothwell, and Wildnauer.[32]

Even skin which is unbroken but showing the signs of protracted irritation seems to be relatively permeable. It is clearly established that chemicals which provoke inflammation increase the rate of transepidermal water loss.[35,36] Increases in transepidermal water loss have even been reported to occur before there were visible signs of inflammation.[37] Recently, Bronaugh has indicated that even mildly sunburned and inflamed skin exhibits increased permeability to organic substances.[63] It is known that UV light, topical vitamin A, and irritating concentrations of acetic acid increase the permeability of hairless mouse skin to hydrocortisone.[38] Thus, it seems that both actinic and chemical damage to the tissue, if mild, sets the skin on a common response course which includes periods of vasodilitation and hyperplasia. The horny layer undergoing rapid formation as the result of such trauma is measurably less effective in holding water in the body and keeping externally contacted chemicals out.

Much more appears to be known of the mechanistic aspects of trauma-induced alteration of the permeability of the skin than appears to be known about how diseases exert their effects. Three types of trauma can be singled out: (1) mechanical injury, (2) heat damage, or (3) damage by corrosive chemicals. Mechanical injury arises when the skin is abraded, cut, scarified, debrided, or stripped. The stratum corneum is literally shredded, cut through, or peeled off its epidermal moorings. The resulting broken or denuded surface loses much of its ability to retard diffusive penetration. In published work from these labs, scarification with a crisscrossed pattern of two sets of three scratches at right angles caused a several-hundred-fold increase in the permeation of vidarabine through hairless mouse skin. Incrementally stripped skin shows rapidly increasing permeability.[39,40] Fully stripped skin is not much different in permeability than the moist epithelia of the inner body. Permeability coefficients of denuded mouse skin are about 0.1 cm/hr and there is little permselectivity left to it. Thus, it can be seen that when the horny layer is broken up or removed, the essential protection the skin offers is lost. The magnitude of effect possible for a given compound is a function of the degree of stratum corneum damage and the level of permeability when the horny layer is intact.

By definition, burns are insult and damage to living tissue brought about (1) by exposure to excessive heat, cold, wind or radiation, (2) by accidental contact with corrosive chemicals, or (3) by high voltages. When burns are severe, which by definition means extensive and deep, heroic measures are often necessary to save the life, including the use of thick coverages of topical antiseptics. In some well-documented instances,[41-43] such therapy has led to acute systemic toxicity, even death. We have learned in these labs that the time and temperature of exposure of skin to a burning stimulus have as much or more to do with the immediate and intermediate term permeability of the tissues than the depth of destruction.[44-47] From the clinical point of view, an accurate estimate of burn depth and the severity of tissue damage is most important. From the therapeutic standpoint, it is also important to know how permeable such wounds are to assure either that there is adequate local deposition of the drug or to assess the risk of systemic accumulation of toxic drug levels. Recent studies indicate that the permeability of burn wounds right after injury is most related to the temperature and less so to the duration of burning.[44-47] Specifically, it has been shown that scalding of hairless mouse skin for 15 to 30 sec with 60°C water produces only nominal increases in in vitro assessed permeability coefficients for small nonelectrolytes.[44] Water and the polar alkanols, methanol, and ethanol, experienced 25 to 50% increases in permeability, but more hydrophobic alcohols experienced two- to fourfold increases. When the burning was extended beyond 30 sec, no further measurable change in permeability was evident. Similar results were obtained when a stainless steel branding device[45] was used to inflict burns to the mouse carcasses at 60°C. Burns were also inflicted for 60 sec while incrementally increasing the temperature.[46,47] Both scalding and branding techniques were used. Only marginal increases in permeabilities were observed up to 70°C. However, at temperatures higher than 80°C, large increases in permeability were seen for all test permeants except *n*-octanol. The magnitudes of the increases were greater for the more polar compounds. The absolute increases were greater the higher the temperature. Scalding at 98°C for 60 sec rendered the horny layer totally incompetent as a barrier. In our recent work, we found that even neomycin B diffuses through 98°C-scalded skin with great facility.

The change in permeability of the horny layer and consequently whole skin brought about by high temperatures appears to be related to thermal denaturation of the keratin structure. The α-helical structure is believed the principal native crystalline form of the soft keratin of the skin. Upon stretching at room temperature, it can be converted into a β-pleated sheet structure.[48] Heating the β-form[49] or the native form of keratin to a high temperature with or without stretching causes the configuration to change into a cross-β-form. Such mechanically or thermally induced β-forms of keratin are considered denatured states. Both α- and β-forms are energetically favorable conformations of polypeptide chains. The preferential formation of the β-structure in some high molecular weight synthetic polypeptides is associated with the presence of bulky substituents or hetero atoms on the α-carbon of the amino acid side chains.[50]

Baden et al.[48] reported that β-sheet structure of human corneum can be converted into a cross-β-structure by heating the skin sample in water at 85°C. The cross-β-structure formed as the result of heating is very stable and cannot be converted back to original forms of keratin either by stretching or by heating. Possibly, if one burns the mouse skin by holding the mouse body firmly against a hot metal surface, the simple β-keratin may form under limiting burning conditions of time and temperature, but if the temperature is raised and/or the contact time with the heating source lengthened, the cross-β-form is likely to be obtained and the thermal imprint left is permanent. Whether the assignment of the form of keratin is correct or not, it does appear that heating at a high enough temperature induces permanent defects in the intracellular matrix of keratin which opens this regime to diffusion. There appears to be very little in the way of permeability selectivity left after the denaturation has been effected, suggesting that solutes applied to the skin in water are mostly diffusing through a highly hydrated, watery field formed in the tissue.

Some chemicals, notably concentrated aqueous phenol and concentrated hydroxide, rapidly and drastically decrease the barrier properties of the stratum corneum.[9,51] Strong base denatures protein but it also saponifies fatty esters and solubilizes free acid residues and probably both effects on the stratum corneum are important. On the other hand, there is no reason to believe phenol has much of an effect on the intercellular lipid region of the horny layer. Phenol, a powerful protein denaturant, should act selectively on the protein phases of the horny layer.[51] Providing this supposition is true, then denaturation of the phenol represents a second example where selective denaturation of keratin leads to profound increases in the permeability of the skin.

IV. FACTORS ASSOCIATED WITH SKIN CONDITIONING

Little is known concerning the effect of bathing or other cosmetic practices on the barrier state of the skin. It is known that soap and water scrubbing removes surface grime and the natural sebaceous residues which are leaked out onto the skin. Excess exposure to harsh detergent solutions or excessive bathing leave the skin dry and pruritic and, in extreme situations, highly irritated. Soaps and detergents also denature the proteins of the horny layer. Skin, in this state, is presumably more permeable than normal skin. The suggestion is that the "oily substance" of the skin is necessary to help hold water in the stratum corneum, which, in turn, is essential for its proper pliability and function. The use of bath oils and of lotions and creams seems to quickly restore the general function and it would be interesting to know how this relates to barrier function.

V. PENETRATION-ENHANCING SOLVENTS

Skin penetration enhancers are yet another form of chemical treatment which increases permeability. The old concept that these carry drugs through the skin is naive, as is evident in the thorough discussion found in a following chapter on this topic. Rather, irrespective of their detailed mechanism(s) of action, they all chemically impair one or another of the phases of the stratum corneum. Solvents with known ability to enhance percutaneous absorption include low molecular weight, volatile solvents such as ether, chloroform, and hexane. Also included are certain solvent combinations containing both a polar and a nonpolar constituent as, for example, chloroform-methanol (2:1) and ether-ethanol (10:1). The mixed solvents have exaggerated effects. For instance, immersion of human stratum corneum in chloroform-methanol (2:1) for 1 hr results in a 100-fold increase in the diffusion coefficient for water.[52] Yet, after this treatment, the gross appearance of stratum corneum, its mechanical strength, and the birefringence of the keratin filaments remained unchanged, collectively suggesting that the structural protein meshwork of the horny layer remained essentially unchanged. However, the dry weight decreased by 20% due to the extraction of substances (presumably lipids) soluble in this medium. The activation energy for diffusion of water decreased from 14.3 to 6.3 kcal/mol, the latter of which is close to that for self-diffusion of liquid-state water, 4.6 kcal/mol. On this basis, Scheuplein and Ross postulated the formation of water-filled, submicroscopic interstices in the delipidized tissue with liquid-like diffusion occurring through these watery channels.[52]

Hydration of the human epidermis can induce manifold increases in its permeability. The degree of increase, of course, depends on the permeant and the duration and nature of the hydration process. It has been shown that the permeability to water can be increased eight-fold through hydration.[52] Similar enhancements were seen with salicylates[53] and an even greater enhancement (20-fold) was seen with cortisone when dry stratum corneum was exposed to water vapor.[54] Clinical advantage of such effects are realized through the use of occlusive dressings, which reportedly increase the absorption of steroids in vivo as much as 100-fold.[55] Part of this occlusive effect may involve retarding evaporation of solvent and removal of the vehicle.

The permeability-enhancing action of aprotic solvents such as dimethyl sulfoxide (DMSO) has been studied extensively. DMSO promotes the penetration of a large variety of substances through human and animal skin in vitro and in vivo.[56] The effective concentration of DMSO as a percentage of binary DMSO-water mixtures[57] appears to be in excess of 50%. DMSO is an extraordinary aprotic solvent. Though incapable of hydrogen-bonding itself, it nevertheless has a high cohesive energy density and is high boiling and viscid. It reacts with water exothermally and is capable of competing for hydrogen donor molecules.[58] The hydrogen bond between DMSO and water is estimated to be 1.3 times as strong as that between two water molecules.[58,59] Due to internal charge separation, it has a quasi-ionic character and is miscible with water as well as many nonpolar solvents. It, therefore, makes a good solvent for a large variety of organic and inorganic substances.

A number of mechanisms have been proposed for the penetration enhancement action of DMSO on the skin. DMSO may increase permeability by increasing hydration of stratum corneum since it is strongly hygroscopic.[60] Here, DMSO is presumed to wick water up through the skin. At high concentrations, DMSO may displace bound water within the organized proteolipid domain of the stratum corneum, possibly to the point where it constitutes a large percentage of the solvated tissue. Forces between DMSO molecules, being weaker than those between water molecules, should result in a looser solvent structure within the tissue and thus, a loosening of the protein organization.[52] Also, at high concentrations, DMSO can extract soluble components (mainly lipids) from the stratum corneum.[60,61] Ultrastructural changes such as enlargement of normal empty spaces seen in the stratum corneum cells were observed in guinea pig skin after 4 hr of treatment with 90% DMSO.[57] These could account for the partial concentration-dependent irreversibility of the action of DMSO. Chandrasekaran et al.[62] found the stratum corneum to be delaminated along its intercellular planes by DMSO, possibly due to the development of osmotic stress within the stratum corneum as the result of the cross current of water and DMSO through the tissue. This was the suggested cause of the marked enhancement of the penetration of scopolamine.

In contrast to the solvent types of permeation enhancers, anionic and cationic surfactants are able to exert their actions at low concentration. A detailed discussion of these surfactant enhancers may be found in the chapter on penetration enhancers.

Presumably, the study of the permeability of skin from its various human sources and in its various states of health is actually a study of how environmental, health factors, and wear and tear factors relate to the structure and composition of the stratum corneum. A high quality, compact stratum corneum is essential to the high state of impermeability associated with normal skin function. To date, all factors which change the cellular organization of the horny layer or the structural qualities of its lipid or keratin regimes represent impairments which open the skin to facile diffusion.

REFERENCES

1. **Elias, P. M., Grayson, S., Lampe, M. A., Williams, M. L., and Brown, B. E.,** The intercorneocyte space in, *Stratum Corneum,* Marks, R. and Plewig, G., Eds., Springer-Verlag, New York, 1983, 53.
2. **Steinert, P. M.,** Epidermal keratin: filiments and matrix in, *Stratum Corneum,* Marks, R. and Steinert, P. M., Eds., Springer-Verlag, New York, 1983, 25.
3. **Elias, P. M. and Friend, D. S.,** The permeability barrier in mammalian epidermis, *J. Cell Biol.,* 65, 185, 1975.
4. **Van Duzee, B. F.,** Thermal analysis of human stratum corneum, *J. Invest. Dermatol.,* 65, 404, 1975.
5. **Yu, C. D., Higuchi, W. I., Ho, N. F. H., Fox, J. L., and Flynn, G. L.,** Physical model evaluation of topical prodrug delivery — simultaneous transport and bioconversion of vidarabine — 5′ valerate. III. Permeability differences of vidarabine and *n*-pentanol in components of hairless mouse skin, *J. Pharm. Sci.,* 62, 210, 1973.
6. **Sheuplein, R. J.,** Mechanism of percutaneous absorption. I. Routes of penetration and the influence of solubility, *J. Invest. Dermatol.,* 45, 334, 1965.
7. **Scheuplein, R. J. and Blank, I. H.,** Permeability of the skin, *Physiol. Rev.,* 51, 702, 1971.
8. **Durrheim, H. H., Flynn, G. L., Higuchi, W. I., and Behl, C. R.,** Permeation of hairless mouse skin. I. Experimental methods and comparison with human epidermal permeation by alkanols, *J. Pharm. Sci.,* 69, 781, 1980.
9. **Roberts, M. S., Anderson, R. A., Swarbrick, J., and Moore, D. E.,** The percutaneous absorption of phenolic compounds: the mechanism of diffusion across the stratum corneum, *J. Pharm. Pharmacol.,* 30, 486, 1978.

10. **Creasy, N. H., Battensby, J., and Fletcher, J. A.,** Factors affecting the permeability of skin, *Curr. Probl. Dermatol.*, 7, 95, 1978.
11. **Arita, T., Hori, R., Anmo, T., Washitake, M., Akatsu, M., and Yajima, T.,** Studies on percutaneous absorption of drugs. I, *Chem. Pharm. Bull.*, 18, 1045, 1970.
12. **Grove, G. L.,** Techniques for substantiating skin care product claims in, *Safety and Efficacy of Topical Drugs*, Kligman, A. M. and Leyden, J. J., Eds., Grune and Stratton, New York, 1982, 157.
13. **Blank, I. H., Moloney, III, J., Emsilie, A. E., Simon, I., and Apt, C.,** The diffusion of water across the stratum corneum as a function of its water content, *J. Invest. Dermatol.*, 82, 188, 1984.
14. **Hammarlund, K., Nilsson, G. E., Oberg, P. A., and Sedin, G.,** Transepidermal water loss in newborn infants. I. Relation to ambient humidity and site of measurement and estimation of transepidermal water loss, *Acta Paediatr. Scand.*, 66, 552, 1977.
15. **Nilsson, G. E.,** Measurement of water exchange through the skin, *Med. Biol. Eng.*, 15, 209, 1977.
16. **Stoughton, R. B.,** Some Bioassays for Measuring Percutaneous Absorption, in *Advances in Biology of Skin*, Vol 12., Montagna, W., Van Scott, E. J., and Stoughton, R. B. Eds., 1969, 537.
17. **Stoughton, R. B.,** Bioassay of antimicrobials, *Arch. Dermatol.*, 101, 160, 1969.
18. **Weingand, D. A., Haygood, C., Gaylor, J. R., and Anglin, Jr., J. H.,** Racial variations in the cutaneous barrier in, *Current Concepts in Cutaneous Toxicity*, Drill, V. A. and Lazar, P., Eds., Academic Press, New York, 1980, 221.
19. **Hammarlund, K. and Sedin, G.,** Transepidermal water loss in newborn infants. III. Relation to gestational age, *Acta Paediatr. Scand.*, 68, 795, 1979.
20. **Wilson, D. R. and Maibach, H. I.,** An in vivo comparison of skin barrier function in, *Neonatal Skin, Structure, and Functions*, Maibach, H. I. and Boisits, E. K., Eds., Marcel Dekker, New York, 1982, 101.
21. **Holbrook, K. A.,** A histological comparison of infant and adult skin in, *Neonatal Skin, Structure, and Functions*, Maibach, H. I. and Boisits, E. K., Eds., Marcel Dekker, New York, 1982, 3.
22. **Schalla, W. and Schaefer, H.,** Mechanism of Penetration of Drugs into the skin in, *Dermal and Transdermal Absorption*, Brandau, R. and Lippold, B. M., Eds., Wissenschaftliche Verlagsgesellschaft mbH Stuttgart, 1982, 41.
23. **Cronin, E. and Stoughton, R. B.,** Percutaneous absorption, regional variations and the effects of hydration and epidermal stripping, *Br. J. Dermatol.*, 74, 265, 1962.
24. **Smith, J. G., Fisher, R. W., and Blank, I. H.,** The epidermal barrier — a comparison between scrotal and abdominal skin, *J. Invest. Dermatol.*, 36, 337, 1962.
25. **Maibach, H. I., Feldman, R. J., Milby, T. H., and Serat, W. F.,** Regional variation in percutaneous penetration in man, *Arch. Environ. Health*, 23, 208, 1971.
26. **Feldman, R. J. and Maibach, H. I.,** Regional variations in the percutaneous absorption of ^{14}C-cortisol in man, *J. Invest. Dermatol.*, 48, 181, 1967.
27. **Maibach, H. I., Feldman, R. J., Milby, T. H., and Serat, W. F.,** Regional variation in percutaneous penetration in man — pesticides, *Arch. Environ. Health*, 23, 208, 1971.
28. **Tregear, R. T.,** Relative permeability of hair follicles and epidermis, *J. Physiol.*, 156, 307, 1961.
29. **Feldman, R. J. and Maibach, H. I.,** Penetration of ^{14}C-hydrocortisone through normal skin, *Arch. Dermatol.*, 91, 661, 1965.
30. **Keys, A., Brozek, J., Henschel, A., Mickelsen, O., and Taylor, H. L.,** *The Biology of Human Starvation*, The University of Minnesota Press, Minneapolis, Minn., 1950.
31. **Kligman, A. M.,** Systemic toxicity in, *Safety and Efficacy of Topical Drugs and Cosmetics*, Kligman, A. M. and Leyden, J. J., Eds., Grune and Stratton, New York, 1982, 239.
32. **Frost, P., Weinstein, G. D., Bothwell, J., and Wildnauer, R.,** Ichthyosiform dermatoses. III. Studies of transepidermal water loss, *Arch. Dermatol.*, 98, 230, 1968.
33. **Carr, R. D. and Tarnowski, W. M.,** Percutaneous absorption of corticosteroids, *Acta Dermatol. Venerol.*, 48, 417, 1968.
34. **Grice, K. A. and Bettley, F. R.,** Skin water loss and accidental hypothermia in psoriasis, ichthyosis, and erythroderma, *Br. Med. J.*, 4, 95, 1967.
35. **Rollins, T. G.,** From xerosis to nummular dermatitis: the dehydration dermatosis, *JAMA*, 206, 637, 1966.
36. **Spruit, D.,** Evaluation of skin function by the alkali application technique *Curr. Probl. Dermatol.*, 3, 148, 1970.
37. **Malten, K. E. and Thiele, F. A. J.,** Evaluation of skin damage. II. Water loss and carbon dioxide release measurements related to skin resistance measurements, *Br. J. Dermatol.*, 89, 565, 1973.
38. **Solomon, A. E. and Lowe, D. J.,** Percutaneous absorption in experimental epidermal disease, *Br. J. Dermatol.*, 100, 717, 1979.
39. **Flynn, G. L., Durrheim, H. H., and Higuchi, W. I.,** Permeation of hairless mouse skin. II. Membrane sectioning techniques and influence on alkanol permeabilities, *J. Pharm. Sci.*, 70, 52, 1980.
40. **Behl, C. R., Flynn, G. L., Linn, E. F., and Smith, W. M.,** Percutaneous absorption of corticosteroids: age, site, and skin-sectioning influences on rates of permeation of hairless mouse skin by hydrocortisone, *J. Pharm. Sci.*, 73, 1287, 1984.

41. **Marsicano, A. R., Hutton, J. J., and Byrant, W. M.,** Fatal hemolysis from mafenide treatment of burns in a patient with glucose-6-phosphate dehydrogenase deficiency, *Plast. Reconstr. Surg.*, 46, 458, 1970.
42. **Banford, M. F. M. and Jones, L. F.,** Deafness and biochemical imbalance after burn treatment with topical antibiotics in young children, *Arch. Dis. Child.*, 53, 326, 1978.
43. **Lavelle, K. J., Doedens, D. J., Kleit, S. A., and Forney, R. B.,** Iodine absorption in burn patients treated topically with povidone-iodine, *Clin. Pharmacol. Thera.*, 17, 355, 1975.
44. **Behl, C. R., Flynn, G. L., Kurihara, T., Smith, W. M., Giatmaitan, O. G., Higuchi, W. I., Ho, N. F. H., and Pierson, C. L.,** Permeability of thermally damaged skin. I. Immediate influences of 60°C scalding on hairless mouse skin, *J. Invest. Dermatol.*, 75, 340, 1980.
45. **Behl, C. R., Flynn, G. L., Barrett, M., Walters, K. A., Linn, E. E., Mohamed, Z., Kurihara, T., Ho, N. F. H., Higuchi, W. I., and Pierson, C. L.,** Permeability of thermally damaged skin. II. Immediate influences of branding at 60°C on hairless mouse skin permeability, *Burns*, 7, 389, 1981.
46. **Flynn, G. L., Behl, C. R., Walters, K. A., Gatmaitan, O. G., Wittkowsky, A., Kurihara, T., Ho, N. F. H., Higuchi, W. I., and Pierson, C. L.,** Permeability of thermally damaged skin. III. Influence of scalding temperature on mass transfer of water and *n*-alkanols across hairless mouse skin, *Burns,* 8, 47, 1981.
47. **Behl, C. R., Flynn, G. L., Barrett, M., Linn, E. E., Higuchi, W. I., Ho, N. F. H., and Pierson, C. L.,** Permeability of thermally damaged skin. IV. Influence of branding iron temperature on the mass transfer of water and *n*-alkanols across hairless mouse skin, *Burns*, 8, 86, 1981.
48. **Baden, H. P., Goldsmith, L. A., and Bonar, L.,** Conformational changes in the α-fibrons proteins of epidermis, *J. Invest. Dermatol.*, 60, 215, 1971.
49. **Van Duzee, B. F.,** Thermal analysis of human stratum corneum, *J. Invest. Deermatol.*, 65, 404, 1975.
50. **Barrow, G. M.,** *Physical Chemistry,* 3rd ed., McGraw-Hill, New York, 1973, 761.
51. **Behl, C. R., Linn, E. E., Flynn, G. L., Pierson, C. L., Higuchi, W. I., and Ho, N. F. H.,** Permeation of skin and eschar by antiseptic. I. Baseline studies with phenol, *J. Pharm. Sci.*, 72, 391, 1983.
52. **Scheuplein, R. J. and Ross, L.,** Effects of surfactants and solvents on the permeability of epidermis, *J. Soc. Cosmet. Chem.*, 21, 853, 1973.
53. **Wurster, D. E. and Kramer, S.,** Investigation of some factors influencing percutaneous absorption, *J. Pharm. Sci.*, 50, 288, 1961.
54. **Scheuplein, R. J., Blank, I. H., Brauner, G. J., and MacFarlane, D. J.,** Percutaneous absorption of steroids, *J. Invest. Dermatol.*, 52, 63, 1969.
55. **McKenzie, A. and Stoughton, R.,** Methods for comparing percutaneous absorption of steriods, *Arch. Dermatol.*, 86, 608, 1966.
56. **Allenby, A. C., Creasey, N. H., Edgington, J. A. G., Fletcher, J. A., and Schock, C.,** Mechanism of action of accelerants on skin penetration. *Br. J. Dermatol.*, 4 (Suppl. 81), 47, 1969.
57. **Montes, L. F., Day, J. L., Wand, C. J., and Kennedy, L.,** Ultrastructural changes in the horny layer following local application of dimethyl sulfoxide, *J. Invest. Dermatol.*, 48, 184, 1967.
58. **Schuplein, R. J. and Bronaugh, R. L.,** Percutaneous absorption in, *Biochemistry and Physiology of the Skin,* Vol. 2, Goldsmith, L. A., Ed., Oxford University Press, New York, 1255, 1983.
59. **McGregor, W. S.,** The chemical and physical properties of DMSO, *Ann. N. Y. Acad. Sci.*, 141, 3, 1967.
60. **Kurihara, T.,** Physicochemical Study of the Accelerant Effects of DMSO on Percutaneous Absorption of an Antiviral Drug and Other Chemical Prototypes, Ph.D. thesis,University of Michigan, Ann Arbor, 1983.
61. **Embrey, G. and Dugard, P.,** The isolation of dimethyl sulfoxide soluble components from human epidermal preparations: a possible mechanism of action of dimethyl sulfoxide in effecting percutaneous absorption phenomena, *J. Invest. Dermatol.*, 57, 308, 1971.
62. **Chandrasekaran, S. K., Campbell, P. S., and Michaels, A. S.,** Effect of dimethyl sulfoxide on drug permeation through human skin *A.I.Ch.E.J.*, 23, 810, 1977.
63. **Bronaugh, R. L.,** personal communication.

Chapter 2

EXPERIMENTAL SKIN MODELS

David Yeung, Walter P. Smith, and Sergio Nacht

TABLE OF CONTENTS

I. INTRODUCTION

Perhaps one of the biggest challenges faced by pharmacologists and toxicologists in the last 30 years has been the measurement and the prediction of the percutaneous absorption of topically applied drugs and chemical compounds. Since the first publication of acceptable experimental data on the transepidermal penetration of chemical compounds about 40 years ago, various investigators have studied a large number of compounds under different experimental conditions. A variety of animal species have been used as a source of skin for experimental models, and the usefulness of these are treated elsewhere in this volume. Most investigators agree that human skin is unique among mammalian species in its permeability characteristics and have preferred to utilize this tissue for experimental purposes.

However, even among those who used human skin as a diffusional membrane, there has been a large number of experimental set-ups utilized, each one of them offering different advantages and, naturally, disadvantages.

Our purposes in preparing this chapter have been first, to describe our techniques and experience in the measurement of transepidermal and intrafollicular penetration of drugs using excised human skin as an experimental model, since we believe that this tissue provides the most valid and relevant measurement to predict the in vivo situation, and then, we present a novel technique which employs a reconstituted membrane that mimics intact stratum corneum. This work will illustrate the importance of lipids in the skin-barrier function and describes a possible model membrane. Finally, we describe an artificial membrane system which, while simple and reproducible, succeeds in duplicating some of the more complex physical-chemical behavior of human stratum corneum as a permeability barrier and thus allows the quick screening of a large number of compounds, vehicles, and formulations, without the limitations usually imposed by the availability of the human tissue.

We should emphasize, however, that our purpose has not been to present an exhaustive review of either the scientific literature or the methodologies available and, for that, we refer the reader to several excellent reviews available. Instead, our intention has been to relate our personal experiences in this field and to provide the interested reader and experimenter with a few practical techniques useful in this type of research.

II. EXCISED HUMAN SKIN

A. Transepidermal Penetration

The use of excised human skin to study the skin penetration of chemicals has been widespread,[1-6] trying to measure the penetration of drugs into excised human skin under conditions that would closely resemble real-life usage. Virtually all investigators use some type of diffusion cell in which animal or human skin is mounted in a two-compartment chamber and the diffusion of compounds through the full thickness of skin or stratum corneum sheets into a buffer system is measured.

Early models of diffusion cells such as those used by Lyman et al.[7]; Garrett et al.[8] and Kooten et al.[9] are all designed to measure drug diffusion through a membrane system into a receptor solution. Further modification by Coldman et al.,[10] Menczel and Maibach,[11] Wolejsza et al.,[12] and Franz[13] have made considerable improvements in the diffusion cells design. However, they all share one or more of the following disadvantages:

1. Most of the cells are designed for steady-state flux experiments wherein an infinite dose of test solution or product is applied to the skin surface. This certainly does not duplicate the real-life usage of topical products in which constant evaporation of volatile components and, consequently, a change in the concentration of drug occurs.
2. The cells have a small effective diffusional area and this can affect the reproducibility of experimental results.

3. Both the donor and receptor solutions are maintained at a similar temperature by various temperature-regulating devices, while in real-life conditions the donor compartment, namely the skin surface, is constantly exposed to the ambient environment. This tends to create a real-life skin temperature gradient that does not exist in the diffusion cell arrangement.

The diffusion cell design that we have found most satisfactory holds the sample of skin horizontally, with the stratum corneum side exposed to the air. Formulations can be applied to it at rates between 3 and 10 mg/cm^2, which closely resemble real-life conditions. If desired, this design also allows the study of skin penetration at steady-state conditions by placing an excess dose of donor solution or formulation on the skin surface, with the donor compartment stoppered to prevent solvent evaporation.

1. Methodology

Strips of normal human skin, 700- to 800-μm thick, were obtained from the abdominal area of adult individuals as plastic surgery specimens and were either used immediately or stored in such a manner as to maintain their integrity.[14] Circular discs, 4.3 cm in diameter, were punched from these strips and were equilibrated for 12 to 20 hr in phosphate-buffered Ringer's solution containing streptomycin and penicillin. All in vitro permeation studies were performed at least in duplicate.

The diffusion cells consisted of two chambers (Figure 1): the lower one made of Plexiglass®, the upper one of Teflon® or Delrin®. Each skin disc, with its stratum corneum side exposed to the air, was mounted horizontally across the upper chamber of the diffusion cell and held in place with an O-ring, providing an effective diffusional area of 5.08 cm^2.

When mounted, 40 mℓ of physiologic buffer was added to the lower chamber. This buffer solution bathing the dermal (receptor) side of the skin disc was mixed continuously by a Teflon®-coated magnetic rod driven by a 120-rpm electric synchronous motor located below the cell bath.

The cell was equilibrated for 30 min in a water bath maintained by an immersion thermostatic pump at 30° ± 0.4°C. The product was applied by the stratum corneum side of the skin disc in a dose of approximately 3 mg/cm^2 and spread evenly with a Teflon® policeman. This amount of the preparation provided adequate coverage of the entire skin disc. In most instances, the drug of interest was radiolabeled with either ^{14}C or tritium to increase the sensitivity of detection of the permeant in the receptor side buffer.

When an infinite dosing experiment was performed, excessive amounts of the test solution or product were applied to the skin surface. The cell was stoppered to prevent vehicle evaporation, thus maintaining a steady-state delivery of drug to the skin. At selected time intervals, aliquots of the receptor solution were withdrawn through a side tubing and analyzed for radioactivity by liquid scintillation counting. Care was taken to maintain "sink" conditions by diluting the buffer to prevent significant accumulation of tracer on the receptor side of the disc, a condition which could lead to a backflow of radioactivity.

To study the possible skin metabolism of the penetrating drug, the following procedure was conducted. At the end of the experiment, the receptor buffer solution was quantitatively transferred to a separation funnel and extracted a number of times with a suitable organic solvent. The skin surface was then rinsed with an appropriate solvent to remove any material that had not penetrated; then, the skin was extracted with a suitable solvent to recover the penetrated drug. The extract was then concentrated under vacuum in a rotary evaporator and analyzed by appropriate analytical techniques and by autoradiography.[15]

2. Results and Discussion

Table 1 presents data from a study on the percutaneous penetration of benzoyl peroxide

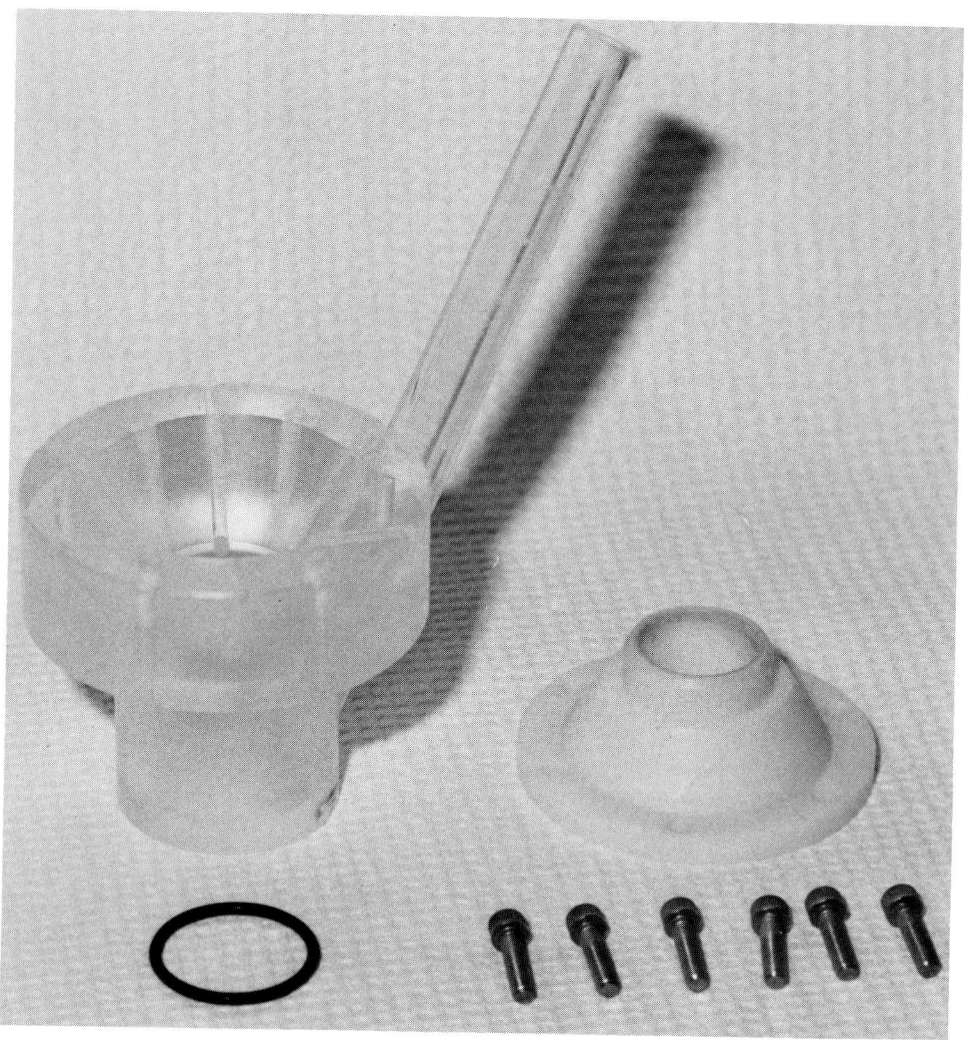

FIGURE 1. Disassembled diffusion cell used with excised human skin.

Table 1
PERCUTANEOUS PENETRATION OF BENZOYL PEROXIDE THROUGH EXCISED HUMAN SKIN

	μg*	%+	
Rinse (skin surface)	4350	95.5	Benzoyl peroxide
Soaks (skin layers)	120	2.6	Benzoyl peroxide and benzoic acid
Buffer (dermal side)	86	1.9	Benzoic acid
Total	4556	100.00	

Note: *, Average of two diffusion cells; +, percent of the total amount recovered.

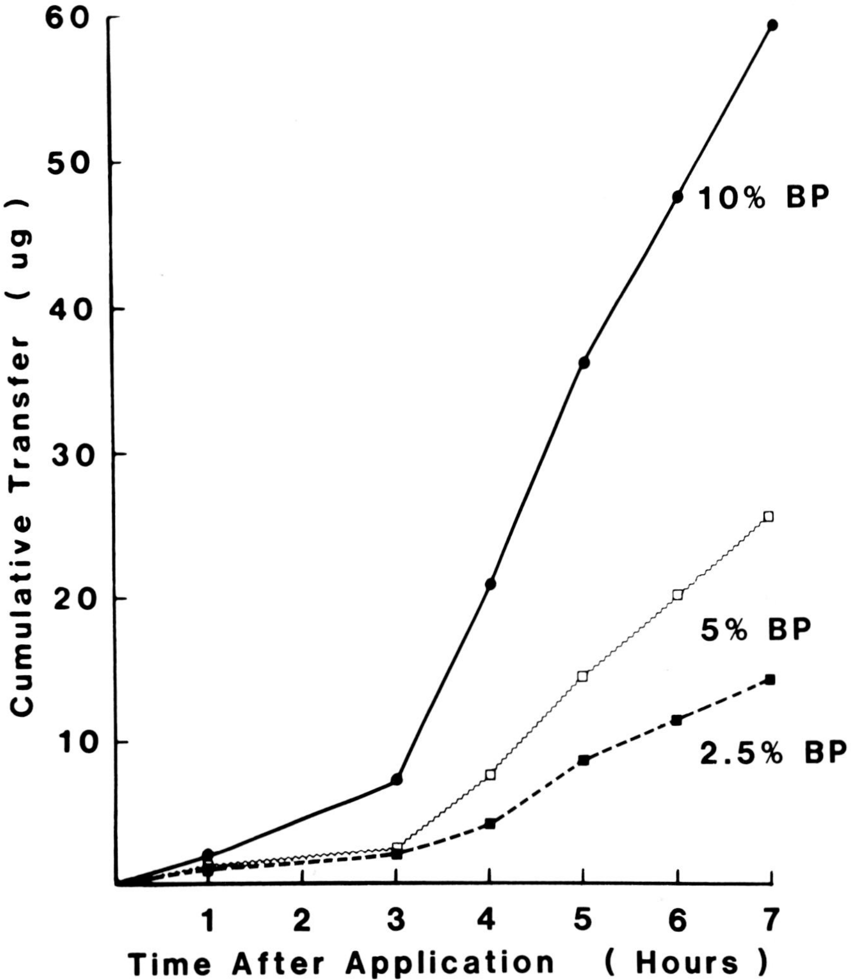

FIGURE 2. Penetration of benzoyl peroxide at different concentrations in a lotion vehicle, through human skin in vitro.

through excised human skin under steady-state conditions.[15] Of the 4.556 μg of radiolabeled benzoyl peroxide in acetone applied to the surface of the skin, 1.9% (86 μg) penetrated through the skin and was recovered as benzoic acid from the receptor buffer solution. The amount of drug retained within the skin layers was 120 μg or 2.6% of the total amount applied. Approximately one half of this was benzoyl peroxide and the other half, benzoic acid. Additionally, from the total amount of drug recovered in the receptor buffer and inside the skin layers, the maximal skin penetration rate of benzoyl peroxide could be calculated (5.1 μg/cm^2/hr).

Thus, the skin penetration of topically applied drugs can be determined quantitatively and also, whether there is any metabolic transformation of the penetrating compound inside the skin layers can be assessed. In vivo studies in rhesus monkeys confirmed the conversion of benzoyl peroxide to benzoic acid after intramuscular or topical administration of the drug,[15] since at least 95% of the radioactivity in urine following either mode of administration was recovered as benzoic acid.

The diffusion cell technique with excised human skin can also be utilized to predict the skin penetration of drugs from various formulations under real-life usage conditions.[5] Results presented in Figure 2 indicate that the total amount of drug that penetrated into the skin is

Table 2
PERCUTANEOUS PENETRATION OF BENZOYL PEROXIDE AS A FUNCTION OF DRUG CONCENTRATION IN THE VEHICLE

Benzoyl peroxide concentration in vehicle (%)	Human skin in vitro (rate [flux],* μg/cm²/hr)	Rhesus monkey in vivo (total urinary excretion, μg)
2.5	0.60⁺	951
5	1.13	1584
10	2.56	1876

Note: *Average of three cells; ⁺ significance levels: 10% vs. 5%, $p = 0.008$; 10% vs. 2.5%, $p = 0.005$; 5% vs. 2.5%, $p = 0.120$.

Table 3
CORRELATION BETWEEN IN VIVO AND IN VITRO SKIN PENETRATION OF RESORCINOL FROM A HYDRO-ALCOHOLIC VEHICLE

	In vivo*	In vitro⁺
Dosage	800 mg/2600 cm² or 0.30 mg/cm²**	2 mg/5.1 cm² or 0.39 mg/cm²
Flux (μg/cm²/hr)	0.37	0.86

Note: *Subchronic topical administration of a 2% resorcinol hydroalcoholic solution to three human subjects; ⁺Skin diffusion cells set up; **Total area of application, average of three subjects.

related to the drug concentration in the vehicle. The penetration rate was significantly higher with the 10% preparation of benzoyl peroxide than at 5% ($p = 0.008$) or at 2.5% ($p = 0.005$) drug concentration (Table 2). These findings correlated well with those obtained in an in vivo model (rhesus monkey).

Thus, the penetration of benzoyl peroxide was concentration dependent, both in rate and amount; namely, the higher the concentration of drug applied, the greater the amount absorbed. Since it is generally accepted that the therapeutic efficacy of many topically applied drugs is dependent upon their ability to penetrate below the stratum corneum, these findings are of clinical interest because they support the common practice of using a higher drug concentration for the more severe acne conditions.

Using the same diffusion cell technique, we have also found good correlation between the in vitro skin penetration of resorcinol and that measured in vivo following repeated topical applications.[6] As indicated in Table 3, the percutaneous absorption rate or resorcinol calculated from the in vivo excretion data correlates well with that determined on excised human skin.

Thus, the usefulness of this in vitro skin diffusion cell model was demonstrated in the study of:

1. The skin penetration of compounds under steady-state conditions
2. The transepidermal delivery of drugs and their skin metabolism, under conditions closely resembling "real life"
3. The effects of drug concentration and vehicle composition on topical drug penetration

B. Intrafollicular Penetration

This technique can measure the amount of a given drug that penetrates into the follicular duct, in many instances, the molecular species present can also be identified. In contrast to the well-studied transepidermal delivery of compounds, this route of skin penetration has been mostly unexplored since it is considered to be relatively unimportant. This may be due in part to the lack of methodology sensitive enough to detect the minute amounts of materials that penetrate into the follicle.

Recent advances in analytical instrumentation and the use of radioactive techniques have rendered possible the identification and measurement of the amounts of materials that penetrate into a single follicle. Examples of such techniques include high performance liquid chromatography, gas chromatography — mass spectrometry, autoradiography, and scintillation counting. The following is a description of the techniques routinely used in our laboratory to evaluate intrafollicular penetration.

1. Methodology and Results

The most useful technique to determine the primary route of skin penetration of compounds is autoradiography. The theory and application of this technique have been extensively reviewed by Rogers.[16] In our studies, we applied to excised human skin products containing the compound radiochemically labeled with a suitable isotope (usually carbon-14 or tritium). After a given contact time, the excess material is removed from the skin surface without adequate solvent and the epidermis is separated from the underlying layers either by heat separation[17] or by cyanoacrylate biopsy.[18] The separated epidermal sheet is then exposed to X-ray film for an appropriate period of time and the film is developed using standard photographic procedures. In so doing, compounds that penetrate primarily transepidermally, produce a rather uniform exposure of the film. On the other hand, discrete patterns are obtained with compounds that penetrate through the follicular ducts. When the radioautograph is compared to the actual stratum corneum sheet under a low-power stereoscope, it can be seen that the dark spots in the X-ray film (indicating accumulation of radio-label) coincide well with the follicular openings in the tissue.

Figure 3 demonstrates the transepidermal penetration of salicylic acid while Figure 4 clearly indicates that the penetration of sulfur is primarily intrafollicular. There are drugs like benzoyl peroxide that can be absorbed through both routes (Figure 5), and therefore produce a combination of a rather uniform background and a discrete pattern of drug localization at the follicular openings.

In addition to examining the primary route of skin penetration of drugs, in many instances we can also determine the chemical specie present in the follicle and measure the amount that penetrated using appropriate analytical techniques. For this purpose, individual follicular fragments are recovered from the treated area of skin using the aforementioned cyanocrylate biopsy procedure. The individual follicles are carefully dissected from the cyanoacrylate biopsy under a stereoscope, pooled, homogenized, and extracted with an appropriate solvent. The amount of drug in the extract is then determined by adequately sensitive analytical techniques or radioactivity counting, if radiolabeled compounds were used. Table 4 presents results indicating the follicular penetration of benzoyl peroxide from two lotion vehicles tested.

In conclusion, this skin penetration technique allows the study of the route of drug penetration and, therefore, provides a better understanding of the mechanism of action of topically applied drugs.

III. RECONSTITUTED SKIN

The barrier function of the skin is extraordinarily important for limiting the absorption of inappropriate materials from the environment and for controlling the loss of both solutes and solvent (water) from the internal milieu. Despite its importance, this barrier function is still poorly understood.

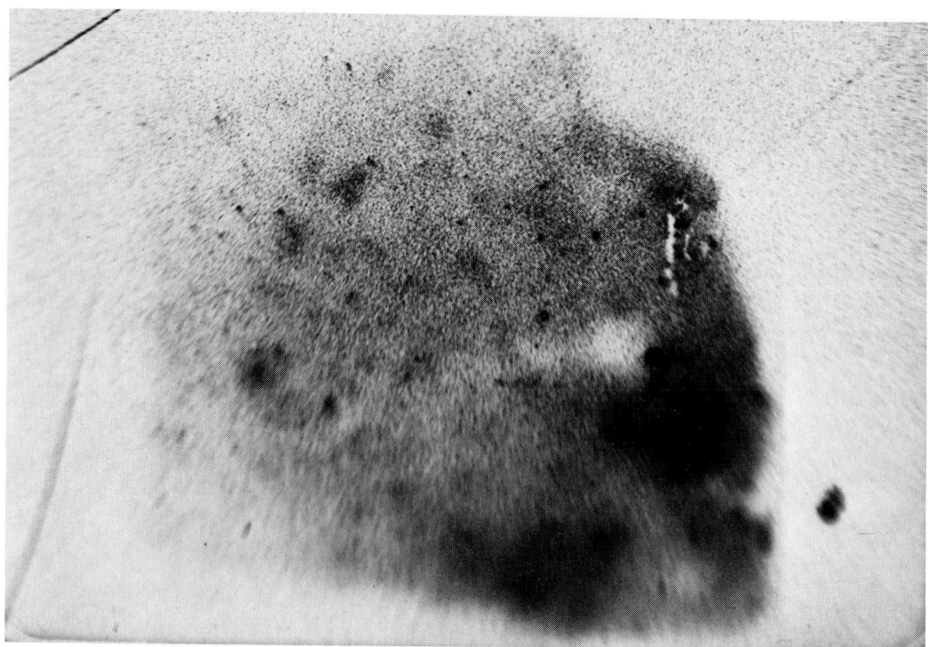

FIGURE 3. Autoradiograph of excised human skin showing the transepidermal penetration of salicylic acid.

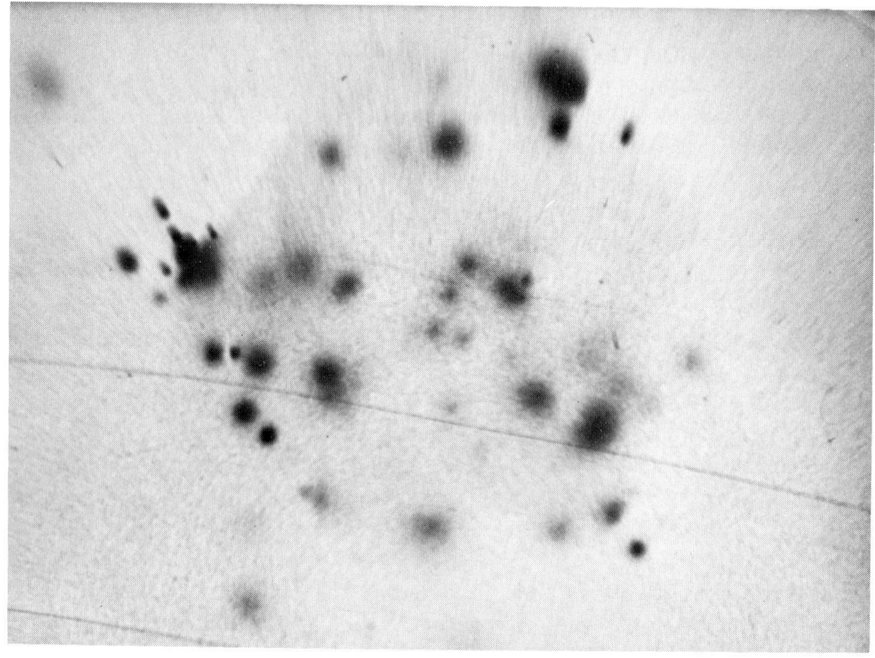

FIGURE 4. Autoradiograph of excised human skin showing the intra-follicular penetration of sulfur.

Although the use of excised human skin or synthetic membranes provide the capability of examining comparative rates and kinetics of penetration of topically applied materials, it cannot yield fundamental information regarding factors controlling permeability at the microscopic level.

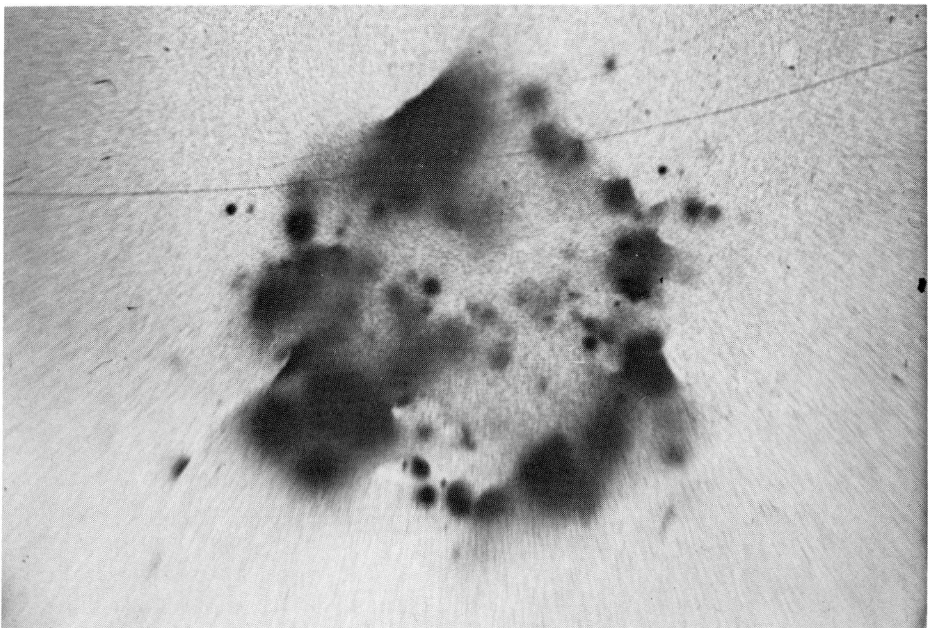

FIGURE 5. Autoradiograph of excised human skin showing transepidermal and intrafollicular penetration of benzoyl peroxide.

Table 4
FOLLICULAR PENETRATION OF BENZOYL PEROXIDE (BP) FROM LOTION VEHICLES

Subject	Number of product applications	Ng BP recovered* per microcomedo	
		Lotion A	Lotion B
1	4	94	55
2	4	55	48
3	8	50	48
4	8	93	105

Note: *Benzoyl peroxide recovered from the follicular extracts was chemically converted to benzoic acid and quantified by high pressure liquid chromatography.

In recent years, the importance of the structural integrity of the stratum corneum has been clarified. Elegant studies by Elias and co-workers[19,20] have demonstrated that when topically applied, some hydrophobic materials pass through the stratum corneum, apparently via the intercellular spaces. The results obtained with hydrophillic materials are not so clear cut.

Earlier investigators[4] demonstrated that solvent-extracted stratum corneum had poorer barrier properties than the intact tissue. Polar solvents were more effective than nonpolar solvents in modifying barrier integrity.

With the recent clarification of the structure of epidermal lipids by Downing and co-workers,[21] and Grey and Yardley[22], the importance of certain polar lipids in controlling permeability has become apparent.

However, studies attempting to correlate permeability with lipid amount or composition have yielded little reliable information due to the complexity of the system being dealt with.[20]

To obviate these problems, we have established an in vitro system of reconstituted skin, in which stratum corneum cells and lipids are first separated and then added back together under defined conditions, forming a reaggregated tissue with varying barrier properties. By modulating lipid quantity and composition we have established a clear relationship between lipid type and amounts and stratum corneum permeability.

A. Methodology

1. Isolation of Lipid-Depleted Corneocytes and Stratum Corneum (SC) Lipids

Fragments of SC, usually less than 0.5 mm in diameter (about 600 cells), were scraped with a scalpel from the calf or sole (plantar callous) of volunteers. Scraping the skin in such a manner may result in removal of cells from a variety of depths within the SC. In fact, upon examination of the lipids obtained from such fragments we found a good amount of glucosylceramides, usually present in the lower layers of the SC.[23] However, no phospholipids could be detected, indicating the absence of stratum granulosum.

The fragments (usually pooled from several volunteers) were ground in a mortar and pestle, suspended in either anhydrous ether or in chloroform:methanol:water (2:1:0.2 vol), and reduced to individual cells. The ground cells were lipid-depleted by stirring for 30 min at room temperature with the above solvents, using a ratio of approximately 1 mℓ solvent per 10 to 15 mg cells.[24] The tissue then was transferred to a ground glass homogenizer and further extracted with gentle homogenization with an aliquot of fresh solvent. After homogenization, the suspension was agitated for 30 min at room temperature. The centrifuged pellet (2000 rpm × 10 min) was collected and used as a source of SC cells. Complete delipidation (greater than 95%) of the cells was verified by the absence of staining with Oil Red O of the extracted cells. Moreover, further exhaustive extractions of the cells (1 to 2 days in chloroform-methanol 1:2) yielded less than 5% of the previously extracted lipid.

The extraction media were pooled and separated into a two-phase system by the addition of equal volumes of chloroform and water; the two phases were separated by centrifugation (2000 rpm × 10 min), and the upper aqueous phase was discarded. The combined lower phases were washed twice with water and they were then evaporated to dryness under nitrogen at 45°C. The dry lipids were then resuspended in chloroform-methanol (2:1) and stored at −20°C.

2. Isolation of Disrupted Corneocytes

Corneocytes were disrupted by grinding then with dry ice in a mortar and pestle and passing through a French-type press at 20,000 p.s.i. Cell clumps and large membrane fragments were precipitated and discarded after low speed centrifugation.

3. Preparation of Protein Fractions

Keratin was prepared as described previously or obtained commercially as a protein hydrolysate.[25]

Reaggregation of SC — For reaggregation studies, about 200 mg of extracted cells were suspended in about 100 μℓ of ether or chloroform:methanol (2:1) and gently pipetted onto a thin water film confined within the boundaries of a 1.3 cm diameter Teflon® O-ring. Immediately after the solvent had evaporated and the cells had settled into a thin film, lipid (about 1 to 10 mg in 10 μℓ of the same solvent) was gently layered onto the cells. The films, which were very fragile after solvent evaporation, were teased off with a scalpel and a fine stream of water and hydrated overnight at 0°C in phosphate-buffered Ringer's solution (pH 7.2) prior to mechanical manipulation. After hydration, the discs were much more coherent and could be examined under a 40 × stereo microscope for obvious flaws, holes, etc., and prepared for physical-chemical analysis. Reaggregation was termed successful if, after overnight hydration, the disc of reformed tissue suspended in water would not break down upon mixing with a Vortex for 1 min. The nature of the reaggregated tissue was such that this assay, although not quantitative, could distinguish between successful and unsuccessful reaggregation.

Permeation Studies — Reaggregated SC discs, free of visible flaws, were equilibrated at room temperature in phosphate-buffered Ringer's solution for 20 hr before their use in permeation studies. The reaggregated SC discs were mounted between two plastic wells with an effective diffusional area of ca. 2 cm^2.[26] A perfect seal between the wells was achieved by tightening a clamp on the wells and applying a thin boundary of cyanoacrylate to the periphery of the discs.

Once the reaggregated SC membrane had been mounted in the permeation cell, the receptor side of the membrane was constantly bathed by filling the receptor compartment with 40 mℓ of physiological saline (pH 7.6).

The cell was equilibrated at 30°C ± 0.5° C for 20 min. Then, 2 mℓ of the donor solution containing a radioactive tracer (^3H_2O, specific activity 2300 μC/mg, New England Nuclear) was accurately measured and applied to the membrane surface. The cell was stoppered with a glass stopper to prevent fluid evaporation, thus maintaining steady-state conditions. Standards were taken from this donor solution at the beginning and the end of the experiment to insure that the concentration of tracer had not changed during the experiment. At selected time intervals, an aliquot of the receptor buffer was withdrawn through the side arm of the lower compartment and analyzed for radioactivity content by liquid scintillation counting.

Flux Determination — The flux of water was calculated by determining the amount of water transferred per unit time and expressed as: μg/cm^2/hr/unit membrane thickness. Membrane thickness was estimated with a micrometer or by microscopy of transverse sections. In most cases, the thickness of the various membranes varied from 0.08 to 0.12 mm. The variation among measurements taken from different locations within a single reaggregated disc was usually less than 0.02 mm. To further standardize these permeation experiments, reaggregated discs were formed with identical surface areas and with the same weight of extracted cells.

B. Results and Discussion

1. Water Permeation Across Reaggregated Stratum Corneum

Discs of reaggregated SC were mounted in the diffusion apparatus, tritiated water was applied to the surface of the discs, and water permeation across the discs was measured. Permeation was linear for at least 48 hr indicating that the discs remained cohesive throughout the test period.

In Figure 6, water fluxes normalized for thickness (each had the same fixed diffusional area) are presented for a variety of discs. There is a definite relationship between water permeation and the amount of calf lipid added to reaggregate the calf SC cells. At the lowest amount of lipid tested (0.01 mg lipid per milligram cells), discs frequently became leaky or lost integrity, and no meaningful fluxes could be measured. At higher lipid/cell ratios, water flux was inversely proportional to the amount of lipid added until a plateau was reached at about 0.04 mg lipid per milligram cells, whereupon additional lipid had no influence on water flux. At the plateau, reaggregated calf SC had a flux of 1.0 ± 0.5 mg/hr/cm^2/mm path length (average ± range). This is close to the values obtained for intact SC.[4,14]

On the other hand, when plantar lipid was added to calf SC, a similar relationship between lipid and water flux was observed (Figure 6), but a plateau occurred at a higher flux — approximately 2.5 ± 0.8 mg/hr/cm^2/mm length. (Intact plantar SC has a flux of about 10 mg/cm^2/hr.[4])

2. Effect of Cellular Fraction on Water Permeation

Discs of reaggregated SC were formed with extracted epidermal lipids, and intact corneocytes, fragmented corneocytes or partially purified keratin and examined for water per-

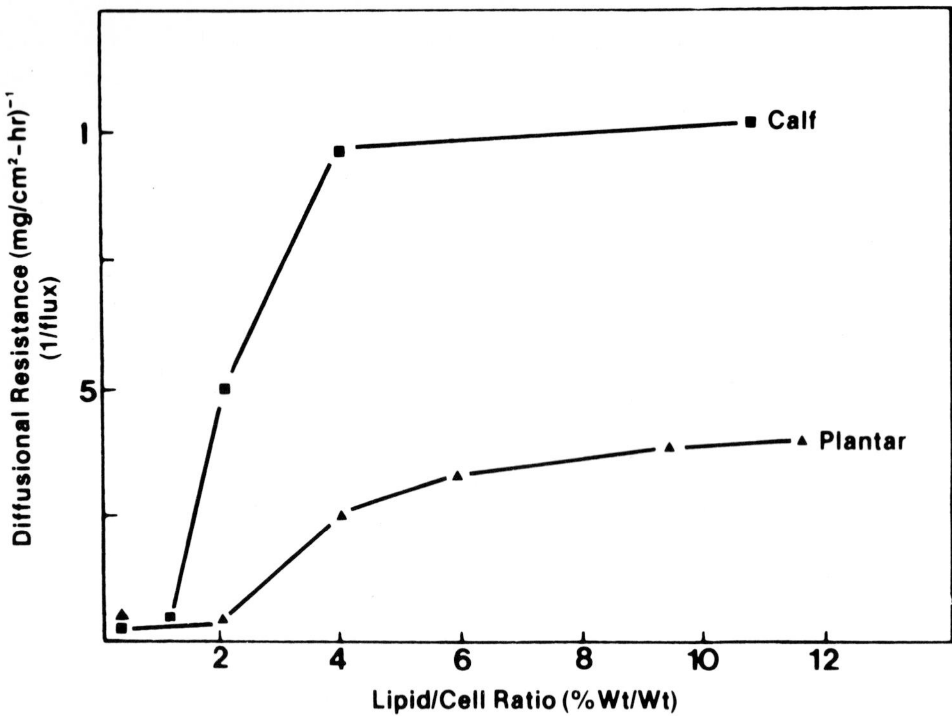

FIGURE 6. Dose response curve: lipid vs. diffusional resistance. The membrane used was calf stratum corneum cells reaggregated with varying amounts of calf (■) lipid (0.1, 1, 2, 4, 7, 10%) or plantar (▲) lipid (0.5, 2, 4, 6, 10%).

Table 5
EFFECTS OF LIPID ON DIFFUSIONAL RESISTANCE

System tested	Water flux mg/cm²/hr*
Intact SC	1.0
Isolated corneocytes +5% epidermal lipids (EL)	1.1
Fragmented corneocytes +5% EL	1.1
Purified keratin +5% EL	0.9
Purified keratin plus no lipid	10.2

Note: *Fluxes determined as in Figure 6. Results obtained are averages of at least three separate experiments. Results are normalized for SC thickness. Average of at least five determinations.

meation characteristics as above. Lipid concentration was 5% w/w in all cases. As Table 5 indicates, each of the systems tested had essentially identical fluxes, approximately 1.0 mg/hr/cm^2/mm path. Reducing the lipid content to 1% w/w in each of the systems had similar effects, namely, a substantial increase in water fluxes to approximately 7 mg/hr/cm^2/mm path (data not shown).

3. Effect of Lipid on Water Permeation

To assess the effect of the lipid material utilized for reaggregating isolated corneocytes on barrier function, reaggregated discs of SC were formed with or without epidermal lipids,

Table 6
EFFECTS OF LIPID ON STRATUM CORNEUM BARRIER QUALITY

Lipids used+	Water flux mg/cm²/hr*
Intact SC	1.0
Chloroform-methanol extracted SC	12.5
Ether extracted SC	2.5
Reaggregated SC	
With no lipids	11.5
With true epidermal lipids	1.1

Note: + All lipids used at 5% total weight of SC; * determined as described in Figure 6.

and their permeability characteristics were compared to those of intact or solvent extracted SC.

As Table 6 demonstrates, true epidermal lipids provided the corneocytes with the best barrier properties, which were similar to those seen in intact skin.

It is generally accepted that in the epidermis, cellular adhesion is maintained by desmosomes which provide rigid connections between cells; additional connections may be mediated by intercellular lipids.[19,27-31] Within the SC, most of the desmosomal connections have lessened and adhesion is therefore more dependent upon lipoidal intercellular cement. The study of isolated SC and of the intercellular lipids can provide a model for examining events leading to the ultimate dyshesion of SC cells (desquamation), as well as clarifying the role that lipids play in establishing the water barrier.

In this study, we have examined reaggregation and barrier properties of reconstituted membranes. Calf SC and plantar SC were utilized as representatives of barriers with either low or relatively high water permeability properties, respectively.[4]

After dissociating the SC fragments into individual cells by homogenization and extraction in organic solvent, calf SC was capable of spontaneous reaggregation only if lipid was added back to the cells. The lipid utilized seemed to have little or no specificity in modulating reaggregation, since individual lipids worked as effectively as the extracted total epidermal lipids. Plantar cells were incapable of such reassociation, whether their own lipids or other lipids were added back to them. No gross differences were observed by phase-contrast microscopy between extracted calf and plantar cells, and no major differences were found by TLC between calf and plantar lipids, except for the sparcity of sebaceous lipids in the plantar extract (data not shown).

When calf cells were trypsinized, no reaggregation could be obtained. Evidence obtained by light microscopy suggests that the trypsinization (at least at 4°C) was mild and produced no gross structural changes. It seems possible that the proteolytic treatment hydrolyses protein linkages necessary to stabilize cellular adhesion. Similarly, treatment of cells with a mix of glycolytic enzymes eliminated all but the most weak interactions between the SC cells and prevented any significant reaggregation.

Since calf cells aggregated poorly when little or no lipid was added back to the extracted cells, it seems likely that lipids nonspecifically provide the proper environment for surface proteins (presumably desmosomal proteins) to orient themselves and form membranes through cell-cell interactions.

Reaggregation did occur, however, if mechanically disrupted cells or partially purified keratin was mixed with the appropriate lipid mixtures. Evidently in plantar cells or with trypsinization, a component necessary for lipid mediated reaggregation is masked or lost.

With this in vitro technique we could dissect and reform SC membranes; thus, we examined some of the manipulations which could affect water permeability of the reaggregated membrane. When the lipid/cell ratio was varied, an inverse relationship was observed between amount of lipid added and water permeability. These results correspond well with recent observations of Elias et al.[32] This relationship was noted when either calf or plantar lipid was added to the calf cells; however, consistently higher fluxes were observed with the plantar lipid, and the plateau (where minimum flux was obtained) was reached at a somewhat higher lipid/cell ratio than with calf lipid.

In conclusion, this system is useful to probe in detail the barrier properties of the SC. With this system we have shown the importance of lipids, qualitatively and quantitatively, in modulating the barrier properties of the SC and differences in cellular contact mechanisms between plantar and calf SC.

IV. ARTIFICIAL MEMBRANES

Skin permeation studies conducted primarily with excised human skin specimens obtained at autopsy have demonstrated that the SC is the rate limiting membrane which behaves like a passive diffusion barrier.[4,33] Recently, Nacht et al.,[15] Yeung et al.,[5,6] and Franz[13] have shown good correlation between results obtained with excised human skin in diffusion cells and those obtained in vivo, supporting the use of excised human skin in vitro as a model to predict percutaneous absorption in vivo. However, this tissue is not readily available and, when obtained, it has a limited viability.[14]

The use of animal skin as a human model has been considered by several investigators.[12,14,33,34,35,36] It has been generally concluded that the skin of the miniature swine most closely resembles the permeability characteristics of human skin, at least for those compounds tested.[34] But even this animal model is far from convenient and it is subject to considerable biologic variation. A synthetic membrane that could mimic the permeability characteristics of human skin would provide a convenient, accessible, and reproducible experimental model without the inconveniences and limitations of the animal ones.

Synthetic membrane models have been used to study drug diffusion kinetics. Early studies using dimethylpolysiloxane membranes were conducted by Garrett and Chemburkar.[8] Barry et al.[37,38] used a cellulose acetate membrane to study the influence of temperature and nonionic surfactants on the permeation rate of various steroids. However, while the use of synthetic membranes in studying drug diffusion kinetics has not been unusual, no correlation has yet been established between the permeability characteristics of any such membranes and that of human skin.

Obviously, there are significant differences between a structurally simple synthetic membrane and the highly complex human skin. Even if we focus just on the SC, the effective permeability barrier of the skin, it is a multilayered membrane of considerable complexity. Recent electron microscopy studies conducted by Lavker[39] and Elias[40] have shown that the SC layers are held together by multilaminar sheets of lipids exquisitely organized to form a water barrier, as well as to provide cellular adhesion. Downing and Wertz[41] have proposed mechanisms for these lipids to organize themselves structurally as a sequence of hydrophobic and hydrophillic regions, while providing the necessary bridging between cell membranes. Thus, it seems logical that multilaminated membranes consisting of alternate hydrophillic and hydrophobic polymeric materials could provide a permeation model that would resemble the properties of human skin more closely than any of the individual materials per se. This model is examined from a theoretical viewpoint in the chapter by Berner and Cooper. To explore the use of synthetic membranes as a model for the study of drug permeation through human skin, we decided to use the compounds listed in Table 7 as model compounds.

These compounds have been widely studied in studies of skin permeability, they cover a

Table 7
PERMEANTS USED TO EVALUATE ARTIFICIAL MEMBRANE SYSTEMS

	Compound	Water solubility (mg/mℓ)
Polar		
	Water	∞
	Salicylic acid	2.0
	Hydrocortisone	0.53
Nonpolar		

reasonably wide range of polarity, and measurements of their relative permeability through the various membranes considered, compared to that through excised human skin, can be helpful to design a suitable model to mimic the permeability characteristics of human skin.

A. Methodology

The sources and preparation of the excised human skin and synthetic membranes are described in detail elsewhere.[42] The design of the diffusion cells used in all the synthetic membranes permeation studies is shown in Figure 7. These cells are similar to those used in skin permeation studies except that the Teflon® top is cylindrical instead of conical and fits snugly into the receptor compartment. A flat rubber O-ring is placed on top of the membrane and a perfect seal between the two compartments is achieved by tightening the set screws in the top. These diffusion cells have a larger effective diffusion area (8.03 cm^2) than those used with human tissue and a receptor volume of 45 mℓ. Other experimental conditions for the synthetic membranes permeation studies are similar to those previously described for human skin.

1. Experimental Procedure

Once the membrane is mounted between the two cell compartments, phosphate buffer pH 7.2 is added to the receptor side and the cell is equilibrated in the water bath at 30°C ± 0.5°C for 20 min. Then, 2 mℓ of the donor solution containing a radioactive tracer is accurately measured and applied to the membrane surface. The cell is then stoppered with a glass stopper to prevent fluid evaporation and to maintain steady-state conditions. At selected time intervals, an aliquot of the receptor buffer is withdrawn through the side arm of the lower compartment and analyzed for radioactive content by liquid scintillation counting.

B. Results

Table 8 summarizes the steady-state fluxes and permeability coefficients measured for different membranes with a saturated solution of salicylic acid in a 50% alcohol/water vehicle on the donor side. Of the various synthetic membranes tested, no single polymeric membrane was found to mimic the permeability of human skin. The Silastic® sheeting was found to yield fluxes and permeability coefficient which are closer to that of excised human skin than the other membranes tested. Cellulose acetate membranes annealed at different temperatures show notably higher fluxes than Silastic® sheeting, Diaflo®-ultrafiltration membrane and excised human skin. The annealing temperature has little or no effect on the permeability characteristics of the membranes, as all three cellulose acetate membranes, annealed at 60, 70, and 90°C, resulted in similar steady state diffusion rates for salicylic acid. On the other hand, a surprisingly slow steady-state flux rate (48 $\mu g/cm^2/hr$) for salicylic acid was observed for the noncellulose microporous Diaflo®-ultrafiltration membrane, probably because its superfine pore size might prevent adequate wetting of the membrane.

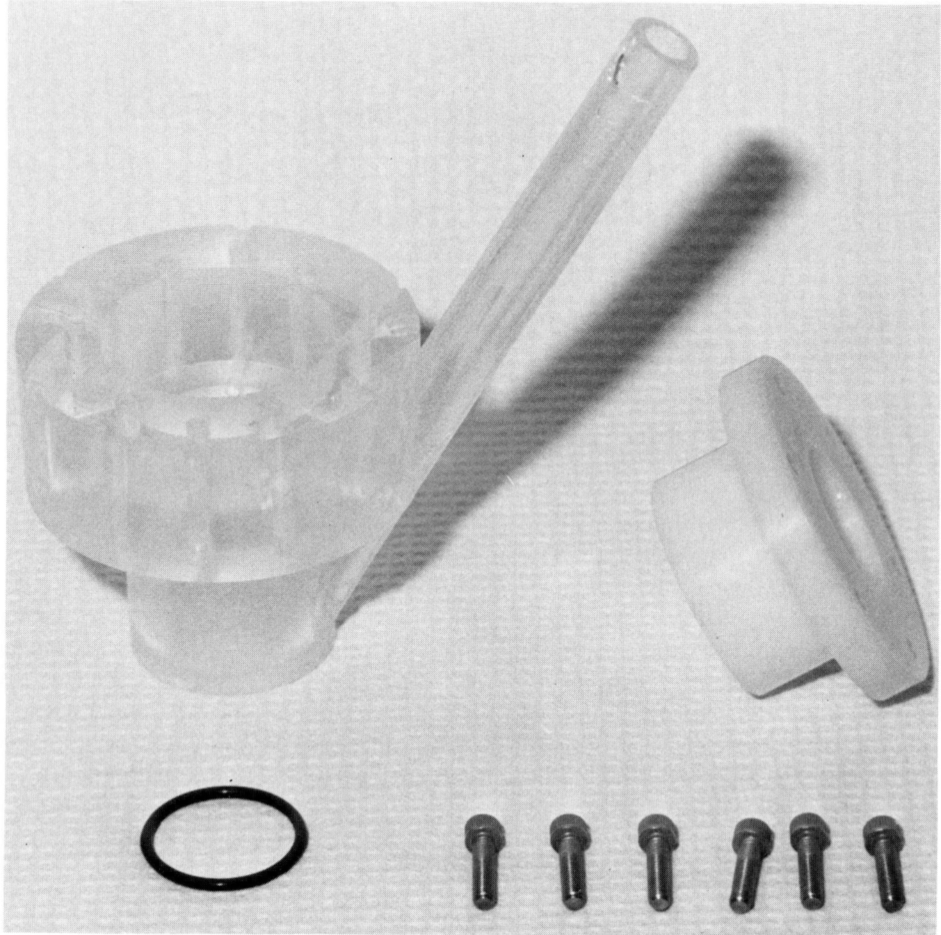

FIGURE 7. Disassembled diffusion cell used with synthetic membranes.

When three Silastic® sheetings or cellulose acetate membranes (annealed at 60°C) were stacked together to form a multilaminate membrane system, the steady-state fluxes of salicylic acid through these trilaminar membranes were significantly lower than through the single membrane, as expected, and close to those through human skin.

But when both types of membranes were combined to form a multimembrane with the Silastic® membrane sandwiched between two cellulose acetate membranes (CSC), the values obtained for the flux (402 μg/cm^2/hr) and permeability coefficient (6.38×10^{-3} cm/hr) were almost identical to those obtained with excised human skin (409 μg/cm^2/hr and 6.36×10^{-3} cm/hr).

Hydrocortisone, a much slower permeating specie, was also used for the evaluation of permeability characteristics of different membranes. Table 9 presents the steady-state flux and permeability coefficient of hydrocortisone from a 50% ethanol/water vehicle through each of the two artificial membranes and through the composite.

Cellulose acetate membrane alone, was found to be extremely permeable to hydrocortisone, with steady-state fluxes about 10^3 times faster than excised human skin. With Silastic® sheeting, the flux is about 8.8 times faster than excised human skin.

Again, the multimembrane sandwich system (CSC) yielded the closest steady-state flux (0.25 μg/cm^2/hr) and permeability coefficient (2.3×10^{-5} cm/hr) to those of excised human skin (0.07 μg/cm^2/hr and 0.7×10^{-5} cm/hr, respectively).

Table 8
STEADY STATE FLUX OF SALICYLIC ACID⁺ THROUGH VARIOUS MEMBRANES

Membrane	Flux ($\mu g/cm^2/hr$)	Ps* (cm/hr)
Cellulose acetate at		
60°C**	1124	1.83×10^{-2}
70°C**	1132	1.84×10^{-2}
90°C**	1079	1.76×10^{-2}
Diaflo® — ultrafiltration	48	7.80×10^{-4}
Silastic® surgical sheet	703	1.14×10^{-2}
Trilaminar cellulose acetate	421	6.85×10^{-3}
Trilaminar Silastic® surgical sheet	167	2.72×10^{-3}
Multimembrane system (cellulose acetate-Silastic® sheet-cellulose acetate)	402	6.38×10^{-3}
Human skin	409	6.36×10^{-3}

Note: ⁺ In all cases, the donor was a saturated solution of salicylic acid in ethanol/water (50/50); * Ps = permeability coefficient (standardized flux); ** annealing temperature.

Table 9
STEADY STATE FLUX OF HYDROCORTISONE⁺ THROUGH VARIOUS MEMBRANES

Membrane	Flux ($\mu g/cm^2/hr$)	Ps* (cm/hr)
Cellulose acetate	73.9	6.4×10^{-3}
Silastic® sheeting	0.61	5.3×10^{-5}
Multimembrane system (cellulose acetate-Silastic® sheet-cellulose acetate)	0.25	2.3×10^{-5}
Human skin	0.07	7.0×10^{-6}

Note: ⁺ In all cases, the donor was a saturated solution of hydrocortisone in ethanol/water (50/50); * Ps = permeability coefficient (standardized flux)

Water permeation through various model membrane systems and excised human skin was measured. As results summarized in Table 10 indicate, while the water fluxes and permeability coefficients through the trilaminated cellulose acetate or Silastic® surgical sheet are quite different from excised human skin, those through the CSC membrane system are quite similar, with permeability coefficient only 1.5 times higher than that of human skin.

To further test the validity of the CSC model in the evaluation of drug-release from different vehicles and to better correlate the diffusion characteristics of this membrane system with those of human skin, the permeation of salicylic acid from saturated solutions in different hydroalcoholic vehicles was assessed. The steady-state flux of salicylic acid from each vehicle was determined for both membranes and the apparent permeability coefficients were calculated; the results are summarized in Table 11. The ratio of the permeability coefficient obtained with the CSC membrane (Pm) to that obtained with human skin (Ps) was found to be fairly constant, ranging from 1.5 to 1.8. Thus, in all cases salicylic acid penetrated

Table 10
PERMEABILITY OF WATER THROUGH EXCISED HUMAN SKIN AND THROUGH THE CSC MULTIMEMBRANE SYSTEM

	Flux ($mg/cm^2/hr$)
Excised human skin	0.62
CSC multimembrane	0.42
Trilaminated cellulose acetate	4.62
Silastic® surgical sheeting	0.06

Table 11
SALICYLIC ACID PENETRATION — EFFECT OF VEHICLE⁺ (MULTI-MEMBRANE SYSTEM VS. HUMAN SKIN)

	CSC Multimembrane		Excised human skin		
Vehicle	Flux ($\mu g/cm^2/hr$)	Pm* (cm/hr)	Flux ($\mu g/cm^2/hr$)	Ps* (cm/hr)	Pm/Ps**
Deionized H_2O	43	2.40×10^{-2}	28	1.32×10^{-2}	1.8
30% EtOH	136	1.04×10^{-2}	92	6.13×10^{-3}	1.7
50% EtOH	402	9.44×10^{-3}	409	6.40×10^{-3}	1.5
70% EtOH	642	3.96×10^{-3}	523	2.55×10^{-3}	1.5
EtOH	1571	2.68×10^{-3}	638	1.55×10^{-3}	1.7

Note: ⁺ In all cases, the donor was a saturated solution of salicylic acid in the indicated vehicle; * Pm = Permeability coefficient for the multimembrane system; ** Ps = Permeability coefficient for excised human skin.

Table 12
HYDROCORTISONE PREPARATION — EFFECT OF VEHICLE (MULTI-MEMBRANE SYSTEM VS. HUMAN SKIN)

	CSC Multi-membrane		Excised human skin		
Membrane	Flux ($\mu g/cm^2/hr$)	Pm* (cm/hr)	Flux ($\mu g/cm^2/hr$)	Ps** (cm/hr)	Pm/Ps
Saturated in saline	1.56×10^{-2}	2.97×10^{-5}	6.90×10^{-3}	1.31×10^{-5}	2.3
1% in a hydroalcoholic vehicle***	1.46×10^{-1}	1.42×10^{-2}	6.13×10^{-2}	5.96×10^{-6}	2.4
0.5% in polymeric vehicle****	2.65×10^{-2}	4.65×10^{-6}	8.99×10^{-3}	1.58×10^{-6}	2.9

Note: *Pm = Permeability coefficient for the multimembrane system; **Ps = Permeability coefficient for excised human skin; ***Vehicle used was ethanol/water (50/50); ****Vehicle contains 5% hydromethacrylate polymer in ethanol/water (50/50).

through the artificial membrane system approximately 1.6 times faster than through human skin. Table 12 summarizes the steady-state permeation rates of hydrocortisone from different vehicles through the CSC membrane and through excised human skin. The Pm/Ps ratios were also computed and again were found to be rather constant, ranging from 2.3 to 2.9.

C. Discussion and Applications

The SC is the protective epithelial membrane of the body and consists of an aggregate lamellae of cornified cells composed mainly of keratin. These keratinized layers of cells are held together by polar lipids which constitute the effective water barrier of the skin. These lipids can be pictured as a multilaminate of alternate hydrophilic and lipophilic regions.

Therefore, a multilayered membrane with both hydrophilic and lipophilic properties can be rationalized *a priori* as mimicking the critical permeation paths of the stratum corneum.

The compounds selected as model permeants in this investigation, salicylic acid and hydrocortisone, are of interest in topical pharmacology and, although both are capable of permeating into human skin, they do so at significantly different rates. Water was also used, since it could probably be considered the standard for human skin permeability studies.

In the present investigation, the type of membranes employed in the initial screening has been previously used by other researchers to study drug diffusion kinetics.[39,40,43] Confirming the previous findings of Garrett and Chembuker,[8] the diffusion and permeation characteristics of salicylic acid and hydrocortisone through Silastic® medical grade sheeting indicate that this membrane acts as a lipid-like barrier and that the diffusion kinetics through this membrane are in accordance with Fick's law.

Conversely, the different types of cellulose acetate membranes tested behaved as a hydrophilic barrier, and the annealing temperature of the cellulose acetate did not alter the permeability characteristic of the membranes.

Of the membranes tested, the cellulose acetate and the Silastic® sheeting show some permeability characteristics similar to those of excised human skin. However, these membranes are either hydrophilic or lipophilic in nature and thus, they are only suitable for screening either hydrophilic or lipophilic compounds. The concurrent use of both types of membrane provides the capability of screening a wider range of compounds for their permeability characteristics, offering distinct advantages over a single membrane system.

When studied both with salicylic acid and with hydrocortisone as model drugs, the CSC multimembrane was found to yield fluxes and permeability coefficients very close to those of intact excised human skin, even though it was consistently found to be somewhat more permeable than SC. Perhaps even closer values to those of human skin could be obtained with a multilaminated membrane composed of more than three layers or with a combination of different hydrophilic and lipophilic membranes. However, from a practical point of view, this would only make the experimental set-up more cumbersome while probably, it would not significantly increase the relative validity of the data obtained, compared to real-life situations.

Further support for the usefulness of this multimembrane system as a model for excised human skin is provided by the apparent permeability coefficients of water through these two models. The remarkably close permeability coefficients for water found with the two membrane systems indicate they share very similar permeability characteristics. We also compared the permeability coefficients of the CSC multimembrane and excised human skin for salicylic acid, using simple alcohol-water donor solutions with different ethanol concentrations. As predicted by the theory, the flux of salicylic acid through either membrane system increases with the increase of ethanol (and drug) concentration in the donor solution. This further extends the observation that the permeation through the CSC membranes is Fickian in nature.

The relatively constant ratio obtained between the permeability coefficient of salicylic acid and hydrocortisone through the multimembrane systems and excised human skin over a wide range of ethanol concentrations supports the similarity in the permeability characteristics of the two membrane models. Thus, the rank orders of drug permeation through the CSC membrane and through excised human skin were the same. A useful membrane model system should exhibit the same permeability to different drugs as excised human skin, or at least it should exhibit a constant ratio of these permeabilities; the observed 1.6 times and 2.5 times higher permeability determined for salicylic acid and hydrocortisone, respectively, represent an acceptable multiple. Since the same multiple was obtained with drug permeability coefficients which ranged from 10^{-3} to 10^{-5} cm/hr, it is reasonable to expect that a 2 to 3 times higher flux will be obtained for all drugs or delivery systems. Optimally, this small discrepancy in flux might be corrected by using a somewhat thicker or more complex membrane system.

In summary, the results obtained suggest the usefulness of the CSC multimembrane system as a permeability model for excised human skin and as a suitable model for the preliminary screening of drug release from different vehicles and formulations, to predict their relative ability to deliver drug for skin penetration. However, further experimental and theoretical studies of such membrane models are required.

REFERENCES

1. **Chowhan, Z. T. and Pritchard, R.,** Effect of surfactants on percutaneous absorption of naproxen, *J. Pharm. Sci.,* 67, 1272, 1978.
2. **Bettley, F. R.,** The influence of soap on the permeability of the epidermis, *Br. J. Dermatol.,* 73, 448, 1961.
3. **Bronaugh, R. L., Congdon, E. R., and Scheuplein, R. J.,** The effect of cosmetic vehicles on the penetration of *N*-nitrosodiethanolamine, *J. Invest. Dermatol.,* 76, 94, 1981.
4. **Scheuplein, R. J. and Blank, I. H.,** Permeability of the skin, *Physiol. Rev.,* 51, 702, 1971.
5. **Yeung, D., Nacht, S., Bucks, D., and Maibach, H. I.,** Benzoyl peroxide: percutaneous penetration and metabolic disposition, *J. Am. Acad. Dermatol.,* 9, 920, 1983.
6. **Yeung, D., Kantor, S., Nacht, S., and Gans, E. H.,** Percutaneous absorption, blood levels, and urinary excretion of resorcinol applied topically in humans, *Int. J. Dermatol.,* 22, 321, 1983.
7. **Lyman, D. J., Loo, B. H., and Crawford, R. W.,** New synthetic membranes for dialysis. I. A copolymer-ester membrane system, *Biochemistry,* 3, 985, 1964.
8. **Garrett, E. R. and Chemburkar, P. B.,** Evaluation, control, and prediction of drug diffusion through polymeric membranes, *J. Pharm. Sci.,* 57, 944, 1968.
9. **Kooten, W. J. and Mali, J. W. H.,** The significance of sweet ducts in permeation experiments on isolated cadaverons human skin, *Dermatology,* 132, 141, 1966.
10. **Coldman, M. F., Poulsen, B. J. and Higuchi, T.,** Enhancement of percutaneous absorption by the use of volatile and nonvolatile systems as vehicles, *J. Pharm. Sci.,* 58, 1098, 1969.
11. **Menczel, E. and Maibach, H. I.,** In vitro percutaneous penetration of benzyl alcohol and testosterone, *J. Invest. Dermatol.,* 54, 386, 1970.
12. **Wolejsza, N. F. and Verar, V.,** Comparison of guinea pig and fetal hog skin, *J. Soc. Cosmet. Chem.,* 30, 375, 1979.
13. **Franz, T. J.,** Percutaneous absorption. On the relevance of in vitro data, *J. Invest. Dermatol.,* 67, 190, 1975.
14. **Galey, W. R., Lonsdale, H. K., and Nacht, S.,** The in vitro permeability of skin and buccal mucosa to selected drugs of tritiated water, *J. Invest. Dermatol.,* 67, 713, 1976.
15. **Nacht, S., Yeung, D., Beasley, J. N., Anjo, M. A., and Maibach, H. I.,** Benzoyl peroxide: percutaneous penetration and metabolic disposition, *J. Am. Acad. Dermatol.,* 4, 31, 1981.
16. **Rogers, A. W.,** *Techniques of Autoradiography,* Elsevier/North Holland, Amsterdam, 1979.
17. **Scheuplein, R. J.,** Mechanism of percutaneous absorption, *J. Invest. Dermatol.,* 45, 344, 1964.
18. **Marks, R. and Dawber, R. P. R.,** Skin surface biopsy: an improved technique for the examination of the horny layer, *Br. J. Dermatol.,* 84, 117, 1971.
19. **Elias, P. M. and Friend, D. S.,** The permeability barrier in mammalian epidermis, *J. Cell. Biol.,* 65, 105, 1975.
20. **Elias, P. M., Goerke, J., and Friend, D. S.,** Permeability barrier lipids: composition and influence on epidermal structure, *J. Invest. Dermatol.,* 69, 535, 1977.
21. **Wertz, P. W. and Downing, D. T.,** Glycolipids in mammalian epidermis, structure and function as water barrier, *Science,* 217, 1261, 1982.
22. **Grey, G. M. and Yardley, H. J.,** Lipid composition of cells isolated from pig, human, and rat epidermis, *J. Lipid Res.,* 16, 434, 1975.
23. **Yardley, H.,** personal communication.
24. **Bligh, E. G. and Dyer, W. J.,** A rapid method of total lipid extraction and purification, *Can. J. Biochem. Physiol.,* 37, 911, 1959.
25. **Widra, A.,** Ascosporogenesis by *Nannizzia Grubyia* on a soluble fraction of keratin, *Mycopathologia,* 30, 141, 1966.
26. **Smith, W. P., Christensen, M. S., Nacht, S., and Gans, E. H.,** Effects of lipids on the aggregation and permeability of human stratum corneum, *J. Invest. Dermatol.,* 78, 7, 1982.

27. **Stachelin, L. A.,** The structure and function of intercellular junctions, *Int. Rev. Cytol.*, 39, 191, 1974.
28. **Elias, P. M., McNutt, N. S., and Fend, D. S.,** Membrane alterations during cornification of mammalian squamons epithelia, *Anat. Rec.*, 189, 577, 1977.
29. **Holubar, K. and Wolff, K.,** Keratinosomenals epidermale lysosomen, *Arch. Klin. Exp. Dermatol.*, 231, 1, 1967.
30. **Weinstock, M. and Wilgram, G. F.,** Fine structural observations on the formation and enzymatic activity of keratinosomes in mouse filiform papillae, *J. Ultrastruct. Res.*, 30, 362, 1970.
31. **Hashimoto, K.,** Cementsome, a new interpretation of the membrane-coating granule, *Arch. Dermatol. Forsch.*, 240, 349, 1971.
32. **Elias, P. M., Cooper, E. R., Korc, A., and Brown, B. E.,** Importance of stratum corneum structural parameters vs. lipid composition for percutaneous absorption, *Clin. Res.*, 28, 134, 1980.
33. **Idson, B.,** Percutaneous absorption, *J. Pharm. Sci.*, 64, 901, 1975.
34. **Bartek, M. J., LaBudde, J. A., and Maibach, H. I.,** Skin permeability in vivo: comparison in rat, rabbit, pig, and man, *J. Invest. Dermatol.*, 58, 114, 1972.
35. **Wester, R. C. and Maibach, H. I.,** Percutaneous absorption in the rhesus monkey compared to man, *Toxicol. Appl. Pharmacol.*, 32, 394, 1975.
36. **Reimenratch, W. B., Shellquist, E. M., Shipwash, E. A., Jeberberg, W. W., and Krueger, G. G.,** Percutaneous penetration in the hairless dog. Weanling and grafted Athymic nude mouse. Evaluation of models for predicting skin penetration in man, *Br. J. Dermatol.*, 3(27), 1123, 1984.
37. **Barry, B. W., Brace, A. R.,** Permeation of oestrone, osteradiol, osteriol, and dexamethasone across cellulose acetate membrane, *J. Pharm. Pharmacol.*, 29, 397, 1977.
38. **Barry, B. W. and El Eini, D. I. D.,** Influence of non-ionic surfactants on permeation of hydrocortisone, dexamethasone, testosterone, and progesterone across cellulose acetate membrane, *J. Pharm. Pharmacol.*, 28, 219, 1976.
39. **Lavker, R. S.,** Membrane coating granules: the fate of the discharged lamallae, *J. Ultrastruct. Res.*, 55, 79, 1976.
40. **Elias, P. M.,** Epidermal lipids, membranes, and keratinization, *Int. J. of Dermatol.*, 20, 1, 1981.
41. **Wertz, P. W. and Downing, D. T.,** Glycolipids in mammalian epidermis: structure and function in the water barrier, *Science*, 217, 1261, 1982.
42. **Yeung, D. and Nacht, S.,** Artificial membranes and skin permeability in, *Percutaneous Absorption, Mechanisms-Methodology-Drug Delivery*, Bronaugh, R. and Maibach, H., Eds., Marcel Dekker, 1985.
43. **Herzog, K. A. and Swarbrick, J.,** Drug permeation through thin-model membranes, *J. Pharm. Sci.*, 60 1666, 1971.

Chapter 3

MODELS OF SKIN PERMEABILITY

Bret Berner and Eugene R. Cooper

TABLE OF CONTENTS

I. INTRODUCTION

The skin is widely recognized for its outstanding barrier properties compared with other biological membranes. Although the skin is a good barrier, molecules are absorbed percutaneously and dermal toxicity is a consideration for all agents contacting the skin. Coupled with this concern for toxicity is the increasing demonstration that the skin can be used as a port of entry for drugs. These factors have greatly increased the need for information regarding percutaneous absorption. Skin transport experiments are time consuming, however, and it is not practical to obtain transport on every molecule of interest. Thus arises the need for modeling skin penetration to guide in the design of experiments and hopefullly to reliably predict cutaneous transport.

From existing skin transport data, it is reasonable to assume that there are at least two parallel pathways for diffusion. The flux (at constant concentration), of polar molecules is independent of partition coefficient[1] and can be enhanced by surfactant treatment.[2] This pathway is often referred to as the polar or aqueous pathway. As the polarity is decreased, the flux becomes a function of partiton coefficient,[3] and this pathway is referred to as the nonpolar or lipophilic pathway.

The first part of this chapter treats these two pathways as parallel and independent and then, a synthesis of the two pathways is presented. The value of looking at these two pathways separately is that the analysis is simpler and one can individually examine those properties that will increase the flux through the pathway.

To model skin permeation more realistically, these pathways need to be combined. In a later section, the skin is modeled as two parallel pathways (1) a continuous polar pathway and (2) a continuous lipophilic pathway. Although this two parallel pathway model has not been rigorously tested, many predictions of this model are quite successful.

To agree with the laminated anatomical structure of the stratum corneum and to determine the area fraction of each of the parallel pathways, one should also include a third parallel pathway: a heterogeneous pathway consisting of alternating hydrophobic and hydrophilic membranes. However, steady-state skin permeation data are rather insensitive to the existence of this third pathway. For simplicity, the two-parallel pathway model is studied in the body of the paper, and the three-parallel pathway model is relegated to Appendix C. Discussions of water permeation and the diffusion constant for flexible molecules are also included in the appendices.

The above two-parallel pathway model is studied for steady-state permeation, and the steady state is rather insensitive to the actual geometry of the heterogeneous media in the stratum corneum. While this insensitivity allows one to obtain reasonable predictions from a steady-state model, nonsteady-state diffusion is highly sensitive to the arrangment of the heterogeneous media. An example of this sensitivity, presented in Appendix D, is the remarkable nonsteady-state permeation of oil-water multilaminates. It is through such nonsteady-state analysis that details of the pathways through the stratum corneum may be elucidated.

II. POLAR PATHWAY

In this analysis, we study the fully hydrated stratum corneum. Permeants through the polar portions of the stratum corneum must partition into regions swollen with water (see Appendix A). Consequently, the partition coefficient for these aqueous regions should be near unity and the steady-state flux through this polar pathway, J_p, is approximately

$$J_p = D_p C_w / l \tag{1}$$

where D_p is the effective diffusion constant in this pathway, l is the thickness of the stratum corneum, and C_w is the concentration in water. Compounds which permeate predominantly through this polar pathway should penetrate independent of partition coefficients.

In contrast, the diffusion coefficient will be a function of the size and shape of the molecule and as a first approximation for rigid molecules the free-volume theory of Bueche[4] can be used to write

$$D_p = D_p^{(0)} e^{-B_p M} \tag{2}$$

where M is the molecular weight and B_p and D_p^0 are constants. Although there are not sufficient data on polar molecules to demonstrate the utility of Equation 2, an equation of this form will be shown to apply for the lipophilic pathway.

Equation 1 indicates that to increase the flux through this polar pathway, one must increase the solubility in water. Yalkowsky[5] has derived an equation for water solubility as a function of partition coefficient and melting point, but this equation is limited to molecules with partition coefficients greater than unity. Thus, for polar molecules one must modify the equation or measure the solubility. Equation 2 predicts that the diffusion coefficient and, hence, the flux will decrease exponentially with size. If this prediction is true, then only relatively small molecules will cross the skin via this pathway. Chemical agents which can alter the conformation of the proteins which determine D_p^0 and B_p should increase the penetration of polar molecules.[2,6] It has been previously mentioned that surfactants are quite effective at altering this pathway and we have also observed tha' heat denaturation (100°C) will have dramatic effects on the penetration of polar molecules.[2]

The transport of water is a special case since it is a very small molecule and because it alters its own penetration.[7] In fact, water can affect the penetration of other molecules as well.[8] A separate discussion of water transport is given in Appendix A, where evidence is presented that diffusion is a solution-diffusion process and does not just involve aqueous pores.

III. THE NONPOLAR PATHWAY

A. An Overview

The majority of cosmetic agents and drugs are lipophilic and thus transport across the nonpolar or lipophilic pathway is perhaps the most important topic for practical applications. As in the previous section, we consider the flux at steady state, J_L, and write

$$J_L = \frac{D_L C_L}{l} \tag{3}$$

where D_L is the lipid diffusion coefficient, l is the thickness of stratum corneum, and C_L is the concentration in the lipid at the outer interface of the stratum corneum.

From a saturated solution, the maximum flux of drug across skin is determined by (1) C_L, the solubility of the lipophilic drug in the stratum corneum lipids and by (2) D_L, the mobility of the drug in these lipids. For crystalline drugs, the solubility of a lipophilic material in lipid is largely given by the ideal solution theory.[9] That is, the solubility of a drug in skin is predominantly determined by how much the drug likes itself — the crystalline lattice energy or drug melting point,[5] T_m.

The diffusion constant of the drug, D_L, may be related to the activation energy required to open a hole in the skin lipids sufficiently large enough to allow the permeant molecule to make a diffusional jump. This activation energy used to create the hole is basically the surface tension of the skin lipids times the surface area of the hole.[4] The surface area is determined by the molecular weight. Thus, the molecular weight, M, of rigid drug molecules should determine the activation energy and D_L should be exponentially related to M.

The predicted rule of thumb is that the maximum flux of drug through skin should decrease by factors of 5 and 10, respectively, for an increase in molecular weight by 100 or 100°C in melting point.

B. The Theory

As before, D_L for rigid molecules is written as[5]

$$D - D_L^{(O)}e^{-B_L M} \tag{4}$$

where D_L^O and B_L are constants. The diffusion constant for flexible molecules is discussed in Appendix B.

To maximize the flux, one needs to keep the size of the molecule to a minimum and to maximize C_L. (The converse holds for reducing the flux, which is often the case for cosmetic ingredients, pesticides, etc.) Since one does not usually measure C_L in skin lipids, it can be approximated by determining the solubility in a lipophilic solvent. If the drug is lipophilic, then a reasonable assumption is that C_L^{max}, the solubility in the lipid, is governed by the ideal solution theory. This assumption has been shown to be quite good for predicting the maximum flux of benzoic acid derivatives[10] and will be employed here to arrive at some useful generalizations.

For a lipid continuous pathway, X_s, the mole fraction solubility of a crystalline drug, is given by the ideal solution theory as:[5,9]

$$X_s = \exp[\Delta H_f(T - T_m)/RTT_m] \tag{5}$$

where ΔH_f is the heat of fusion, T is the absolute temperature, and R is the gas constant. ΔH_f may be related to the entropy of fusion, ΔS_f, by:[5]

$$\Delta H_f = T_m \Delta S_f \tag{6}$$

To a good approximation for rigid aromatics,[5]

$$\Delta S_f \simeq 13.5 \text{ e.u.} \tag{7}$$

(While this chapter will concern itself with rigid aromatics, Yalkowsky has derived another useful relationship for ΔS_f for flexible solutes.[5] Substituting Equations 6 and 7 for rigid aromatics into Equation 5, we find that

$$X_s = \exp[6.79(1 - T_m/T)] \tag{8}$$

The drug solubility in g/mℓ, is

$$C_L^{max} = \frac{MW \exp[6.79(1 - T_m/T)] \times 10^{-3}}{1 - \exp[6.79(1 - T_m/T)]} \tag{9}$$

where W is a constant (the molecular weight of the lipid component in skin). Thus, the solubility of drug in stratum corneum decreases exponentially with T_m and increases linearly with the molecular weight M. Note that this M dependence is small compared to the M dependence of D_L.

Equations 4 and 9 point to two key variables in maximizing or minimizing the flux across

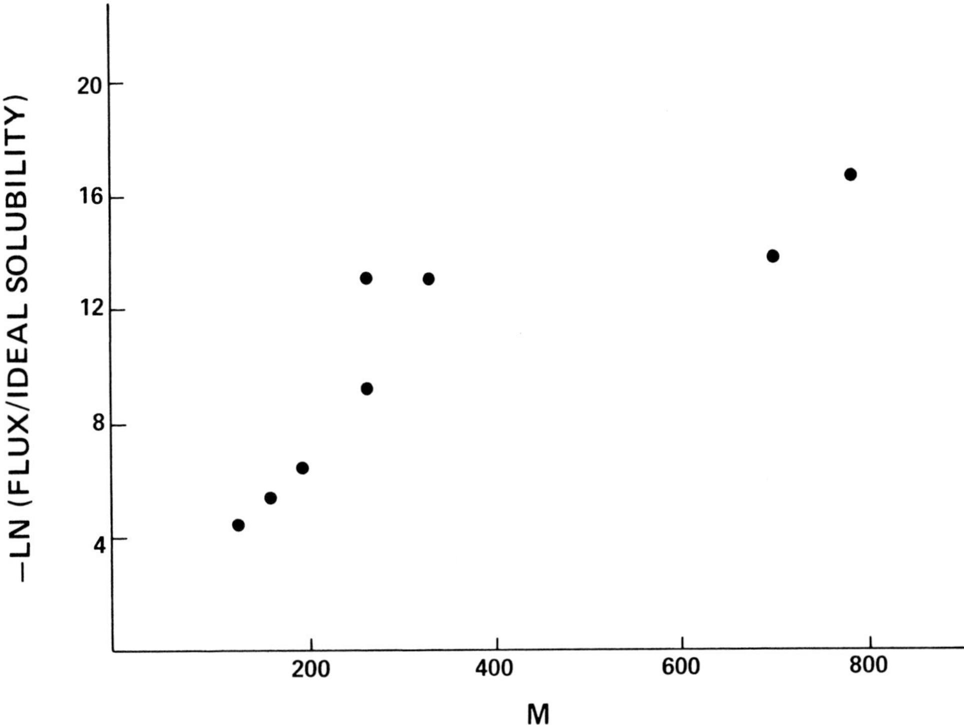

FIGURE 1. The logarithm of the diffusion constant (the experimental flux/ideal solution solubility) is plotted vs. molecular weight.[12]

the nonpolar pathway: the molecular weight or size and the melting point. The reduction of such a complex problem into two common variables is an oversimplification, but it does factor out the main processes that are at work. As mentioned before, the melting point variable has been shown to be the dominant factor for benzoate flux where the size and, hence, D_L is essentially constant. A recent study of the cutaneous flux of 36 compounds of various sizes and melting points[11] has shown that the model accounts for much of the data for fluxes ranging over six orders of magnitude. Molecular volume was used instead of molecular weight, but since the two quantities are highly correlated either one may be used. The quantity B_L is a fundamental property of the skin and is related to the energy required to make a hole in the lipids or the internal pressure of the lipids.

Additonal support for this model can be obtained by applying it to existing data in the literature.[12] A plot of ln $[J/C_L^{max}]$ vs. M (where C_L^{max} is calculated from Equation 9) for these data is shown in Figure 1. The correlation coefficient is 0.87 and $B_L = 0.016$. This value of B_L compares with $B_L = 0.014$ obtained for the set of molecules described earlier.[11] The results are almost identical and are promising, considering the fact that the molecules, the tissue, and the investigators are different. Thus, it seems that the model can be quite useful in estimating the maximum flux of lipophilic cosmetic ingredients, pesticides, drugs, etc. If more accuracy than an order of magnitude is needed, a multiple pathway theory is required, or it is necessary to perform the experiment.

IV. THE TWO-PARALLEL PATHWAY MODEL FOR SKIN PERMEATION

A. An Overview

The detailed geometry of the pathways in stratum corneum is unknown and thus, the appropriate boundary-value diffusion equations cannot be written down. As a first approximation, one may consider a two-parallel pathway model consisting of (1) a continuous polar pathway and (2) a continuous nonpolar pathway.

For these two parallel pathways, the flux of drug through stratum corneum is the sum of the fluxes from the continuous polar and nonpolar regions. That is [13]

$$J = J_p + J_L \tag{10}$$

or

$$J = (A_p D_p + A_L P D_L)\, C_w \tag{11}$$

Here, A_p and A_L are the area fractions of the polar and nonpolar pathways, respectively. From fitting water penetration data,[7] one finds that $A_p \approx 0.1$. P, is the partition coefficient of the nonpolar phase (for simplicity, the octanol-water partition coefficient) and D_p and D_L are given by Equations 2 and 4, respectively. For lack of information, we assume that $B_L = B_p$. While the data of Scheuplein and Blank for long-chain alcohols would suggest a factor of two difference between B_L and B_p, the two-parallel pathway model treats these long-chain alcohol data by the extended free-volume theory presented in Appendix B. Further studies are required to fit separately B_L and B_p. The water solubility, C_w, may either be measured or for $P \geqslant 1$ may be predicted by the theory of Yalkowsky,[5] using the equation:

$$C_w = \frac{M \exp[-(0.023\, T_f + 1.59)]\, 5.5 \times 10^{-2}}{P[1 - \exp[-(0.023\, T_f + 1.59)]/P]} \tag{12}$$

where T_f is the melting point of the drug in degrees Celsius. Thus, there are three key parameters of the drug to predict skin penetration: M, P, and either C_w or T_f.

The beauty of this two parallel pathway approach is the ability to predict a wide variety of skin penetration data with a knowledge of P and M in addition to T_f for $P \geqslant 1$ or C_w for $P < 1$. By inserting these variables into Equation 11, one can estimate the maximum skin permeation within a factor of four (Figure 2). Thus, this theory may be used (1) to estimate the flux of drug and consequently, to determine whether a drug is a reasonable transdermal candidate, (2) to compare probable fluxes of a series of congeners of a drug, or (3) to predict the dominant transport pathway.

This theory still requires rigorous experimental testing including (1) proper choice of molecules to span P, M, and C_w space and (2) nonlinear curve fitting of the five adjustable parameters. Currently, this model is best regarded as a method of obtaining surprisingly good "ballpark" calculations for skin permeation. The mathematical presentation of a more complex three-parallel pathway model is included in Appendix C.

B. The Predictions of the Two-Pathway Model

The predictions of the two-pathway model for (1) drug permeability, (2) the flux of ionized vs. unionized forms of salicyclic acid, and (3) the selective penetration enhancement of highly polar molecules by surfactants will now be considered. Clearly, the predictions of the model for water permeation are accurate since the model is fit to these data.

Using Equations 11 and 12 and the appropriate values of the constants, one may predict the flux of crystalline drug from saturated aqueous solution. A plot of ln J_{max} (experimental) vs. ln J_{max} (theory) for compounds from References 1 and 10 is shown in Figure 2. For this plot, $r^2 = 0.92$. To set the proper perspective, $r^2 = 0.46$ for J_{max} (experimental) vs. J_{max} (theory). That is, the good fit is an artifact of the natural logarithms, but is excellent

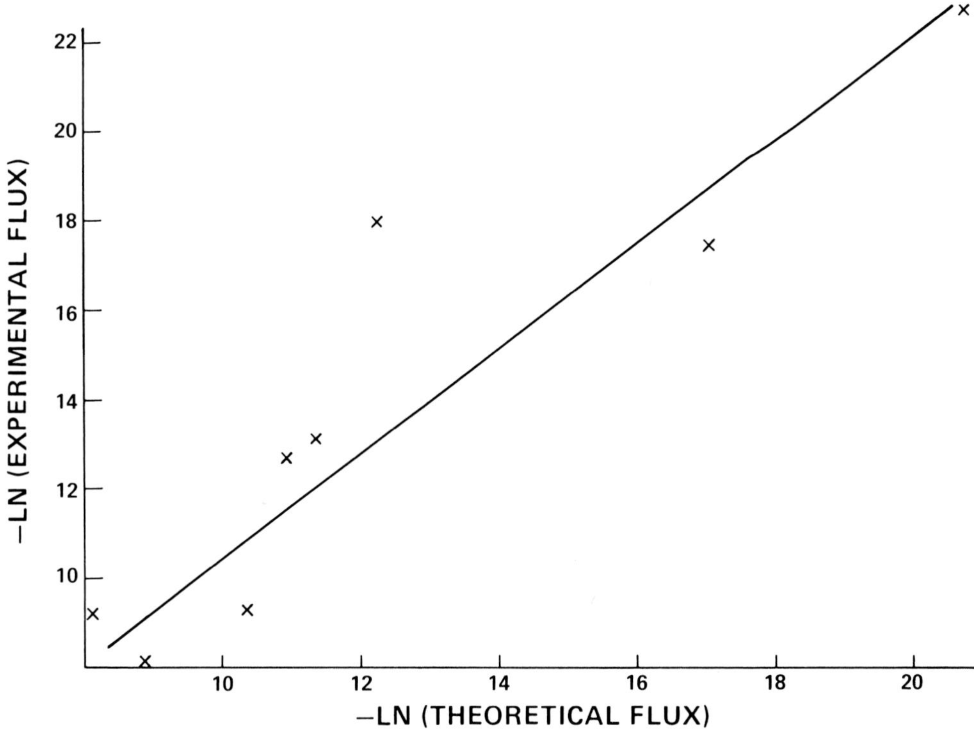

FIGURE 2. A plot of the experimental and theoretical skin permeation as predicted by the two-pathway model.[12]

compared to other theories for skin permeation. Consequently, this two-parallel pathway model only estimates the flux of drug through skin within a factor of four.

The qualitative difference between the single nonpolar pathway and the two-parallel pathway models' treatment of data is the suggestion that drugs with high molecular weight and small P are more accurately treated by the latter model. One test to distinguish between the models occurs when the conversion of a drug-free base to a hydrochloride results in a small decrease in melting point and a large increase in water solubility. The single-pathway theory predicts that the free base should penetrate better than the hydrochloride. Under these unusual conditions, the two-parallel pathway model can predict the reverse relationship or equal penetration.

The flux of unionized drugs are generally much larger than that for the ionized form of the same drug[2,12] For example, at constant concentration (2 g/ℓ) the predicted fluxes of salicylate ion (pH 9.9) vs. salicylic acid (pH 2.65) are 1.4×10^{-7} g/cm^2/hr and 2.5×10^{-5} g/cm^2/hr, respectively. That is, the ionized form penetrates some 200 times slower than the unionized form. These fluxes at the two pHs were observed experimentally.[2] This difference in penetration is due to a difference in the driving force of the salicylic acid at the two pHs and to a difference in the area fraction of the two pathways. If the experiment were performed at high pH with a higher concentration of salicylate ion, the difference in flux should be much less.

The two-pathway model may also be used to interpret the selective enhancement of polar vs. nonpolar molecules. Cooper reports that decylmethyl sulfoxide enhances the penetration of salicylate ion by some 100-fold, but only enhances salicylate ion by some twofold.[2] As a simple approximation, we assume that D in the aqueous phase is enhanced some 100-fold, but that the nonpolar phase is unaffected. This might be accounted for by the decylmethyl sulfoxide interacting with stratum corneum proteins in the aqueous phase.[2,6] Given this 100-fold change in D for the aqueous phase, the two-pathway model predicts a 100-

fold enhancement for the flux of salicylate ion and from one- to twofold enhancement for salicylic acid. The agreement between theory and experiment is again excellent.

The prediction of this model for the flux through skin as a function of P at constant M and C_w is for small P independent of P, but for large P, is linear with P. This independence of flux for small P has been observed by Cooper.[1] The independence of P at short chain lengths and the linearity at large P has been observed for the series of alcohols.[3] A plateau region was also observed at very large P due to an unstirred boundary layer.

The ability of this two-pathway model to predict a wide range of skin permeation data makes this an exciting tool to interpret and estimate the skin permeability of drugs. Nevertheless, thorough experimental testing of the model should be performed.

V. APPENDIX A

A. The Continuous Polar Pathway Through Stratum Corneum: Water Permeation

The ability to enhance selectively the penetration of the ionized vs. unionized forms of drugs[1] and the different temperature dependences of the penetration of polar and nonpolar solutes[3] have led to the hypothesis of a separate continuous polar "shunt" pathway through the stratum corneum. Water, which has a solubility of approximately 0.1 to 1 mg/g in oils,[14] is the permeant through the stratum corneum about which the most data are available.[3,7] Due to its low solubility in oils, water permeation undoubtedly is through this polar pathway. We have consequently chosen water permeation to elucidate the nature of this continuous polar pathway.

Recently, Wu[7] has measured the changes in water flux, membrane thickness, and the equilibrium sorption of water in the membrane for fetal hog skin as a function of small increments in water activity. We will fit Wu's data to two models for skin permeation: (1) a nonporous solution-diffusion mechanism and (2) a porous diffusion pathway. The nonporous model is the one considered by Wu.[7] In the nonporous solution-diffusion model, there is a partitioning step between the applied aqueous source and the skin. For this model, the partition coefficients, P_w, diffusion constant, D_w, and the membrane thickness, all depend on the water activity. On the other hand, in the porous diffusion model there is a network of aqueous pores which swell with increasing water activity. These changes with water activity are reflected in D_w and l because there is no partitioning step. That is, the concentration of water in the source compartment and in the pores are identical. In the porous model, changes in the equilibrium sorption of water only reflect changes in pore lengths and diameters. For the nonporous model, C is related to the concentration of water inside the stratum corneum while for the porous model C is related to the water concentration in the surrounding solutions.

In the following sections, we derive the theoretical results for the two models and use the data of Wu to fit the parameters. These results are then used to predict the fluxes and time lags for stratum corneum under specified experimental conditions. While Wu's data are for fetal hog skin and the fluxes and time lags are for human stratum corneum, the data more closely agree with the nonporous solution-diffusion model. In both models, the keratinous membrane is assumed to be homogeneous.

B. The Nonporous Solution-Diffusion Model

The flux, J, through the keratin membrane is the product of "the driving force," the gradient in the chemical potential, μ, and the mobility. That is[16]

$$J = -(D_w/RT)\, C \frac{\partial \mu}{\partial x} \tag{13}$$

where C is the permeant concentration, R is the gas constant, T is the absolute temperature, and x is the distance across the membrane. The chemical potential, μ, may be written as:

$$\mu = \mu_o + RT \ln a \tag{14}$$

where μ_o is the chemical potential of the standard state and a is the thermodynamic activity. We define the partition coefficient, P_w, as

$$a = C/P_w \tag{15}$$

Note that P_w is a reciprocal activity coefficient and not the standard partition coefficient. Substituting Equations 2 and 3 into Equation 1, one finds that:

$$J = -P_w D_w \frac{\partial a}{\partial x} \tag{16}$$

Equation 16 is the basic relationship between the flux and thermodynamic activity.

In the experimental method of Wu,[7] steady-state measurements of J_s are made for small increments in thermodynamic activity. At steady state, we may integrate both sides of Equation 16 over the entire membrane to obtain:

$$J = -1/l \int_0^l dx\, P_w D_w \frac{\partial a}{\partial x} = \frac{1}{l} \int_{a_o}^{a_i} da\, P_w D_w \tag{17}$$

where a_i and a_o are the water activities on the inside and outside of the membrane, respectively. Note that l is the membrane thickness under these conditions. To determine D_w as a function of a, we assume that over the small increment in activity, P_w and D_w are independent of a. With this assumption,

$$D_w = \frac{J\, l}{P_w(a_i - a_o)} \tag{18}$$

J, l, and P_w were obtained from the measurements of Wu[7] for fetal hog skin and small $a_i - a_o$. For the sake of analytical simplicity, we fit P_w and D_w to simple functions and obtain reasonable correlation coefficients. The functions chosen by Wu are more accurate, but not as simple. It was found that P_w may be represented as

$$P_w = 0.19 + 0.003 \exp[3.56\, a] \tag{19}$$

and

$$D_w = 4.0 \times 10^{-10} + 3.25 \times 10^{-9}\, a \tag{20}$$

The correlation coefficient for D_w (cm²/sec) is 0.94. Using Equations 19 and 20 for P_w and D_w and the measurements for l, one may predict the steady-state fluxes for a_o and a_i.

To solve for the time lag, t_L, we use Equation 16 and the method of Frisch[13] to find that:

$$t_L = \frac{l^2 \int_{a_o}^{a_i} da P_w\, D_w \int_{a_o}^{a} da^l\, P_w^2\, Da_w^l}{\left[\int_{a_o}^{a_i} da\, P_w\, D_w\right]^3} \tag{21}$$

C. The Porous-Diffusion Model

The key feature which distinguishes the porous model from the solution-diffusion model is the absence of a partitioning process. That is, Equation 18 for the solution-diffusion model relates fluxes to concentrations inside the stratum corneum. On the other hand, Equation 23, for the porous-diffusion model, relates fluxes to the concentration in the solutions surrounding the skin. Changes in the equilibrium sorption of water reflect changes in the volume fraction and length of the porous pathway, which are the relevant parameters for the flux. The relevant flux equation is Fick's law.

$$J = -D_w \frac{\partial C}{\partial x} \tag{22}$$

The steady-state flux, J and D_w may be obtained in an analogous manner to Equations 17 and 18. We find that provided D_w is constant for small changes in activity,

$$D_w = \frac{J\,l}{C_i - C_o} \tag{23}$$

where C_i and C_o are the concentrations of water in the saturated salt solutions on the inside and outside of the keratin membrane, respectively. Using this approach to fit the data of Wu[7]

$$D_w = 2.5 \times 10^{-10}C - 1.6 \times 10^{-11} \tag{24}$$

with a correlation coefficient of 0.96, and D_w is expressed in cm²/sec.

An expression for t_L may be obtained by the method of Frisch[13] and

$$t_L = \frac{l^2 \int_{C_o}^{C_i} dC D_w \int_{C_o}^{C} dC' \, D_w C'}{\left[\int_{C_o}^{C_i} dC \, D_w \right]^3} \tag{25}$$

D. A Comparison of the Predictions for the Two Models of The Polar Pathway

To study the predictions of (1) the nonporous solution-diffusion model and (2) the porous diffusion model, we consider two different experimental conditions. In the first variable activity experiment,[15] there is neat water on the inside of the stratum corneum and sink conditions on the outside of the stratum corneum ($a_i = 1$ and $a_o = 0$). In the second tracer diffusion experiment,[3] ^3H_2O is used on one side of the stratum corneum and neat water is used on the other side ($C_i = 1$ and $C_o = 0$ but the stratum corneum behaves as if the activity of water were unity throughout it).

A comparison of the predicted t_L and J as well as data for these two experiments is shown in Table 1. In all four cases, the predictions of the nonporous solution-diffusion model are more consistent with the experimental data. Note that one of the four data points may be forced to agree with either model by using A_p as an adjustable parameter. However, the remaining three data points still favor the solution-diffusion model. These results are only ballpark calculations and more vigorous experimental testing is still required.

While solution diffusion models as well as a porous model lead to Equation 1, the two models lead to far different predictions. In particular, the porous model predicts that the flux should increase linearly with pressure while the solution-diffusion model predicts the flux should be nearly independent of pressure. Secondly, the porous model predicts that at

Table 1
THE WATER PERMEATION THROUGH SKIN

	Experimental data	Porous model	Nonporous model
Flux for variable activity	4×10^{-7} g/cm²/sec	7×10^{-8} g/cm²/sec	3×10^{-7} g/cm²/sec
Flux for tracer diffusion	10^{-6} g/cm²/sec	10^{-7} g/cm²/sec	5×10^{-7} g/cm²/sec
Time lag for variable activity	0.2 hr	3 hr	0.1 hr
Time lag for tracer diffusion	0.2 hr	0.8 hr	0.5 hr

saturation, the flux through the polar pathway should vary with the solubility in the solvent vehicle for the drug while the solution-diffusion model states that the flux through the polar pathway is a constant from saturated solutions. Note these predictions assume constant hydration of the skin with different vehicles.

VI. APPENDIX B

A. On The Diffusion Constant of Flexible Molecules in Polymers and Stratum Corneum

The diffusion constant, D, will be studied for flexible molecules (1) with chain lengths $n \geq 4$ or 5 where 4 or 5 segments is the segment-to-segment correlation length and (2) with n sufficiently small that entanglement effects are negligible. From the free-volume theory, D should have the form:[4]

$$D = D' \exp[-aV_m] \tag{26}$$

where V_m is the hole volume required for a diffusional jump. For a flexible molecule, V_m should be the volume of the number of segments in the correlation length, e.g., $n = 4$ or 5. Consequently, D should be independent of chain length for $n \geq 5$. This behavior of D has been observed for *n*-paraffins in polyisobutylene.[17] The independence of D on chain length in stratum corneum has also been observed for alcohols[3] and has been suggested for alkanoic acids.[18] For very long chain lengths, however, the flexible permeant and the molecule may become entangled[19] and D may be proportional to n^{-2}.

For a combination of a rigid molecule with a long-chain attachment, one might expect V_m to reflect the combined rigid group with four or five carbon segments. The independence of D on M for flexible molecules has scarcely been examined and requires careful study.

VII. APPENDIX C

A. The Three-Parallel Pathway Model: The Theory

The permeation through three pathways, (1) a continuous polar pathway, (2) a continuous lipophilic pathway, and (3) a heterogeneous pathway (an oil-water multilaminate) is modeled (Figure 3). Thus, J_{max}, the maximum flux of drug through skin, is proportional to C_w, the water solubility of the drug. We assume that (1) C_{Lmax}, the drug solubility in the nonpolar phase equals PC_w, where P is the octanol-water partition coefficient and (2) the partition coefficient in the fully hydrated polar pathway is unity. The diffusion constants for the three pathways are modeled by free-volume theory. For $P \geq 1$, the water solubility C_w, is modeled by the method of Yalkowsky,[5] who derived a relationship for C_w in terms of partition coefficient and melting point. C_w must be measured for $P < 1$.

The heterogeneous diffusion model is extremely complex to solve, but one can obtain an upper and lower bound to the steady-state problem by the series-parallel and parallel-series approximations.[20] These bounds are, respectively:

Barrier Pathways for Skin

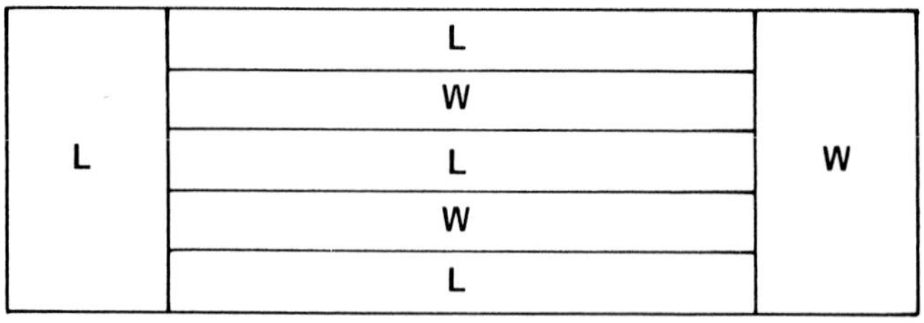

L | L / W / L / W / L | W

FIGURE 3. The three-parallel pathway model for skin transport consisting of a continuous lipid pathway, an oil-water multilaminate, and a continuous aqueous pathway.

$$J^{u}_{max} = \frac{2\exp[-BM]\,C_w}{l}\left[\frac{(A_L\,PD_L^{(o)} + (1 - A_L)\,D_p^{(o)})\,(A_p\,D_p^{(o)} + (1 - A_p)\,PD_L^{(o)})}{(1 - A_L + A_p)\,D_p^{(o)} + (1 - A_p + A_L)\,PD_L^{(o)}}\right] \qquad (27)$$

and

$$J^{L}_{max} = \frac{\exp[-BM]\,C_w}{l}\left[A_L\,PD_L^{(o)} + A_p\,D_p^{(o)} + \frac{2\,(1 - A_L - A_p)\,PD_L^{(o)}\,D_p^{(o)}}{D_p^{(o)} + PD_L^{(o)}}\right] \qquad (28)$$

When $P \geqslant 1$ for rigid aromatics, C_w is given by:[5]

$$C_w = \frac{M\exp[-(0.023\,T_f + 1.59)]\;5.5 \times 10^{-2}}{P(1 - \exp[-(0.023\,T_f + 1.59)]/P)} \qquad (29)$$

T_f is the melting point in degrees Celsius; A_L and A_P are the area fractions of the nonpolar (lipid) and polar (water) continuous pathways, respectively. For the cases considered, the fluxes predicted by Equations 27 and 28 never differ by more than a factor of two. Note that for simplicity equal thicknesses of oil and water barriers in the oil-water multilaminate have been selected.

The problem arises of evaluating the constants l, D_L^O, D_p^O, B_p, B_L, A_p, and A_L. Let $B_L = B_p = B$. $B = 0.016$ after fitting $\ln[J_{max}/C_L^{max}]$ vs. M for the data from References 10 and 12. If a large data base on skin permeation were available, the constants could be fit to the data. In the absence of this data base, we estimated D_p^O, A_p, and A_L from water permeation data,[7] and D_L^O from salicylic acid data.[2]

As an estimate, $A_L \approx 0.5$ and an upper limit for $A_p = 0.1$. The value of A_p is probably somewhat large and the effects of area fractions and diffusion constants are difficult to separate with the amount of skin transport data available. While these estimates are properly viewed as an "order of magnitude calculation", (and rigorous curve-fitting to a wide range of data is required), the predictions from these estimates of skin permeation are surprisingly good.

Note that Equations 27 and 28 have more adjustable parameters than one could ever fit usefully with steady-state skin transport data. By comparing the predicted skin fluxes between the two- and three-parallel pathway, the similarity makes it clear that steady-state skin transport is insensitive to the existence of the lipid-water multilaminate pathway. To understand the geometry of the heterogeneous stratum corneum media, one must consider nonsteady-state transport such as that discussed in Appendix D.

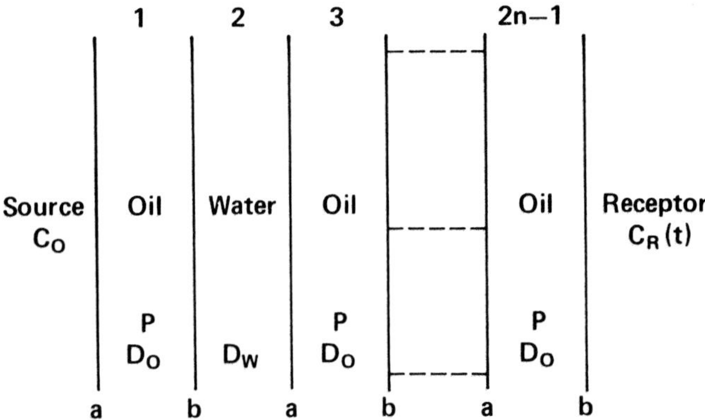

FIGURE 4. A model for permeation through a series of 2n − 1 oil-water multilaminates.

VIII. APPENDIX D

A. An Oil-Water Multilaminate: The Need for Shunt Pathways in the Model for Stratum Corneum

Photomicrographs of the stratum corneum reveal a multilayered structure and perhaps an intuitive first model for skin permeation is a series of oil and water multilaminates (Figure 4). In this section, nonsteady-state permeation through and desorption from oil-water multilaminates are studied and the predictions of this model are found to be at variance with corresponding data for skin permeation and desorption. In particular, oil-water multilaminates have the extraordinary capability of separating permeants exponentially based on the partition coefficient and diffusion constant and skin does not exhibit this selectivity. Continuous lipophilic and hydrophilic shunt pathways are suggested as a means of rectifying the model.

We now consider nonsteady-state permeation through oil-water multilaminates. A well-stirred aqueous source compartment of constant solute concentration, C_o, and a well-stirred aqueous receptor compartment of volume, V_R, are separated by a series of alternating n oil and n − 1 water membranes (Figure 5). Fick's law diffusion of the permeant is assumed in each oil or water slab and the diffusing solute has a partition coefficient, P, and diffusion constants, D_o and D_w in the oil and water membranes, respectively. The thicknesses of each oil and water slab are l_o and l_w, respectively. Asymptotic solutions for nonsteady-state diffusion may be obtained[21,22] and these solutions are for $C_R(t)$, the concentration of solute in the aqueous receptor compartment at time, t.

The nonsteady-state permeation of solutes with P are very different from P_{max} (the optimal P for transport through these oil-water multilaminates) and displays the most interesting features of these oil-water multilaminates. In the large n limit, it may be shown that[21]

$$P_{max} = (D_w/D_o)^{1/2} \tag{30}$$

For a homologous series of compounds, the compound with P given by Equation 30 will exhibit maximum transport. The time lag, t_L, for these multilaminates[22] is greatly extended by P, and consequently, t_L for such multilaminates as thick as stratum corneum (10 to 20 μ) may be of the order of hours to months while t_L for a membrane of equal thickness in a configuration which is not laminated may be of the order of minutes. By comparison, t_L for diffusion through stratum corneum ranges from some 15 min for water to 16 hr for progesterone.[3]

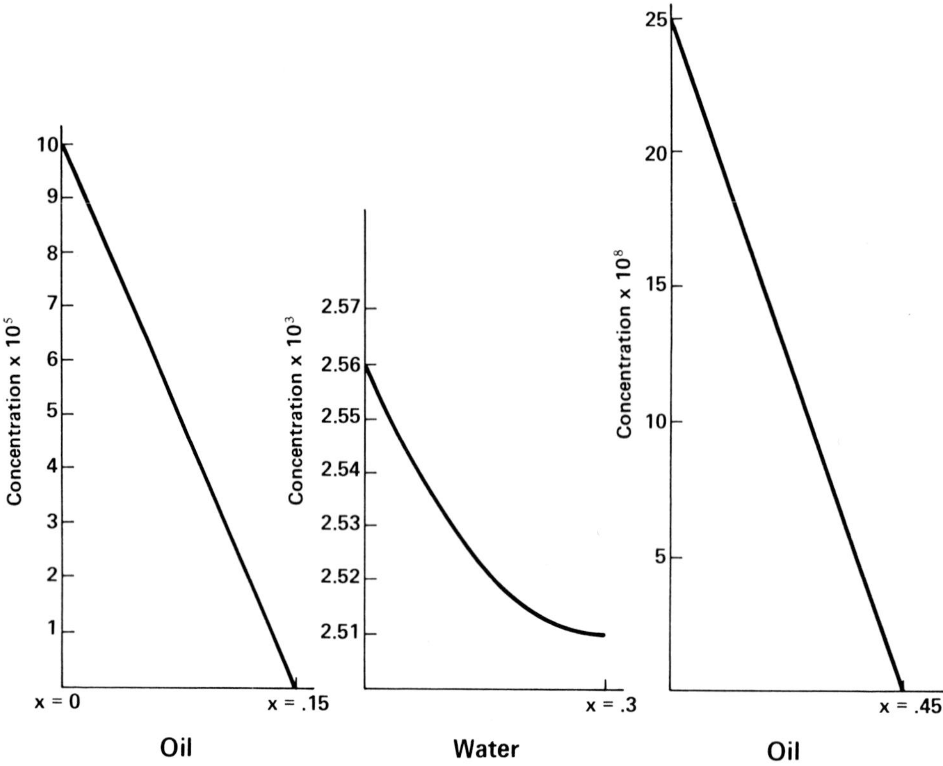

FIGURE 5. Concentration profile across oil-water multilaminate for $n = 2$, $P = 10^{-4}$, and $t = 71390$ sec.

For solutes for which $P << P_{max}$ and $t < t_L$, one finds that:[21]

$$C_R(t) = (Al_w/V_R n!)(PD_o t/l_o l_w)^n C_o \tag{31}$$

where A is the area of the membrane. Note that for small P, these oil-water multilaminates separate solutes exponentially (to the power of n) based on P and D_o. This extraordinary selectivity in the nonsteady-state for small P solutes is most easily understood by realizing that when P is small, oil membranes act as a barrier and water membranes act as a sink. Before steady state obtains, the solute concentration profile in the oil membranes are at steady state (linear with distance) and the profile in the water membranes are at nearly constant concentration (Figure 5). Thus, the extension of the time lag by P reflects the time to fill up the water sinks with the rate of ''trickling'' determined by the oil barrier. Similarly, the exponential separation is due to n ''sequential separations'' based on P and D_o. In an analogous fashion, the result for $P \gg P_{max}$ and $t < t_L$ is[21]

$$C_R(t) = (D_w t/Pl_o l_w)^{n-1} C_o/(n - 1)! \tag{32}$$

In the large P limit, there is exponential separation based on P and D_w to the power of the number of water barriers $(n - 1)$.

If stratum corneum were such an oil-water multilaminate, skin permeability should demonstrate this exponential separation based on P. Since the stratum corneum has some 15 cell layers, one might choose $n = 15$ and expect a selectivity of the order of P^{15}. The selectivity of skin falls far short of this extraordinary value[2] and as has already been demonstrated for intestinal and vaginal absorption,[24,25] a multilaminate model may not be suitable for biological tissues due to hydrophilic and hydrophobic shunt pathways.

Desorption out of an oil-water multilaminate membrane also predicts results that are at variance with skin permeability. To study desorption, the source and receptor compartments used for permeation experiments (Figure 5) are replaced with two infinite well-stirred aqueous receptor compartments which act as sinks (C = 0). Provided $P << 1$, the amount released from the multilaminate membrane, N_{OUT}, is [26]:

$$N_{OUT} = \frac{2D_o \, PC_o t}{l_o} \tag{33}$$

Similarly, for $P >> 1$,

$$N_{OUT} = \frac{2\,D_w\,C_o t}{l_w} + 2\,PC_o l_o \tag{34}$$

Thus, desorption from an oil-water multilaminate acts like steady-state permeation through a single outer membrane with a ''burst effect'' due to initial dumping of solute from the outermost membrane. More importantly, desorption from an oil-water multilaminate is linear with time. This behavior is in contrast to desorption from a monolith,[13] which is linear with $t^{1/2}$. Desorption from the stratum corneum [27] is linear with $t^{1/2}$. Consequently, shunt pathways are required as an addition to the multilaminate model to correct the variance from the behavior of the stratum corneum.

Oil-water multilaminates are an appealing, simple model for skin permeability, due to (1) the resemblance to the photomicrographs, (2) the ability to explain the good barrier properties of stratum corneum, and (3) the ability to explain separate polar and nonpolar pathways for permeation through stratum corneum. However, the predictions for nonsteady-state permeation and desorption from oil-water multilaminates do not agree with the results for stratum corneum and shunts should be added to the model. The shunts and dependence of the nonsteady-state with respect to arrangment of materials within the membrane could provide avenues for exploring the heterogeneity of skin. However, the models become extremely complex and are at present not as useful as the simpler models considered in earlier sections.

REFERENCES

1. **Cooper, E. R.,** Increased skin permeability for lipophilic molecules, *J. Pharm. Sci.,* 73, 1153, 1984.
2. **Cooper, E. R.,** Effect of decylmethyl sulfoxide on skin penetration, *Solution Behavior of Surfactants,* Mittal, K. L. and Fendler, E. J., Eds., Plenum Press, New York, 1982, 1505.
3. **Scheuplein, R. J. and Blank, I. H.,** Permeability of the skin, *Physiol. Rev.,* 51, 702, 1971.
4. **Kumins, C. A. and Kwei, T. K.,** Free volume and other theories, *Diffusion in Polymers,* Crank, J. and Park, G. S., Eds., Academic Press, New York, 1968, 107.
5. **Yalkowsky, S. H.,** Solubility and solubilization of nonelectrolytes, *Techniques of Solubilization of Drugs,* Yalkowsky, S. H., Ed., Marcel Dekker, New York, 1981, 1.
6. **Oertel, R. P.,** Protein conformation changes induced in human stratum corneum by organic sulfoxides: an infrared spectroscopic investigation, *Biopolymers,* 16, 232, 1977.
7. **Wu, M. S.,** Determination of concentration — dependent water diffusivity in a keratinous membrane, *J. Pharm. Sci.,* 72, 1421, 1983.
8. **Idson, B.,** Percutaneous absorption, *J. Pharm. Sci.,* 64, 901, 1975.
9. **Denbigh, K.,** *The Principles of Equilibrium,* Cambridge University Press, London, 1981, 244.
10. **Cooper, E. R.,** Effect of substituents on benzoic acid transport across human skin *in vitro, J. Controlled Rel.,* 1, 153, 1984.
11. **Kasting, G., Cooper, E. R., and Smith, R. L.,** Effect of lipid solubility and molecular size on percutaneous absorption, to be submitted.

12. **Michaels, A. S., Chandrasekaran, S. K., and Shaw, J. E.,** Drug permeation through human skin: theory and in vitro experimental measurement, *A. I. Ch. E. J.* 21, 985, 1975.
13. **Crank, J.,** *The Mathematics of Diffusion,* Clarendon Press, Oxford, 1975.
14. **Lang, J.,** personal communication.
15. **Berner, B.,** unpublished observations.
16. **Katchalsky, A. and Curran, P. F.,** *Nonequilibrium Thermodynamics in Biophysics,* Harvard University Press, Cambridge, Mass. 1965.
17. **Stannett, V.,** Simple gases, *Diffusion in Polymers,* Crank, J. and Park, G. S., Eds., Academic Press, New York, 1968.
18. **Liron, Z. and Cohen, S.,** Percutaneous absorption of alkanoic acids. II. Application of regular solution theory, *J. Pharm. Sci.,* 73, 538, 1984.
19. **DeGennes, P. G.,** *Scaling Concepts in Polymer Physics,* Cornell University Press, Ithaca, New York, 1979.
20. **Bell, G. E. and Crank, J.,** Influence of imbedded particles on steady-state diffusion, *J. Chem. Soc. Faraday Trans. 2,* 70, 1259, 1974.
21. **Berner, B. and Cooper, E. R.,** Asymptotic solution for nonsteady-state diffusion through oil-water multilaminates, *J. Membr. Sci.,* 14, 139, 1983.
22. **Berner, B. and Cooper, E. R.,** Application of diffusion theory to the relationship between partition coefficient and biological response, *J. Pharm. Sci.,* 73, 102, 1984.
23. **Hwang, S., Owada, E., Yotsuyanagi, T., Suhardja, L., Ho, N. F., Flynn, G. L., and Higuchi, W. I.,** Systems approach to vaginal delivery of drugs. II. *In situ* vaginal absorption of unbranched aliphatic alcohols, *J. Pharm. Sci.,* 65, 1574, 1976.
24. **Yalkowsky, S. H. and Flynn, G. F.,** Transport of alkyl homologs across synthetic and biological membranes: a new model for chain length-activity relationships, *J. Pharm. Sci.,* 62, 210, 1973.
25. **Berner, B. and Cooper, E. R.,** Desorption out of an oil-water multilaminate membrane, *J. Controlled Release,* 1, 149, 1984.
26. **Cooper, E. R. and Berner, B.,** Skin permeability, *Methods in Skin Research,* Skerrow, D. and Skerrow, C. Eds., John Wiley & Sons, New York, 1985, 407.

Chapter 4

PENETRATION ENHANCERS

Eugene R. Cooper and
Bret Berner

TABLE OF CONTENTS

I. INTRODUCTION

The low permeability of the skin relative to other biological tissues is well known and it is perhaps this fact that has kept the skin as a minor port of entry for drugs. As compared to the oral or gastric mucosa, the stratum corneum is compact and highly keratinized. The lipids and proteins of the stratum corneum provide a complex structure that is quite impermeable. Despite the complexity of the stratum corneum and the difficulty of accurately modeling the heterogeneity of the barrier, the basic concepts for altering transport can be understood and are the subjects of this chapter.

For some time it has been recognized that surface active agents such as soaps[1] can enhance the permeation of skin. Apart from detergents, dimethyl sulfoxide (DMSO)[2] is perhaps the most widely known penetration enhancer. This solvent is so good at enhancing penetration that it is really the standard to which everything else is compared. Except for the recent introduction of 1-dodecylazacycloheptan-2-one (Azone®),[3] very few new penetration enhancers have been reported. This paucity of penetration enhancers will soon be remedied, however, since transdermal drug delivery has become an accepted mode of drug delivery.

While the ability to enhance penetration is important, it is critical that this task be accomplished without skin irritation or sensitization. On the surface, it seems almost impossible to find an agent that will disrupt such an impermeable barrier as the stratum corneum without altering the more fragile living tissue below. The large concentration drop across the stratum corneum will make this task easier, but it remains a formidable challenge nonetheless. For some situations, such as skin cancer, irritation will not be as significant a factor as it will be for chronic usage and thus, a spectrum of penetration enhancers can be envisioned.

This chapter will not deal with the biological consequences of penetration enhancers, but will focus on creating options to increase penetration. In the early stages of the development of penetration enhancers, however, it is important to obtain skin irritation data to position the utility of the system. The starting point for the discussion of penetration enhancers will be a review of (1) the factors which control diffusion and (2) how the gross composition of skin is related to diffusion. Existing penetration aids will be discussed in light of these considerations and then an approach for new enhancers will be proposed.

In the terminology of this chapter, an enhancer is a compound which alters the skin as a barrier to the flux of a desired permeant. The key to finding an enhancer is to compare the flux across skin of the permeant at the same thermodynamic activity in (1) a vehicle with the putative enhancer and (2) a standard vehicle, such as an aqueous solution. Saturated solutions or equal fractions of saturation should be used to obtain constant activity in the two vehicles.

II. DIFFUSION AND MEMBRANE COMPOSITION

The flux, J, of drugs across skin can be written as:

$$J = D \frac{\partial c}{\partial x} \tag{1}$$

where D is the diffusion coefficient, C is the concentration of diffusing species, and x is the position in the membrane. To enhance the flux of the drug, one must either increase D or C. The large enhancements which have been observed suggest that D is the more important parameter.

D is a function of the size, shape, and flexibility of the diffusing molecule as well as the membrane resistance. For rigid permeant molecules, D is given in the chapter on models of skin permeability as:

$$D = D_o \exp[-BM] \tag{2}$$

where D_o is a constant and B is related to the energy to make a hole large enough for a diffusional jump.

D is really only an apparent diffusion coefficient since the stratum corneum is heterogeneous. The stratum corneum as a barrier contains lipids, keratinized proteins, and varying amounts of water.[4] Consistent with this composition is the three-parallel pathway model presented in the chapter on models of skin permeability. The three parallel pathways are (1) a continuous polar or aqueous pathway composed of proteins, (2) a continuous nonpolar pathway consisting of lipids, and (3) a heterogeneous polar-nonpolar multilaminate of lipids and proteins. Thus, the above equations apply to each of the phases in the three parallel pathways. From the nature of polymer diffusion, it seems very likely that solvent swelling or protein conformational change is key to altering the penetration of the polar pathway. The effects of penetration enhancers on flux are generally so great that their effect is more likely on the diffusion coefficient rather than the concentration, since one does not expect 100-fold increases in the concentration in the skin. Experiments with polar molecules of various molecular weights could test the validity of Equation 2 and determine if the enhancer affects D_o and/or B.

The key to altering the nonpolar pathway appears to be fluidizing the lipids. From the differential scanning calorimetry studies of Van Duzee,[5] much of the stratum corneum lipids appear crystalline. Enhancers of the nonpolar pathway apparently fluidize these lipids. Since diffusion through fluids is dramatically larger than diffusion in solids, fluidizing the lipids could substantially increase skin diffusion. Binary vehicles appear to act on both polar and nonpolar regions and may exert their greatest effects on the multilaminate pathway.

III. PENETRATION ENHANCERS

A. Surfactants

With the possible exception of DMSO, the best known penetration enhancers are perhaps surfactants. In the 1960s, Bettley and Donoghue[1] showed that soaps could increase the flux of water across human epidermis and later Bettley[6] showed similar effects for glucose and sodium salicylate.

More recently it has been shown that detergents alter the transport of polar molecules to a much greater extent than the transport of nonpolar molecules. For example, treatment of epidermis with decylmethyl sulfoxide (C_{10}MSO)[7] greatly increased the penetration of ionized salicyclic acid (salicylate), but only marginally increased the penetration of the unionized species. Bettley[8] and later Scheuplein and Ross[9] proposed that surfactants alter the protein conformations and thus, enhance polar pathway transport. Oertel's[10] work with infrared spectroscopy further supports this protein conformational change model.

The ability of a surfactant to alter penetration is a function of the polar head group and the hydrocarbon chain length. In a study of the effects of alkyl sulfates on alternating current (A.C.) conductance Scheuplein and Dugard[11] showed the optimum chain length of alkyl sulfates for increasing conductance was 12 carbons. This optimal chain length may be interpreted as a trade-off between sufficient lipophilicity to partition into the stratum corneum and decreasing water solubility with increasing alkyl chain length.[12] A good illustration of the solubility effect is the great difference between the effect of sodium stearate and sodium oleate. Here, the lipophilicity and head group are the same, but the solubility of the oleate is much greater. Consequently, sodium oleate is an effective enhancer while sodium stearate is ineffective.

The effect of the polar head group on the ability of a surfactant to enhance penetration appears to correlate with Laughlin's[13] concept of surfactant hydrophilicity. Hydrophilic head

Table 1
SURFACTANT HEAD GROUP LISTED IN DECREASING HYDROPHILICITY AND PROTEIN INTERACTION

Head group (example)
Ionic (sodium dodecyl sulfate)
Zwitterionic (dodecyldimethylammoniopropanesulfonate)
Sulfoxide (dodecylmethyl sulfoxide)
Ethoxylate (dodecanol hexaethoxylate)
Alcohol (dodecyl alcohol)

groups such as on sodium lauryl sulfate are very effective at altering the penetration of polar molecules, but alcohols, which have the lowest hydrophilicity are ineffective. The ranking is reproduced in Table 1, where the most hydrophilic polar groups are ranked highest. It may well be that irritation follows a similar ranking and thus, one must pay a price for enhanced penetration. The irritation of sodium lauryl sulfate is well known and it probably is not usable in a practical delivery system. Some of the less hydrophilic head groups might be useful for short exposures or in low concentrations.

B. Solvents

Solvents such as DMSO, 2-pyrrolidone, and dimethylformamide can swell the stratum corneum and may also be able to solubilize or fluidize lipids.

Thus, one might expect that these solvents could increase penetration by swelling the polar pathway and/or by fluidizing lipids. The effect of these solvents on penetration is dependent on the solvent concentration[2] and high concentrations of DMSO are needed to increase the flux. An explanation of the action of DMSO on stratum corneum has been given by Chandrasekaran.[14] He observed a larger increase in flux only when a large gradient (in either direction) of DMSO existed across the stratum corneum. This effect he attributed to the osmotic stresses created in the skin. However, other solvents such as glycerol, propylene glycol, propanol, etc., also create osmotic gradients across skin and yet they do not enhance penetration as DMSO does. Thus, the creation of osmotic gradients is not sufficient for explaining the effect of DMSO on penetration and other factors must be considered. Lipid fluidization resulting from swelling is a reasonable hypothesis.

C. Binary Systems

Polar lipids in combination with propylene glycol can be used to enhance the penetration of nonpolar species like salicylic acid,[15] but are also effective in enhancing the penetration of acyclovir,[16] which is more water soluble than lipid soluble. Apparently, these binary systems open up the heterogeneous multilaminate pathway in the stratum corneum.

One key to this binary vehicle system is the selection of a lipid component which has an unsaturated hydrocarbon chain. Unsaturated fatty acids incorporated in *Escherichia coli*[17] or liposomes[18] are known to enhance membrane permeability and fluidity. Thus, it is reasonable to assume that such systems are changing the fluidity of the stratum corneum lipids. Crude calorimetry measurements[19] are consistent with this hypothesis.

For the binary systems, the head group of the lipid is insignificant compared to the hydrocarbon chain. For example, oleic acid is effective but not stearic acid, and oleyl methyl sulfoxide is effective but not stearyl methyl sulfoxide. Perhaps the saturated chain is just too insoluble to have much of an effect. Even Azone®[3] can fit into this binary system scheme by considering it to be a short-chain lipid which creates a "hole" in the matrix of longer chain lipids of the stratum corneum.

The second key ingredient is the polar solvent. Propylene glycol was one of the best polar solvent enhancers, but other diols were also effective. However, the effectiveness of diols as enhancers in binary systems generally decreases with the number of carbons in the diol.

The necessity for both the diol and lipid components is indicated by the existence of an optimal combination of these components for obtaining maximal enhancement. Perhaps the combined components open up the heterogeneous pathway. Regardless of the mechanism of this synergism, these binary systems bring new opportunities for enhancers.

D. Future Enhancers

The nature of the penetrant must be considered to design a penetration enhancer. If the penetrant is polar, the enhancing material should interact strongly enough with the proteins of the stratum corneum to alter the protein conformation to a more permeable conformation. This effect can be accomplished through swelling (as occurs with hydration) and/or through a direct interaction as with detergents. If the permeant is lipophilic, one can find a system to fluidize the crystalline lipids, as is conjectured for the binary systems.

New penetration enhancers may be discovered by looking for novel ways to alter proteins and fluidize lipids. Examining the effects of penetration enhancers as a function of the molecular size of the permeant might be a useful tool in exploring the mechanism. For example, by using Equation 2, one could learn if D_o and/or B is affected by the penetration enhancer. Thermodynamic techniques such as calorimetry and probes of molecular dynamics such as solid-state ^{13}C NMR might be employed to examine the effects of agents on the viscosity or crystallinity of the stratum corneum components.

Much fundamental work remains to be done with penetration enhancers, especially with solvents like DMSO. The basic parameters of protein conformation and swelling and lipid structure and fluidity will have to be measured more precisely to interpret more accurately the interactions of enhancers with skin. Agents which maximally interact with the stratum corneum and minimally interact with the living tissue are to be desired. This aspect of the problem presents perhaps the greatest challenge for the future.

REFERENCES

1. **Bettley, F. R. and Donoghue, E.,** Effect of soap on the diffusion of water through isolated human epidermis, *Nature (London),* 17, 185, 1960.
2. **Scheuplein, R. J. and Blank, I. H.,** Permeability of the skin, *Physiol. Rev.,* 51, 702, 1971.
3. **Stoughton, R. B.,** Enhanced percutaneous penetration with 1-dodecylazacycloheptan-2-one (Azone), *Arch. Dermatol.,* 118, 474, 1982.
4. **Anderson, R. L. and Cassidy, J. M.,** Variations in physical dimensions and chemical composition of human stratum corneum, *J. Invest. Dermatol.,* 61, 30, 1973.
5. **Van Duzee, B.,** Thermal analysis of human stratum corneum, *J. Invest. Dermatol.,* 65, 404, 1975.
6. **Bettley, F. R.,** The influence of soap on the permeability of the epidermis, *Br. J. Dermatol.,* 73, 448, 1961.
7. **Cooper, E. R.,** Effect of decylmethyl sulfoxide on skin penetration, *Solution Behavior of Surfactants,* Mittal, K. L. and Fendler, E. J., Eds., Plenum Press, New York, 1982, 1505.
8. **Bettley, F. R.,** The influence of detergents and surfactants on epidermal permeability, *Br. J. Dermatol.,* 77, 98, 1965.
9. **Scheuplein, R. J. and Ross, L.,** Effects of surfactants and solvents on the permeability of epidermis, *J. Soc. Cosmet. Chem.,* 21, 853, 1970.
10. **Oertel, R. P.,** Protein conformational changes induced in human stratum corneum by organic sulfoxides: an infrared spectroscopic investigation, *Biopolymers,* 16, 232, 1977.
11. **Scheuplein, R. J. and Dugard, P. H.,** Effects of ionic surfactants on the permeability of human epidermis: an electrometric study, *J. Invest. Dermatol.,* 60, 263, 1973.

12. **Cooper, E. R. and Berner, B.,** Interactions of surfactants with epidermal tissues-physicochemical aspects, *Surfactants in Cosmetics,* Rieger, M. M., Ed., Marcel Dekker, New York, 1985, 195.
13. **Laughlin, R. G.,** Relative hydrophilicities among surfactant hydrophilic groups, in *Advances in Liquid Crystals,* Academic Press, New York, 1978, 41.
14. **Chandrasekaran, S. K.,** Controlled release of scopolamine for prophylaxis of motion sickness, *Drug Dev. Ind. Pharm.,* 9, 627, 1983.
15. **Cooper, E. R.,** Increased skin permeability for lipophilic molecules, *J. Pharm. Sci.,* 73, 1153, 1984.
16. **Cooper, E. R., Merritt, E. W., and Smith, R. L.,** Effect of fatty acids and alcohols on the penetration of acyclovir across human skin *in vitro, J. Pharm. Sci.,* 74, 688, 1985.
17. **Davis, M. D. and Silbert, D. F.,** Changes in cell permeability following a marked reduction of saturated fatty acid content of *Escherichia coli* K-12, *Biochem. Biophys. Acta,* 373, 224, 1974.
18. **DeGier, J., Mandersloot, J. G., and Van Deenen, L. L. M.,** Lipid composition and permeability of liposomes, *Biochem. Biophys. Acta,* 150, 666, 1968.
19. **Wickett, R.,** personal communication.

Chapter 5

AZONE®

R. Vaidyanathan, V. J. Rajadhyaksha, B. K. Kim, and J. J. Anisko

TABLE OF CONTENTS

I. INTRODUCTION

Problems in conventional modes of delivery of biologically active compounds have encouraged development of novel drug delivery systems, including transdermal administration for systemic activity. Since most active drugs do not permeate intact skin in therapeutic amounts, there is a need for compounds which safely and effectively promote the penetration of active drugs into and through the skin. Azone®, the subject of this chapter, is a compound which has shown remarkable penetration enhancing properties.

A. Transdermal Delivery for Systemic Activity

Percutaneous delivery of drugs has been of great interest to physical pharmacists and dermatologists alike for the past 30 years.[1-9] The human skin being readily accessible would desirably be a logical portal of entry for pharmacologically active agents if it were not a functional protective barrier for the body. A thorough understanding of the anatomy, physiology, and molecular biologic functions of the skin along with its barrier properties and putative drug permeation routes, however, has permitted the design of therapeutically effective transdermal delivery systems.

The reason most often cited for clinical ineffectiveness following topical drug application is the poor percutaneous penetrability of the drug itself. The impressive barrier property of the stratum corneum has long been well recognized.[10-14] Methods to enhance the penetration of active drugs across this tissue barrier, a fraction of a millimeter in thickness, would open up a new frontier for drug delivery.

The interest in the study of percutaneous absorption has moved from an enumeration of descriptive details to a correlation of the physicochemical parameters, including consideration of biopharmaceutical aspects, which affect topical and transdermal delivery of drugs.[15-19] In vitro experimental techniques, although not fully predictive of in vivo activity, coupled with in vivo animal studies have proven to be valuable methods for evaluation and development of candidate transdermal therapeutic systems.[20-26]

B. Role of Penetration Enhancers

A large number of pharmacologically active agents are candidates for transdermal delivery. There are examples of active drugs which penetrate the skin at rates high enough to yield therapeutic levels in the plasma, such as scopolamine and nitroglycerin. Such drugs are, however, the exception since most drugs do not permeate intact skin in therapeutic amounts.[7,17] This limitation is particularly evident with hydrophilic drugs.

The literature abounds with information on methods of augmenting percutaneous penetration.[17,27-34] A typical approach includes use of vehicles which modify skin permeability by solvent action on the stratum corneum.[35-38] Although formulation additives and modifications in vehicular compositions have provided some measure of enhancement by their effects on thermodynamic activity of the permeant or on the barrier properties of the skin or both, such effects are often less than satisfactory. However, active drugs which permeate the skin only marginally may show enhanced penetration providing therapeutic levels using such techniques.

In order to allow clinically useful topical application of the vast majority of drugs which show little or no transdermal penetration on their own, ways to enhance and maintain adequate penetration rates must be found. Consequently, there has been an intensive search for compounds which would modify the diffusional resistance of the stratum corneum.

A number of reports exist in the literature about aprotic materials such as dimethyl sulfoxide (DMSO), dimethylacetamide (DMA), and dimethylformamide (DMF), which possess sorption promotion properties.[37,39-45] While such materials have been shown to provide enhancement, many have not been widely accepted either because of suspected pharmacologic activity or unresolved questions about safety.

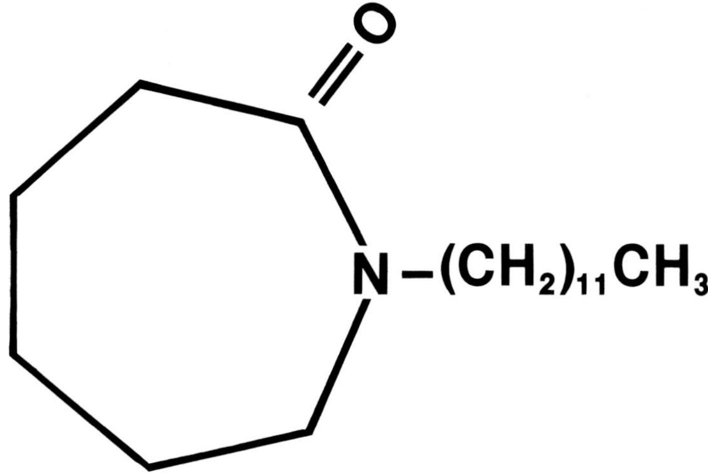

FIGURE 1. Chemical structure of Azone® (1-dodecylhexahydro-2H-azepin-2-one)

An ideal penetration enhancer in addition to being safe, nontoxic, and nonirritating should also be pharmacologically inert while reversibly modifying the barrier properties of the skin.[15,46]

II. AZONE® AS A PENETRATION ENHANCER

A. Properties of Azone®

Azone® is a colorless, odorless, pharmacologically inert liquid which is nonirritating to human skin. A number of studies have demonstrated enhanced penetration of both hydrophobic and hydrophilic drugs when formulated with Azone®; however, more dramatic effects have been reported with hydrophilic drugs.

Azone® (Figure 1) is one of a series of *N*-alkylated cyclic amides which were synthesized to promote the penetration of active compound through biological membranes.[47-54] Azone® has a smooth, oily, nongreasy feel. When incorporated into creams and lotions, Azone® imparts a pleasant emolliency to the product. The technical properties of Azone® are shown in Table 1.

Azone® (1-dodecylhexahydro-2H-azepin-2-one) is prepared by alkylation of caprolactam with 1-bromododecane in the presence of a strong base such as sodium hydride or sodium amide in a hydrocarbon solvent.[55,56] Azone® has also been synthesized by phase transfer catalysis.[57]

Azone® has been assayed by gas chromatography using a 6 ft glass column with 3.5 mm inside diameter (ID) packed with 3% OV-17 or GC Q, 100/120 mesh.[58] The flow rate of the carrier gas, helium, was 30 mℓ/min. The injector and flame ionization detector were maintained at 300°C while the oven temperature was 225°C. Under these operating conditions, the retention time of Azone® was approximately 6 min.

B. Mechanism of Action

Azone®'s precise mechanism of action is not well understood at the present time. There are data available, however, which can be used to make predictions.

Penetration enhancers and vehicles usually impart their effect through a combination of different factors. Three of these are particularly relevant to an understanding of their mechanism of action:

Table 1
TECHNICAL PROPERTIES OF AZONE®

USAN name	Laurocapram
Empirical formula	$C_{18}H_{35}NO$
Formula weight	281.49
Purity	> 99%
Physical form	Clear, colorless liquid
Color, (APHA)	< 50
Moisture, %	< 0.2
Freezing point, °C	−7°
Boiling point, °C	160° at 0.05 mm Hg
Viscosity, cp	45.2
Refractive index, n_D	1.4701
Specific gravity, d^{25}	0.912
Surface tension dy/cm$^{22°}$	32.65
Flash point	100°C no flash
Miscible with	Most organic solvents, including alcohols, ketones, hydrocarbons
Immiscible with	Water
Acute oral toxicity	LD_{50}(rat) > 9 g/kg
Stability	> 7 years

- A solvent action on the stratum corneum usually leading to increased skin hydration and possibly temperature elevation
- A direct, noninvasive action on the diffusional resistance of the stratum corneum
- An increase in the partition coefficient of the permeant promoting its release from the vehicle to the skin

Azone® exhibits, for example, greater solubilizing properties than most solvents. Accordingly, a greater amount of the drug would be dissolved in an Azone® formulation, promoting greater skin penetration.

Inferential techniques can be used to evaluate the mechanism by which substances promote skin penetration. For example, the effect of penetration enhancers and vehicles on the rate and extent of penetration of a homologous series of solutes, which differ in their degree of lipophilicity, can be determined.

An analysis of several recently reported studies, using such techniques, strongly suggests that Azone® and DMSO possess different modes of action.

A study was carried out on the effect of Azone® on the permeability coefficient of alkanols.[59] The results of this study, shown in Table 2, indicate an increased permeability coefficient for lower alkanols, such as methanol and propanol, until an optimum concentration of Azone® is reached. Beyond this, higher concentrations of Azone® do not seem to have an appreciable effect on permeability. For butanol through hexanol, the permeability coefficient values peak at an optimum Azone® concentration and then decline with higher Azone® concentrations. For the higher alkanol, octanol, the permeability coefficient values are inversely related to the concentration of Azone®.

If an applied vehicle is more lipophilic than a membrane, then permeability coefficients of homologous solutes should decrease as solute lipophilicity increases.[60] The results of this study likewise suggest that Azone®, being more lipophilic than the stratum corneum, enhances the permeation of the lower alkanols more than the higher alkanols. As seen in Table 2, for butanol through hexanol this decrease in permeability is seen only beyond an optimum Azone® concentration. If action of Azone® on the stratum corneum were greater than its thermodynamic effects on the permeant, then these results as well as the inverse relationship between the Azone® concentration and the permeability coefficient for the higher alkanol octanol, would be unlikely.

Table 2
EFFECT OF VARYING CONCENTRATIONS OF AZONE® IN NORMAL SALINE. PERMEABILITY COEFFICIENTS OF ALKANOLS, THROUGH FULL THICKNESS HAIRLESS MOUSE SKIN IN TWO-COMPARTMENT DIFFUSION CELLS AT 37°C

	Permeability coefficient [P × 10^3 (cm/hr)]					
% Azone®	*n*-Methanol	*n*-Propanol	*n*-Butanol	*n*-Pentanol	*n*-Hexanol	*n*-Octanol
0	6.23	4.27	10.14	23.83	42.85	66.91
0.1	16.04	25.85	29.45	101.17	89.66	62.96
0.5	14.66	—	46.73	101.11	112.62	27.49
1.0	22.59	28.44	65.11	64.13	96.72	16.43
3.0	16.83	25.88	85.99	39.46	26.31	6.81
5.0	20.77	16.02	78.58	29.81	14.64	5.94
10.0	—	—	42.91	—	12.59	9.36

In practice, it is often difficult to isolate the effect of an agent on a single parameter in the overall process of percutaneous absorption, but these results suggest that Azone®'s permeation enhancing abilities can be better explained by its thermodynamic effects on the permeant rather than its effects on the stratum corneum per se.

Using a similar alkanol model, two other studies evaluating the effects of skin stripping[61] and varying DMSO concentrations[62] have been reported.

The results of the skin stripping study, shown in Figure 2, show a positive correlation between the layers of stratum corneum removed and the degree of permeability for the lower alkanols; but, very little effect on the higher alkanols was observed.

The DMSO results demonstrate a biphasic effect on penetration enhancement. Depending upon solvent composition, control may reside with either the thermodynamic effects on the permeant or on the kinetic influences on the membrane. At DMSO concentrations below 50% the thermodynamic effects of the vehicle on the permeant predominate, i.e., the amount of penetration is a function of the degree of lipophilicity of the permeant. In contrast, at DMSO concentrations above 50%, there appears to be a departure from thermodynamic control since a sharp increase in the permeation of methanol and butanol occurs at these higher concentrations. This kinetic mechanism is similar to that already described in the skin stripping study and suggest that changes in the diffusional resistance of the stratum corneum are operational in this phase. It is interesting to note that DMSO is typically not effective as a penetration enhancer at concentrations below 50%.[46]

C. Formulation Guidelines

Azone® has been successfully formulated into gels, creams, and lotions with both hydrophilic and lipophilic compounds. The penetration enhancing potential of Azone® seems to be maximized in formulations containing predominantly hydrophilic components. Consequently, large amounts of lipophilic agents such as petrolatum, mineral oil, high molecular weight polyethylene glycols, or isopropyl myristate should be avoided since they appear to bind the Azone® and suppress its penetration enhancing activity.

1. Optimum Azone® Concentration

With both hydrophilic and lipophilic drugs, there appears to be an optimum Azone® concentration for maximum skin penetration. For lipophilic drugs, as discussed in the case of the higher alkanols, the determination of this optimum concentration is particularly important for maximum penetration enhancement since higher Azone® concentrations result

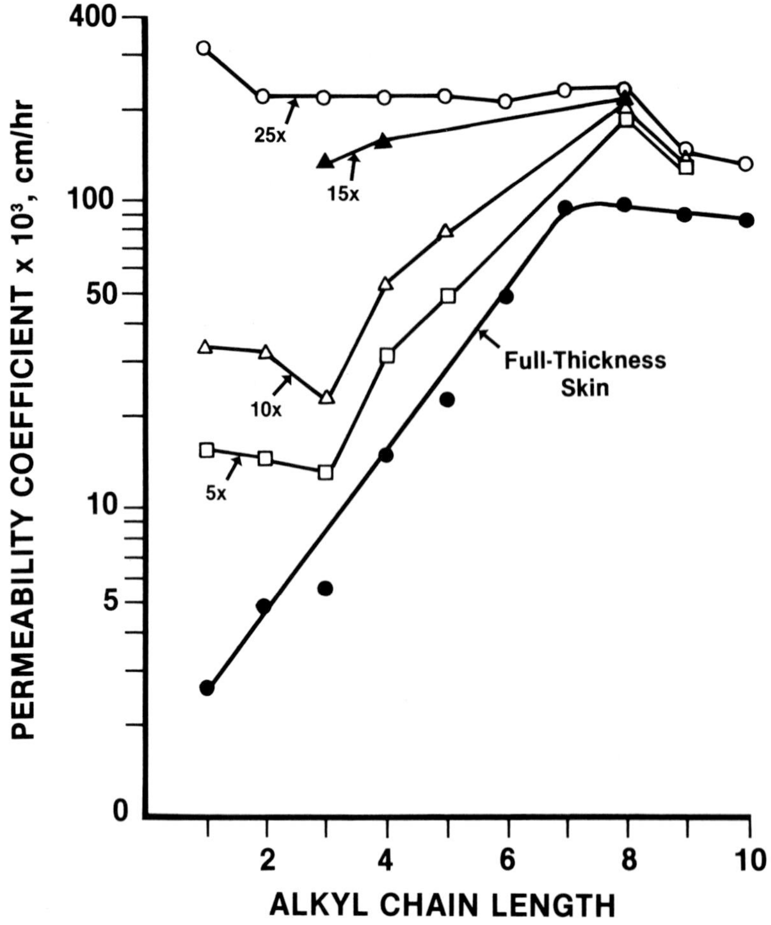

FIGURE 2. Semilog plot of permeability coefficients for stripped hairless mouse membranes and normal hairless mouse skin as a function of alkyl chain length. All data were obtained at 37°. The skin was stripped 5, 10, 15, and 25 times. (From Flynn, G. L., Durrheim, H. and Higuchi, W. I., *J. Pharm. Sci.*, 70, 56, 1981. With permission).

in increasingly lesser effects in penetration. In contrast, for hydrophilic drugs, beyond the optimum Azone® concentration, there is no additional effect on penetration and a plateau is generally seen.

For drugs soluble in Azone®, the solubility value of the drug in Azone® should be determined. Knowing the desired drug concentration in the final formulation, the required concentration of Azone® can be calculated by maintaining the proportion of the drug to Azone® at saturation level. This will favor maximum skin penetration.

For drugs insoluble in Azone®, identification of an Azone® compatible solvent should be the initial step. Glycerol, water, ethanol, isopropanol, or low concentrations of propylene glycol may be effective. By way of caution it should be pointed out that as a penetration enhancer, Azone® may accentuate skin reactions typically seen with some formulation excipients; for example, the skin irritation may occur when Azone® is combined with propylene glycol. This is especially true with high concentrations of propylene glycol. Once the appropriate solvent has been identified, then formulations with predominantly hydrophilic components and varying proportions of Azone® should be evaluated to identify the optimum level of Azone® in the formulation. It is generally seen that Azone® concentrations in the range 1 to 10% are most effective.

2. Sample Formulations

a. Gel formulation

For drugs soluble in Azone®, the following gel formulation serves as an example. This information has been found to work well for both hydrophilic and lipophilic drugs.

Ingredients	Percent
Drug and Azone®	Fixed proportion
Carbopol 930, 940 or 941	1—1.5
Tween-20	3—5
* Preservative	0.2—0.25
** Neutralizing agent	To required pH
Deionized water q.s.	100

For drugs not soluble in Azone®, the above formulation should be modified for the inclusion of the solvent in a fixed proportion to the drug.

b. Cream formulation

Cream formulations seem to be especially useful for lipophilic drugs. Lipophilic drugs in Azone® probably act as a reservoir for the intrinsic partitioning of the drug into the hydrophilic components of the formulation. Lipophilic drugs readily partition from the hydrophilic components into the stratum corneum. This process facilitates further partitioning from the reservoir to the hydrophilic components, maintaining the chemical equilibrium. Therefore, the rate and extent of penetration of lipophilic drugs in Azone® formulations should be maximized when large proportions of hydrophilic components are present in the formulation. The following sample formulation is appropriate for drugs soluble in Azone®.

Ingredients	Percent
Oil Phase	
Cetyl alcohol	8.0—10.0
Stearyl alcohol	1—2
Glyceryl monostearate	3—5
Drug and Azone®	Fixed proportion
Water phase	
***Hydrophilic solvent	5—10
Sodium lauryl sulfate	0.1
Deionized water q.s.	100

For drugs insoluble in Azone®, the above formulation could be modified for inclusion of the appropriate solvent. Depending on whether the solvent is water miscible or not, the saturated solution of the drug in the solvent is added to the water phase or the oil phase.

III. EVALUATION OF TOXICITY POTENTIAL OF AZONE®

A. Preclinical Studies

An extensive program has been conducted in mice, rats, guinea pigs, rabbits, and monkeys to determine the toxicity potential of Azone®.[58] The results of these studies demonstrate that Azone® possesses a safe toxicological profile. A summary of these studies follows.

* Combination preservatives such as methyl and propyl parabens or potassium sorbate and sorbic acid can be used. The oil soluble preservatives are dissolved in Azone®, by warming, if necessary.

** Carbopol solution can be neutralized with triethanolamine, solutions of sodium hydroxide, glycine, or 4-aminobutyric acid in water. Choice of neutralizing agent is based on the desired pH of the final formulation. With triethanolamine or sodium hydroxide the final pH will be neutral to basic while with the amino acid solutions it wil be in the acidic range.

***For example, propylene glycol or glycerine.

- The acute, oral LD_{50} of Azone® is high — more than 9000 mg/kg in rats and more than 7000 mg/kg in mice. The intraperitoneal LD_{50} is more than 4000 mg/kg in both mice and rats.
- In acute eye irritation studies in rabbits, Azone® was found to be nontoxic; Azone® 100% was slightly irritating but not toxic to the eyes of the animals tested.
- The results of acute dermal toxicity studies in animals show that animal models are not predictive of the topical irritability potential of Azone® in humans. Azone® was irritating to the skin of rodents and rabbits at concentrations of 10% or less, but was *not* found to be irritating to human skin (see Clinical Safety Studies below).
- The results of several neurotoxic studies in rodents are consistent with the results of other toxicity studies. The median neurotoxic dose of Azone® was approximately 0.7 mℓ/kg in rats.
- The results of long-term dermal toxicity studies in mice and rats consisting of 6 months of treatment revealed no treatment-related systemic changes and demonstrated the safety of Azone® in chronic administration.
- The results of a fertility and reproduction study in rats showed that dermal administration of Azone® did not interfere with the reproductive capacity of males or females nor were the offspring adversely affected.
- There was no evidence of embryo toxicity or teratogenicity following dermal administration of Azone® to mice.
- Azone® appears to be rapidly and essentially cleared from the circulation. The results of a pharmacokinetic study in monkeys showed that following intravenous administration of labeled Azone®, nearly 90% of the dose was recovered in 120 hr, including more than 75% from the urine. Following percutaneous administration, more than 70% of the administered dose was recovered externally; of the Azone® absorbed, the major route of elimination was urinary, as in the case of intravenous administration. Plasma levels of radioactivity remained very low throughout the study.
- The results of a pharmacokinetic study in mice following topical application are consistent with those in monkeys, approximately 90% of the Azone® absorbed was eliminated in the urine in 48 hr.
- Azone® was nonmutagenic in strains TA-153, TA-100 and TA-98, and was preferentially toxic to TA-1537.

As of this writing, additional long-term toxicologic studies are underway and have shown no untoward reactions or oncogenic potential.

B. Clinical Safety Studies

The results of a thorough program to evaluate its clinical safety have shown that Azone® does not appear to pose any undue risk in clinical use.

1. 21-Day Cumulative Irritancy Studies

Two studies to evaluate the relative irritancy potential of Azone® were performed. In the first study, several Azone® concentrations as well as controls were applied to each of 11 subjects. Materials were applied 5 days weekly for 21 days to the same site according to the method of Phillips.[63] Azone® in concentrations of up to 50% was not irritating. Full strength Azone® was slightly more irritating than its mineral oil control in one of the 11 volunteers.

In the second study, pure Azone® contained in a polymeric matrix delivery system and a control patch were applied to each of 10 subjects. Patches were applied 5 days weekly for 21 days to the same site also according to the method of Phillips.[63] The results of this study demonstrated that even at such high concentrations, Azone® was not irritating.

2. Modified Draize Skin Sensitization Study

Azone® at a concentration of 50% was evaluated for its potential to induce irritation and sensitization. A repeat-insult patch test on 200 human subjects was performed using a modification of the Draize procedure.[64] After the final challenge, retesting was done on subjects in whom erythema was observed; no irritation or sensitization developed. Overall, allergic contact sensitization did not occur at the Azone® concentration tested.

3. Photoirritation (Phototoxicity) Study

A study was done to determine the photoirritation (phototoxicity) potential of Azone® at a concentration of 100%. The study was perfomed using a modification of the Marzulli procedure[65] in ten healthy adults. The test site (upper arm or back) was moistened with approximately 0.2 mℓ of Azone® following cellophane tape stripping and irradiated after 1 hr. Readings of irradiated sites were made 24 hr later. There was no evidence of photoirritation (phototoxicity) in this assay.

4. Modified Photo Draize Skin Sensitization Study

The irritation and photosensitization potential of 100% Azone® was evaluated in a repeat-insult patch test on 25 heatlhy adults according to the Modified Draize procedure.[65] Irradiation was performed after each patch was removed. The challenge patch was removed after 24 hr, the area irradiated, and read 96 hr after application.

No evidence of allergic or photoallergic contact sensitization occurred. There were no dropouts for toxicity-related reasons.

IV. REPRESENTATIVE EXAMPLES OF ENHANCED PERCUTANEOUS ABSORPTION WITH AZONE®

A. Range of Pharmacologically Active Compounds Formulated with Azone®

Azone® has been formulated with hydrophilic and lipophilic compounds from a number of different classes. The list below shows many of the compounds already successfully formulated with Azone® for topical or transdermal application.

Class	Compound
Antibiotics	Clindamycin
	Erythromycin
	Fusidic acid
Antifungals	Griseofulvin
	Tolnaftate
Antivirals	Cytarabine
	Trifluorothymidine
Antimetabolites	5-Fluorouracil
Anthelmintics	Thiabendazole
Depigmenting agents	Hydroquinone
Corticosteroids	Amcinonide
	Desonide
	Desoximetasone
	Diflorasone diacetate
	Fluocinolone acetonide
	Triamcinolone acetonide
Nonsteroidal antiinflammatories	Indomethacin
	Ibuprofen
Nitrates	Isosorbide dinitrate

The partial list above does not include all compounds formulated in each class. Neither does it include all classes for which Azone® has been formulated such as betablockers, antihistamines, peptides, bronchodilators, neuroleptics, and steroidal hormones.

Table 3
BIOASSAY OF ANTIMICROBIAL ACTIVITY IN THE CORIUM AFTER TOPICAL APPLICATION OF CLINDAMYCIN[a]

With Azone®		Without Azone®	
% Clindamycin in vehicle A[b]	Average (range) radius of inhibition of *P. acnes* (mm)[c]	% Clindamycin in vehicle B[d]	Average (range) radius of inhibition of *P. acnes* (mm)[c]
1.0	28 (26—30)	1.0	21 (18—25)
0.5	26 (25—29)	0.5	19 (15—23)
0.1	17 (15—20)	0.1	13 (12—15)
0.02	9 (8—11)	0.02	0 (0)
0.004	6 (5—7)	0.004	0 (0)
0.0008	5 (3—7)	0.0008	0 (0)

[a] Different concentrations of clindamycin phosphate were incorporated into a vehicle with and without 8% 1-dodecylazacycloheptan-2-one (Azone®); 0.005 mℓ was applied to the epidermal surface. With Azone® there is a significant ($p < .001$) increase in antimicrobial activity at every concentration of clindamycin as compared with same concentration of clindamycin without Azone.®

[b] Vehicle A: 8% Azone®, 52% isopropyl alcohol, and 40% water.

[c] Ten specimens of *Propionibacterium acnes* were used.

[d] Vehicle B: 60% isopropyl alcohol and 40% water.

From Stoughton, R. B., *Arch. Dermatol.*, 118, 476, 1982. With permission.

B. Results of Topical Formulations for Localized Action

Using in vitro techniques, the percutaneous penetration of a number of compounds formulated with and without Azone® was evaluated. The results of these studies clearly demonstrate the magnitude of the effect of Azone®. Some of these results are presented in the following subsections.

1. Antibiotics

The penetration of antibiotics was evaluated by applying the formulations to epidermal discs in in vitro glass diffusion cells.[66] These cells were then incubated at 33°C. The receptor compartment was partly filled with saline so that the corium could be bathed with the water vapor. After a predetermined interval, the epidermis was heat separated. The radius of inhibition of organisms was then determined by applying a punch of the corium to an inoculated culture plate.

The results with clindamycin, erythromycin, and fusidate sodium are summarized in Tables 3, 4, and 5, respectively.

2. Corticosteroids

In vivo vasoconstriction was assessed using the methods of Stoughton.[29] Ethanolic solutions of steroids (with and without Azone®) were applied to the forearm of human volunteers without occlusion.[67] Steroid effectiveness was evaluated from the resultant blanching, using a scale from 0 (no vasoconstriction) to 3 (intense vasoconstriction). The vasoconstriction scores produced by five steroids are summarized in Table 6.

Subsequently, triamcinolone acetonide was reformulated as a cream with cetyl alcohol and stearyl alcohol as discussed elsewhere in this chapter. This Azone® optimized formulation was compared with two commercially available triamcinolone acetonide creams using the vasoconstrictor assay. These results are presented in Table 7.

3. Antifungals and Anthelmintics

Azone® optimized and control formulations were applied to the upper arm of human

Table 4
BIOASSAY OF ANTIMICROBIAL ACTIVITY IN HAIRLESS MOUSE SKIN AFTER TOPICAL APPLICATION OF 1% ERYTHROMYCIN[a]

Azone® (%)	Propylene glycol (%)	Isopropyl alcohol (%)	Average (range) radius of inhibition of *P. acnes* (mm)[b]
50	10	40	28 (26—30)
15	10	75	25 (22—28)
8	10	82	22 (18—24)
4	10	86	20 (16—22)
2	10	88	16 (12—19)
0	10	90	14 (10—16)

[a] Erythromycin base was applied to hairless mouse skin on penetration chamber in different concentrations of 1-dodecylazacycloheptan-2-one (Azone®) (0.005 mℓ). There was normal saline in the chamber but the level of the fluid was kept 4 mm below the corium. Specimens were incubated at room temperature for 20 hr. Then, the epidermis was removed and 6-mm punch biopsy specimens were taken and placed on brain-heart infusion agar plates inoculated with *Propionibacterium acnes*. The bioassay shows that (Azone®) concentrations of 2, 4, 8, 15, and 50% increase antimicrobial activity significantly compared with the formulation without Azone® $p < 0.1$; except 2% concentration, $p = .06$).

[b] Eight specimens of *Propionibacterium acnes* were used.

From Stoughton, R. B., *Arch. Dermatol.*, 118, 476, 1982. With permission.

Table 5
BIOASSAY OF ANTIMICROBIAL ACTIVITY IN THE CORIUM AFTER TOPICAL APPLICATION OF 1% FUSIDATE[a]

Azone® (%)	Propylene glycol (%)	Isopropyl alcohol (%)	Average (range) radius of inhibition of *P. acnes* (mm)[b]
50	10	40	2 (0—3)
25	10	65	5 (4—8)
12	10	78	6 (4—9)
6	10	84	11 (9—13)
3	10	87	16 (15—18)
0	10	90	6 (5—7)

[a] Fusidate sodium was applied to the epidermal surface in different concentrations of 1-dodecylazacycloheptan-2-one (Azone®) (0.005 mℓ). The bioassay shows increased antimicrobial activity from the vehicles containing Azone® at lower concentrations; Azone® concentrations of 3% and 6% give greater antimicrobial activity than the formulation without Azone® ($p < .01$).

[b] Ten specimens of *Propionibacterium acnes* were used.

From Stoughton, R. B., *Arch. Dermatol.*, 118, 476, 1982. With permission.

Table 6
EFFECT OF AZONE® ON VASOCONSTRICTION PRODUCED BY STEROIDS

Steroid	Azone® (%)	Ethyl alcohol (%)	Vasoconstriction score (Obs/max)[a]	Vasoconstriction score (%)	Ratio
Triamcinolone acetonide, 0.1%	0	99.9	21/72	29	2.24
	3	96.9	47/72	65	
Amcinonide, 0.1%	0	99.9	13/36	36	2.25
	2	97.9	29/36	81	
Desonide, 0.1%	0	99.9	14/42	33	2.45
	2	97.9	34/42	81	
Desoximetasone, 0.25%	0	99.9	6/30	20	3.65
	1	98.9	22/30	73	
Fluocinolone acetonide, 0.025%	0	99.9	4/45	9	4.44
	2	97.9	18/45	40	

[a] Obs/max = observed score/maximum score possible.

From Stoughton, R. B. and McClure, W. O., *Drug Dev. Ind. Pharm.*, 9(4), 725, 1983. With permission.

Table 7
EFFECT OF AZONE® ON VASOCONSTRICTION OF TRIAMCINOLONE ACETONIDE

Preparation	Vasoconstriction scores (maximum score = 30)
Triamcinolone acetonide 0.1%, Azone® 1.6% in a cream	28
Triamcinolone acetonide 0.1% commercial formulation A	7
Triamcinolone acetonide 0.1% commercial formulation B	3

volunteers according to the method of Knight.[68] The formulations were left in place for 20 min and then washed with soap and water for 60 sec. After the skin was dried, cellophane tape strippings of upper to lower stratum corneum were taken and inoculated with 600 spores of *Tricophyton mentagrophytes*. After 6 days incubation, the amount of growth was scored on a scale of 0 (no growth) to III (heavy growth).

The results of studies with thiabendazole and tolnaftate are represented in Figures 3 and 4, respectively.

4. Other Compounds

The penetration of a variety of compounds from a number of different therapeutic classes formulated with and without Azone® was evaluated. The in vitro flux through full thickness hairless mouse skin was assessed using the Franz diffusion cell assembly.

The results of the study with hydroquinone and indomethacin are shown in Figures 5, and 6, respectively; and the results of the study with 5-FU are summarized in Table 8.

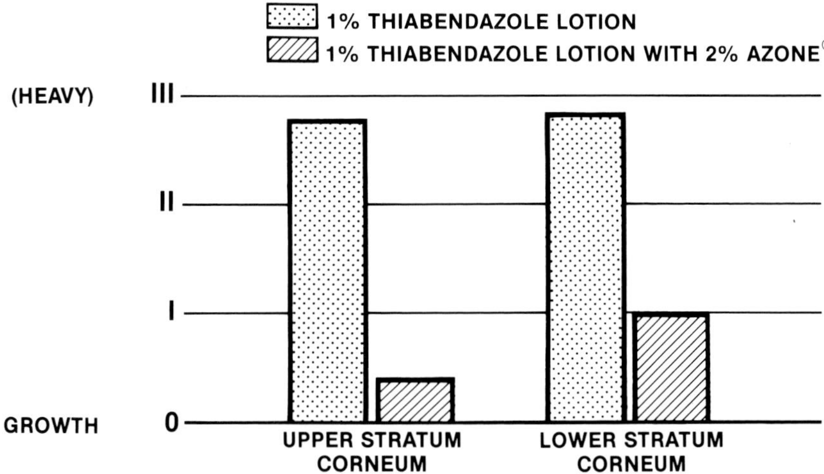

FIGURE 3. **Thiabendazole.** This graph summarizes the mean growth of T. mentagrophytes in upper and lower stratum corneum from 10 human volunteers. The Azone®-optimized thiabendazole formulation shows substantially greater growth inhibition than the thiabendazole formulation without Azone.®

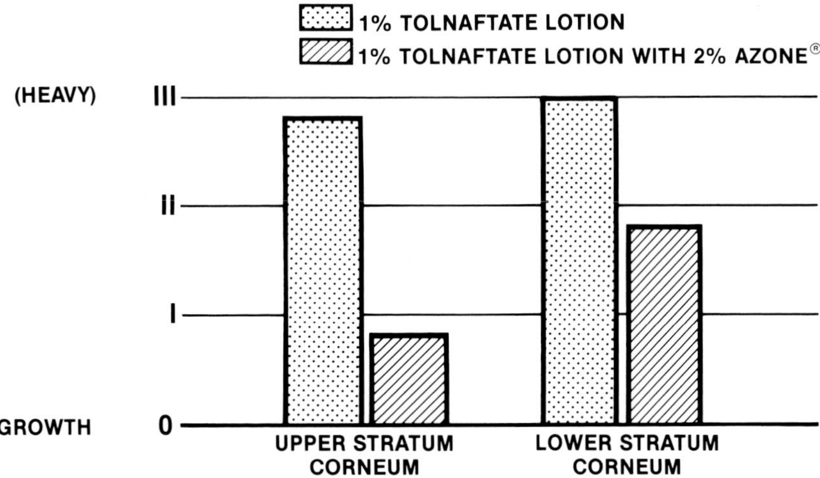

FIGURE 4. **Tolnaftate.** This graph summarizes the mean growth of *T. mentagrophytes* in upper and lower stratum corneum from 10 human volunteers. The Azone®-optimized tolnaftate formulation shows substantially greater growth inhibition than the tolnaftate formulation without Azone.®

In this section, we will report results of these in vivo animal studies for two representative drugs, namely indomethacin and isosorbide dinitrate.[58]

C. Results of Transdermal Formulations for Systemic Activity

To evaluate beneficial effects of Azone® for transdermal delivery, a number of polymeric matrices were evaluated. Both commercially available loading type devices and polymeric devices formulated in-house were used. In vitro hairless mouse skin assay in Franz diffusion cells was employed to evaluate the penetration of drugs from candidate formulations. Following conclusions drawn from in vitro studies, Azone® optimized formulations (along with appropriate control formulations) were evaluated by in vivo bioavailability studies in rhesus monkeys.

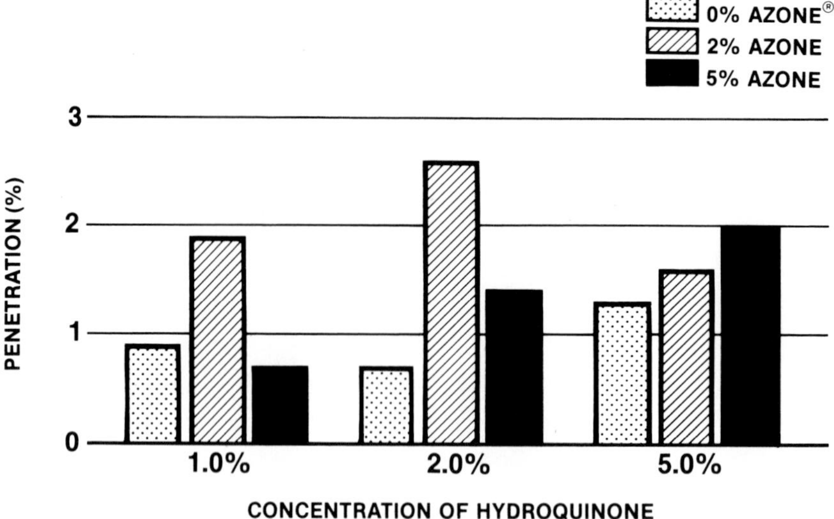

FIGURE 5. **Hydroquinone.** This graph summarizes the in vitro results of 9 formulations of hydroquinone (1, 2, and 5%) and Azone® (0, 2, and 5%) applied to hairless mouse skin. The formulation with 2% Azone® shows substantial penetration enhancement of hydroquinone compared to the formulation without Azone®.

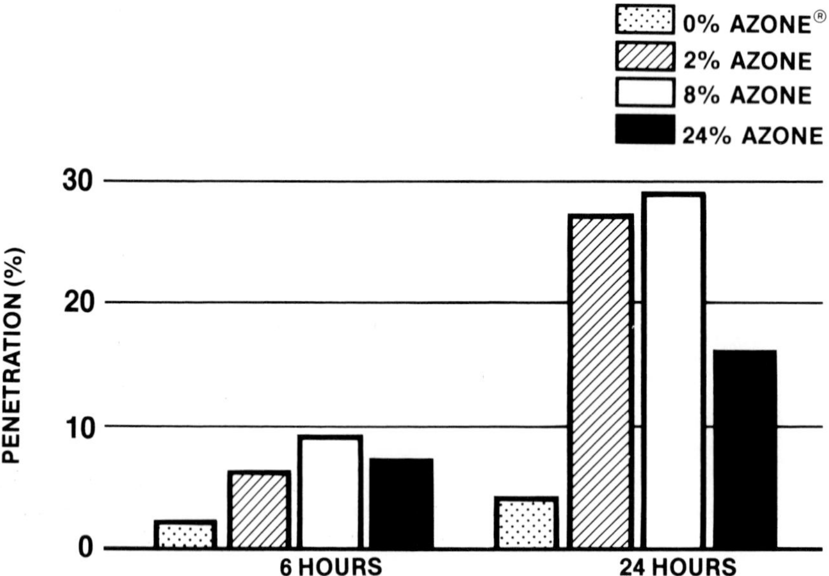

FIGURE 6. **Indomethacin.** This graph demonstrates the *in vitro* penetration of 1% indomethacin through full-thickness hairless mouse skin when formulated with Azone® (0, 2, 8 and 24%). The formulations with 2 and 8% Azone® show substantially more penetration than the formulation without Azone®, especially after 24 hr.

Table 8
PENETRATION OF SKIN BY 2.4% FLUOROURACIL IN DIFFERENT CONCENTRATIONS OF AZONE®[a]

Azone® (%)	Average (range) penetrating skin (%) 7 hr	24 hr
0	0.7 (0.5—1.1)	2.5 (0.9—5.2)
1.8	66.1 (43.0—75.1)	75.7 (62.1—85)
9.0	40.7 (35.1—46.2)	48.5 (40.6—54.2)
45.0	7.0 (4.2—9.3)	17.0 (12.5—23.6)

[a] Ten specimens were used for each concentration.

From Stoughton, R. B., *Arch. Dermatol.*, 118, 476, 1982. With permission.

In this section, we will report results of these in vivo animal studies for two representative drugs, namely indomethacin and isosorbide dinitrate.[58]

1. Indomethacin

The bioavailability of transdermally administered indomethacin in rhesus monkeys was evaluated. Polymeric matrix devices consisting of 1.3% indomethacin and 5% Azone® were used. Each 4-cm^2 patch contained 20 mg of the active drug. The test treatments consisted of transdermal applications at two dose levels, 20 and 40 mg. For the 40-mg dose, two 20-mg patches were applied at different sites. The patches were removed 24 hr after application. A 25-mg oral dose and 10-mg intravenous dose were employed as control treatments. There were three monkeys in each treatment group.

The mean indomethacin plasma concentration for each treatment group is shown in Figure 7. These results clearly demonstrate that plasma indomethacin levels following 40-mg transdermal administration are at least comparable to 25-mg oral dose. Moreover, appreciable plasma levels following 40-mg transdermal dose are maintained through 24 hr.

2. Isosorbide Dinitrate

The bioavailability of isosorbide dinitrate in rhesus monkeys was evaluated. Polymeric matrix devices consisting of 5% isosorbide dinitrate and 7% Azone® were used. Each 16-cm^2 patch contained 40 mg of the active drug. The test treatments consisted of transdermal applications at two dose levels, 40 and 80 mg. For 80-mg dose, two 40-mg patches were applied at different sites. The patches were removed 24 hr after application. A 40 mg oral dose and a 40-mg isosorbide dinitrate matrix formulation without Azone® were employed as control treatments.

The mean plasma concentrations of isosorbide dinitrate and of its metabolites, 2-mononitrate and 5-mononitrate, are shown in Figure 8, 9, and 10, respectively.

Following oral administration, isosorbide dinitrate blood levels are extremely low in contrast to that of its metabolites suggesting the rapid metabolism of this drug when administered by this route. Transdermal administration, on the other hand, is associated with sustained plasma levels over the time of application.

The peak isosorbide dinitrate plasma levels of approximately 160 and 70 ng/mℓ, with the 80- and 40-mg doses of the Azone® optimized formulation, respectively, are in contrast with the peak plasma levels of approximately 7 ng/mℓ for the 40-mg transdermal patch without Azone.® Such results clearly demonstrate the magnitude of Azone®'s penetration

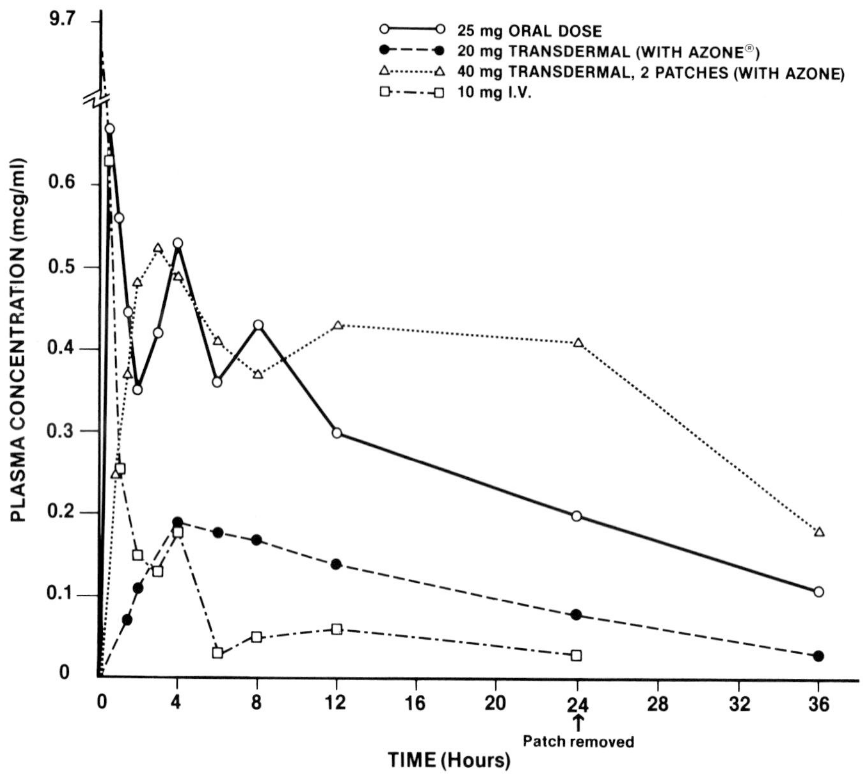

FIGURE 7. **Indomethacin.** This graph summarizes the results of an in vivo bioavailability study in rhesus monkeys. Indomethacin was administered as a 25-mg oral dose, a 10-mg intravenous dose, a 20-mg Azone®-optimized transdermal patch, and as two 20-mg Azone® optimized transdermal patches. The mean plasma levels are presented.

enhancing potential. Moreover, plasma levels of isosorbide dinitrate and its metabolites decline rapidly after removal of the Azone® optimized patches.

V. SUMMARY

The in vitro and in vivo data presented in this chapter demonstrate that Azone® possesses penetration enhancing properties with a wide variety of compounds and classes. Moreover, Azone®'s safety has been demonstrated in an unusually large number of preclinical and clinical safety studies. Heretofore, pharmaceutical excipients have not been studied in such depth.

In conclusion, we feel confident that by adhering to the formulation suggestions presented in this chapter, Azone® can play an important role in facilitating the skin penetration for many of the active drugs.

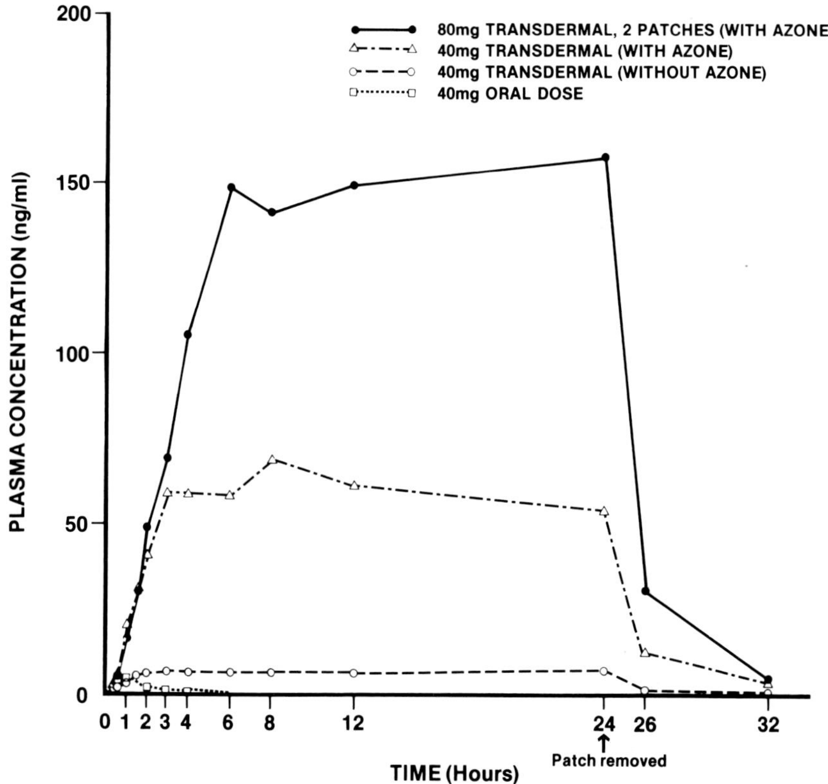

FIGURE 8. **Isosorbide Dinitrate(ISDN).** This graph summarizes the results of an in vivo bioavailability study in rhesus monkeys. ISDN was administered as a 40-mg oral dose, a 40-mg transdermal patch without Azone®, a 40-mg Azone® optimized transdermal patch, and as two 40-mg Azone® optimized transdermal patches. The mean plasma ISDN levels are presented.

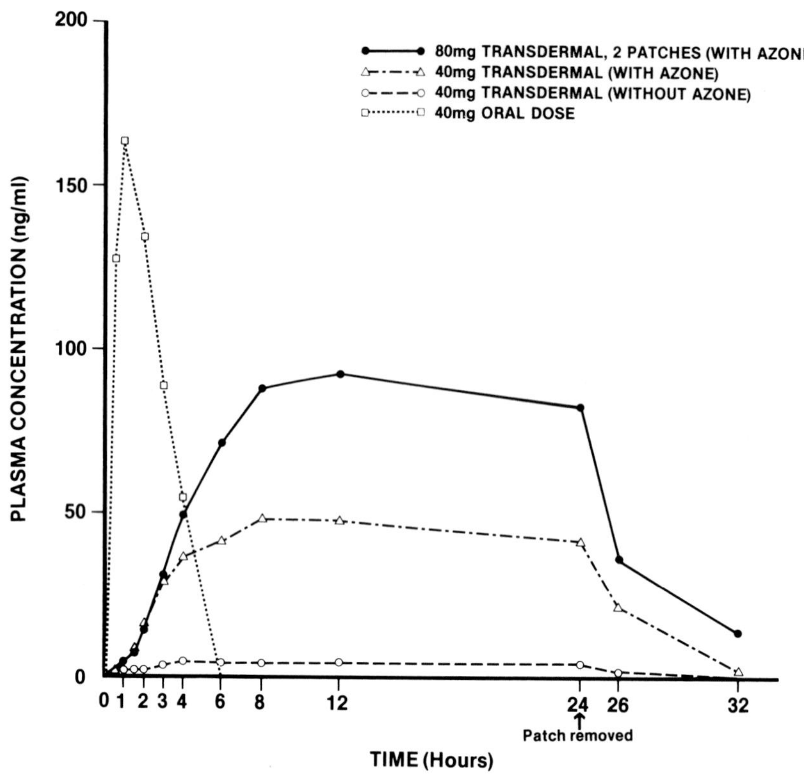

FIGURE 9. **2-Mononitrate.** This graph summarizes the results of an in vivo bioavailability study in rhesus monkeys. ISDN was administered as a 40-mg oral dose, a 40-mg transdermal patch without Azone® a 40-mg Azone®-optimized transdermal patch, and as two 40-mg Azone®-optimized transdermal patches. The mean plasma 2-mononitrate levels are presented.

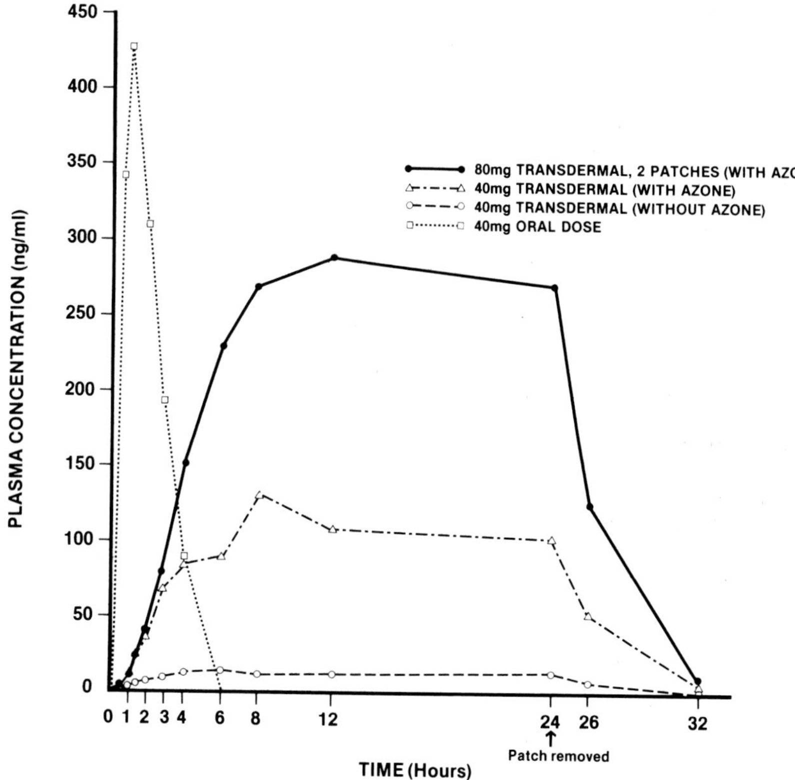

FIGURE 10. **5-Mononitrate.** This graph summarizes the results of an in vivo bioavailability study in rhesus monkeys. ISDN was administered as a 40-mg oral dose, a 40-mg transdermal patch without Azone®, a 40-mg Azone®-optimized transdermal patch, and as two 40-mg Azone®-optimized transdermal patches. The mean 5-mononitrate levels are presented.

REFERENCES

1. **Rothman, S.,** *Physiology and Biochemistry of the Skin,* University of Chicago Press, Chicago, 1954.
2. **Malkinson, F. D. and Rothman, S.,** Percutaneous absorption, in *Handbuch der Haut-und Geschlectskrankheiten: Normal und pathologische Physiologie der Haut.,* Vol. 1, (Part 3), Jadassohn, J., Ed., Springer-Verlag, Basel, 1963, 90.
3. **Malkinson, F. D.,** Permeability of the stratum corneum, in *The Epidermis,* Montagna, W. and Lobitz, W. C., Eds., Academic Press, New York, 1964, 435.
4. **Tregear, R. T.,** The permeability of skin to molecules of widely-differing properties, *Progress in the Biological Sciences in Relation to Dermatology,* Vol.2, Rook, A. and Champion, R. H., Eds., Cambridge University Press, New York, 1964, 275.
5. **Treager, R. T.,** *Physical Functions of Skin,* Academic Press, New York, 1966.
6. **Blank, I. H. and Scheuplein, R. J.,** Transport into and within the skin, *Br. J. Dermatol.,* 81 (Suppl. 4), 4, 1969.
7. **Scheuplein, R. J. and Blank, I. H.,** Permeability of the skin, *Physiol. Rev.,* 51, 702, 1971.
8. **Scheuplein, R. J.,** Skin permeation, *The Physiology and Pathophysiology of the Skin,* Vol. 5, Jarrett, A., Ed., Academic Press, New York, 1978, 1669.
9. **Scheuplein, R. J.,** Percutaneous absorption: theoretical aspects, *Percutaneous Absorption of Steroids,* Mauvais-Jarvis, P., Vickers, C. F. H., and Wepierre, J., Eds., Academic Press, New York, 1980, 1.
10. **Burch, G. E. and Winsor, T.,** Rate of insensible perspiration locally through living and through dead human skin, *Arch. Intern. Med.,* 74, 43, 1944.

11. **Winsor, T. and Burch, G. E.,** Diffusion of water through dead plantar, palmar, and tarsal human skin and through the nails, *Arch. Dermatol.*, 53, 39, 1946.
12. **Blank, I. H.,** Further observations on factors which influence the water content of the stratum corneum, *J. Invest. Dermatol.*, 36, 33, 1953.
13. **Monash, S. and Blank, H.,** Location and reformation of the epithelial barrier to water vapor, *Arch. Dermatol.*, 78, 710, 1958.
14. **Kligman, A. M.,** The biology of the stratum corneum, in *The Epidermis,* Montagna, W. and Lobitz, W. C., Jr., Eds., Academic Press, New York, 1964, 20
15. **Katz, M. and Poulsen, B. J.,** Absorption of drugs through the skin, in *Handbook of Experimental Pharmacology,* Vol. 28, (Part 1), Brodie, B. B. and Gillette, J., Eds., Springer-Verlag, Basel, 1971, 103.
16. **Poulsen, B. J.,** Design of topical drug products: biopharmaceutics, in *Drug Design (Medicinal Chemistry),* Vol. 4, Ariens, E. J., Ed., Academic Press, New York, 1973, 149.
17. **Idson, B.,** Percutaneous absorption, *J. Pharm. Sci.*, 64, 901, 975.
18. **Higuchi, T.,** Prodrug, molecular structure and percutaneous delivery, in *Deisgn of Biopharmaceutical Properties Through Prodrugs and Analogs,* Roche, B., Ed., American Pharmaceutical Association, Washington, D. C., 1977, 409.
19. **Flynn, G. L.,** Topical drugs, in *Modern Pharmaceutics,* Banker, G. S. and Rhodes, C. T., Eds., Marcel Dekker, New York, 1979, chap. 8.
20. **Shaw, J. E. and Chandrasekaran, S. K.,** Transdermal therapeutic systems, in *Drug Absorption: Proceedings of the International Conference on Drug Absorption,* Prescott, L. F. and Nimmo, W. S., Eds., ADIS Press, New York, 1981, 186.
21. **Shaw, J. E., Chandrasekaran, S. K., Michaels, A. S., and Taskovitch, L.,** Controlled transdermal delivery, *in vitro* and *in vivo,* in *Animal Models in Human Dermatology,* Maibach, H., Ed., Churchill Livingstone, Edinburgh, 1975, 138.
22. **Shaw, J. E., Chandrasekaran, S. K., Campbell, P. S., and Schmitt, L. G.,** New procedures for evaluating cutaneous absorption, in *Cutaneous Toxicity,* Drill, V. A. and Lazar, P., Eds., Academic Press, New York, 1977, 83.
23. **Shaw, J. E., Taskovich, L., and Chandrasekaran, S. K.,** Properties of skin in relation to drug absorption *in vitro* and *in vivo,* in *Current Concept in Cutaneous Toxicity,* Drill, V. A. and Lazar, P., Eds., Academic Press, New York, 1980, 127.
24. **Chandrasekaran, S. K., Bayne, W., and Shaw, J. E.,** Pharmacokinetics of drug permeation through human skin, *J. Pharm. Sci.*, 67, 1370, 1978.
25. **Chandrasekaran, S. K., Benson, H., and Urquhart, J.,** Methods to achieve controlled drug delivery — the biochemical engineering approach, in *Sustained and Controlled Release Drug Delivery Systems,* Robinson, J. R., Ed., Marcel Dekker, New York, 1978, 557.
26. **Chandrasekaran, S. K., Theeuwes, F., and Yum, S. I.,** The design of controlled drug delivery systems, in *Drug Design,* Vol. 8, Ariens, E. J., Ed., Academic Press, New York, 1979, 133.
27. **Poulsen, B. J., Young, E., Coquilla, V., and Katz, M.,** Effect of topical vehicle composition on the *in vivo* release of fluocinolone acetonide and its acetate ester, *J. Pharm. Sci.*, 57, 928, 1968.
28. **Coldman, M. F., Poulsen, B. J., and Higuchi, T.,** Enhancement of percutaneous absorption by the use of volatile: non-volatile systems as vehicles, *J. Pharm. Sci.*, 58, 1098, 1969.
29. **Stoughton, R. B.,** Bioassay of formulations of topically applied glucocorticosteroids, *Arch. Dermatol.*, 106, 825, 1972.
30. **Chowhan, Z. T. and Pritchard, R.,** Effect of surfactants on percutaneous absorption of naproxen. I. Comparisons of rabbit, rat, and human excised skin, *J. Pharm. Sci.*, 67, 1272, 1978.
31. **Windheuser, J. J., Haslam, J. L., Caldwell, L., and Shaffer, R. D.,** The use of *N,N*-diethyl-*m*-toluamide to enhance dermal and transdermal delivery of drugs, *J. Pharm. Sci.*, 71, 1211, 1982.
32. **Ostrenga, J., Steinmetz, C., Poulsen, B., and Yett, S.,** Significance of vehicle composition. II. Prediction of optimal vehicle composition, *J. Pharm. Sci.*, 60, 1180, 1971.
33. **Turi, J. S., Danielson, D., and Woltersom, J. W.,** Effects of polyoxypropylene 15 stearyl ether and propylene glycol on percutaneous penetration rate of diflorasone diacetate, *J. Pharm. Sci.*, 68, 275, 1979.
34. **Marion-Landais, G. and Krum, R. J.,** Specialized vehicles to augment percutaneous penetration of topical steroids, *Curr. Ther. Res. Clin. Exp.*, 25, 56, 1979.
35. **Stoughton, R. B.,** Dimethylsulfoxide (DMSO) induction of a steroid reservoir in human skin, *Arch. Dermatol.*, 91, 657, 1965.
36. **Stoughton, R. B. and Fritsch, W. E.,** Influence of dimethylsulfoxide (DMSO) on human percutaneous absorption, *Arch. Dermatol.*, 90, 512, 1964.
37. **Munro, D. D. and Stoughton, R. B.,** Dimethylacetamide (DMAC) and dimethylformamide (DMFA) effect on percutaneous absorption, *Arch. Dermatol.*, 92, 585, 1965.
38. **Sarkany, I., Hadgraft, J. W., Caron, G. A., and Barrett, C. W.,** The role of vehicles in the percutaneous absorption of corticosteroids, *Br. J. Dermatol.*, 77, 569, 1965.

39. **Allenby, A. C., Creasy, N. H., Edgington, A. G., Fletcher, J. A., and Schock, C.,** Mechanism of action of accelerants on skin penetration, *Br. J. Dermatol.*, 81, Suppl. 4, 47, 1969.
40. **Stoughton, R. B.,** Percutaneous absorption, *Toxicol. Appl. Pharmacol.*, 7 (2), 1, 1965.
41. **Allenby, A. C., Fletcher, J., Schock, C., and Tees, T. F. S.,** The effect of heat, pH, and organic solvents on the electrical impedance and permeability of excised human skin, *Br. J. Dermatol.*, 81 (Suppl. 4), 31, 1969.
42. **Baker, H. J.,** The effects of dimethylsulfoxide, dimethylformamide, and dimethylacetamide on the cutaneous barrier to water in human skin, *J. Invest. Dermatol.*, 50, 283, 1968.
43. **McDermot, H. L., Finkbeiner, A. J., Wells, W. J., and Heggic, R. M.,** The enhancement of penetration of an organophosphorous anticholinesterase through guinea pig skin by DMSO, *Can. J. Physiol. Pharmacol.*, 45, 299, 1967.
44. **Kligman, A. M.,** Topical pharmacology and toxicology of dimethylsulfoxide — part 1, *JAMA*, 193, 796, 1965.
45. **Kligman, A. M.,** Dimethylsulfoxide — part 2, *JAMA*, 193, 923, 1965.
46. **Barry, B. W.,** *Dermatological Formulations: Percutaneous Absorption*, Marcel Dekker, New York, 1983, chap. 4.
47. **Rajadhyaksha, V. J.,** U. S. Patent 3,989,815, 1976.
48. **Rajadhyaksha, V. J.,** U. S. Patent 3,991,203, 1976.
49. **Rajadhyaksha, V. J.,** U. S. Patent 4,122,170, 1978.
50. **Rajadhyaksha, V. J.,** U. S. Patent 4,405,616, 1983.
51. **Rajadhyaksha, V. J.,** U. S. Patent 4,415,563, 1983.
52. **Rajadhyaksha, V. J.,** U. S. Patent 4,423,040, 1983.
53. **Rajadhyaksha, V. J.,** U. S. Patent 4,424,210, 1984.
54. **Rajadhyaksha, V. J.,** U. S. Patent 4,444,762, 1984.
55. **Rajadhyaksha, V. J.,** U. S. Patent 3,989,816, 1976.
56. **Rajadhyaksha, V. J.,** U. S. Patent 4,316,893, 1982.
57. **Rajadhyaksha, V. J., Peck, J. V., and Minaskanian, G.,** U. S. Patent 4,422,970, 1983.
58. **Nelson Research & Development Co.,** data on file (Drug master file 4670/ADA), Irvine, Calif.
59. **Vaidyanathan, R., Flynn, G. L., and Higuchi, W. I.,** Azone® Enhanced Delivery of Drugs into the Epidermis. I. Effect of Enhancer Concentration on the Perméability of Select Compounds, Abstract, American Pharmaceutical Association, Academy of Pharmaceutical Society Meeting, San Diego, November, 1982.
60. **Kurihara, T.,** Physicochemical Study of the Accelerant Effects of DMSO on Percutaneous Absorption of an Antiviral Drug and Other Chemical Prototypes, Ph.D. thesis, University of Michigan, Ann Arbor, 1983.
61. **Flynn, G. L., Durrheim, H., and Higuchi, W. I.,** Permeation of hairless mouse skin. II. Membrane sectioning techniques and influence on alkanol permeabilities, *J. Pharm. Sci.*, 70, 52, 1981.
62. **Kurihara, T., Flynn, G. L., and Higuchi, W. I.,** Considerations in Percutaneous Drug Delivery: Influence on Permeant Lipophilicity on DMSO Mediated Mass Transfer Across Skin, Abstract, American Pharmaceutical Association, Academy of Pharmaceutical Society Meeting, San Diego, November, 1982.
63. **Phillips, L., Steinberg, M., Maibach, H. I., and Akers, W. A.,** A comparison of rabbit and human skin response to certain irritants, *Toxic. Appl. Pharmacol.*, 21, 369, 1972.
64. **Marzulli, F. and Maibach, H.,** Contact allergy: predictive testing in humans, *Adv. Mod. Toxicol.*, 4, 353, 1977.
65. **Marzulli, F. and Maibach, H.,** Perfume phototoxicity, *J. Soc. Cos. Chem.*, 21, 695, 1970.
66. **Stoughton, R. B.,** Enhanced percutaneous penetration with 1-dodecylazacyclohepton-2-one, *Arch. Dermatol.*, 118, 474, 1982.
67. **Stoughton, R. B. and McClure, W. O.,** Azone®: a new non-toxic enhancer of cutaneous penetration, *Drug. Dev. Ind. Pharm.*, 9(4), 725, 1983.
68. **Knight, A. G.,** Culture of dermatophytes upon stratum cornium, *J. Invest. Dermatol.*, 59, 427, 1973.

Chapter 6

INFLUENCE OF VEHICLES ON SKIN PENETRATION

Joel L. Zatz and Pramod P. Sarpotdar

TABLE OF CONTENTS

I. INTRODUCTION

While permeation through skin is a passive process, the primary barrier layer of the skin, the stratum corneum, is not inert. Interactions of drugs, solvents, and other substances with the stratum corneum may lead to changes in resistance to diffusional transfer. In general, alterations in vehicle formulations affect one or both of the following:

1. Escaping tendency of the drug from the vehicle
2. Skin membrane resistance

Escaping tendency from the vehicle influences the membrane/vehicle partition coefficient which controls the concentration gradient across the stratum corneum. Thus, a higher escaping tendency is reflected as a higher gradient and therefore leads to faster penetration through the skin.

Skin membrane resistance is usually described in terms of an effective diffusion coefficient. Changes in diffusional path length would also affect membrane resistance, but such changes are not likely to occur when different formulations of a single drug entity are considered.

Differences in escaping tendency are due to changes in the degree of drug-vehicle interaction and do not affect the structure or integrity of the membrane. These are noninteractive effects because the skin is not involved. Changes in skin membrane resistance imply an alteration in the makeup or organization of the stratum corneum.

II. pH

The stratum corneum is a tough, chemically resistant tissue. While it can be damaged by exposure to solutions of extreme pH, moderate pH values (about 3 or 4 to 9) are tolerated. Skin penetration of nonionic compounds is unaffected by pH within this range. The penetration of ionogenic drugs depends on pH because of its effect on the relative concentrations of charged and uncharged species. Each form of the drug has its own solubility and intrinsic permeability.

A discussion of this situation has been given by Michaels et al.[1] On the assumption that each specie permeates the skin at a rate proportional to its concentration gradient and that the diffusion of each specie is independent of the other species present, the following equation was derived for weak bases:

$$\frac{J_{B(o)}\, t_S}{C_{B(o)}} = \frac{P_B + P_{BH^+}(C_{H^+}/K_A)}{(1 + C_{H^+}/K_A)}$$

In this equation, $J_{B(o)}$ is the total drug flux, $C_{B(o)}$ is the total drug concentration, t_s is the stratum corneum thickness, P_B and P_{BH+} are the specific permeability of the unionized, and ionized drug, respectively, C_{H+} is hydrogen ion concentration and K_A is the ionization constant for the drug. The specific permeability is the permeability constant multiplied by t_s. At a fixed pH, all of the terms on the right hand side of the equation are constants, so that flux should be proportional to drug concentration. This was confirmed experimentally for scopolamine, ephedrine, and chlorpheniramine.[1]

If it is assumed that both species have the same diffusion coefficient, the specific permeabilities are in the ratio of the respective partition coefficients. We may anticipate that the unionized form will be the more permeable and the less water soluble specie. Because of both factors, the specific permeability of the unionized form will be greater than the ionized form. The maximum flux that can be obtained (this would occur when saturated solutions are applied to the skin) is a function of both the specific permeability and the solubility (C^0):

Table 1
EFFECT OF IONIZATION ON SKIN PERMEATION

Drug	Skin species	Relative permeability constant[a]	Relative maximum flux[b]	Ref.
Ephedrine	Human	0.06	—	1
Scopolamine	Human	0.06	0.36	1
Chlorpheniramine	Human	0.004	—	1
Methotrexate	Hairless mouse	—	0.1	2

[a] Permeability constant of ionized/unionized specie.
[b] Flux of ionized/unionized specie.

$$\frac{J_{MAX(B)}}{J_{MAX(BH^+)}} = \frac{P_B C_B^0}{P_{BH^+} C_{BH^+}^0}$$

In this equation, J_{MAX} is maximum flux. The subscripts (B) and (BH+) refer to the free base (unionized) and ionized form, respectively.

Table 1 contains some data from several ionogenic compounds. As expected, the permeability constant for the unionized form of each drug is considerably greater than for the ionized form. Experimental values of maximum flux were used to estimate the ratios that are quoted in Table 1. The computations show that the unionized specie is the more permeable. From data presented by Wallace et al.,[2] the maximum flux of the unionized form of methotrexate was about 10 times the maximum flux of the ionized form. This was not accounted for by differences in membrane gradient (estimated as the product of solubility and partition coefficient) leading to the conclusion that differences in diffusivity or diffusional pathway taken by the two forms was responsible.

III. SOLVENTS

Solvents or cosolvents chosen for a formulation affect the escaping tendency from the vehicle and therefore the rate of percutaneous absorption. Solvent molecules may themselves enter the skin and effect changes in structure which, in turn, influence drug permeation. It is well known that the degree of hydration is an important consideration in the penetration of many drugs.

A. Escaping Tendency

Although many types of interactions can occur when drug solutions are applied to the skin, the effect of solvents on escaping tendency must always be considered. Ideally, saturated solutions of the same drug in different solvents should have the same escaping tendency. In saturated solutions, dissolved drug is in equilibrium with excess solid whose thermodynamic activity is assigned a value of unity. Therefore, the activity of dissolved drug is also unity. At lower concentrations, the escaping tendency is reduced. In many cases reported in the literature, flux is proportional to concentration so that the ratio of drug concentration to its solubility in the vehicle may be used as an indication of escaping tendency. Another possibility, based on the regular solution theory, is to relate escaping tendency to the excess free energy of solute in the vehicle.[3] This approach was used to account for differences in steady-state penetration of propionic acid through porcine skin from a series of organic solvents.

A change in vehicle that increases drug solubility leads to a decrease in the percutaneous absorption rate if the drug concentration in the solution is kept constant. For example, the

Table 2
HYDROCORTISONE FLUX THROUGH MOUSE SKIN[6]

Cosolvent	Concentration (%v/v)	Steady-state flux (μg/hr/cm²)	Concentration/ solubility
Propylene	25	0.119	1.1 (supersaturated)
Glycol	40	0.089	0.91
	60	0.078	0.65
Isopropanol	20	0.217	1.1 (supersaturated)
	40	0.214	0.22
	60	0.196	0.11

steady-state penetration flux of diflorasone diacetate through hairless mouse skin from mineral oil (polyoxypropylene 15 stearyl ether) solutions was progressively reduced in the presence of higher quantities of the latter, which acts as a cosolvent for the drug.[4] Similarly, the penetration of butyl paraben through guinea pig skin from aqueous solutions was reduced by the addition of two cosolvents, polyethylene glycol 400 and propylene glycol.[5]

Shahi and Zatz[6] determined the effect of two cosolvents, propylene glycol and isopropanol, on steady-state penetration of hydrocortisone through mouse skin. The data are collected in Table 2. It is evident that in the case of propylene glycol-water solutions, hydrocortisone flux is correlated with escaping tendency, expressed as the ratio of concentration to solubility in the vehicle. In other words, the effects of propylene glycol concentration can be explained in terms of nointeractive vehicle effects. However, this is not the case for penetration from isopropanol-water solutions. The flux varies very little although there are large differences in the concentration-solubility ratio. Clearly, for these solutions, other factors aside from escaping tendency must be operative. It is apparent that isopropanol interacts with mouse stratum corneum and that the effect of this interaction balances that of escaping tendency in this particular group of experiments.

B. Interaction of Solvents with Skin

Although human skin is a passive barrier, there is probably not a single solvent which does not interact in some way with the skin. The stratum corneum in vivo is always partially hydrated and as long as the ambient relative humidity is less than 100%, the transfer of water has to be in an outward direction. At between 40 to 90% ambient relative humidity the amount of water per gram of tissue at 31°C is reported to be 0.2 to 0.7 g.[7] This water content has a significant effect on the permeability of the skin. Scheuplein and Ross[8] showed that the normal hydrated stratum corneum is about 10 times more permeable compared to the dried stratum corneum. When soaked in water, stratum corneum can absorb up to two to three times its own weight, which increases its permeability for water and polar compounds even further.[9] Stoughton[10] showed that the changes in the ambient relative humidity from 50 to 100% increased the flux of glucocorticosteroids by a factor of 10. Based on this property of the skin, it is reasonable to assume that the solvents which increase the hydration of the skin generally will increase its permeability while the hygroscopic solvents like polyethylene glycol or glycerol will decrease the permeability of the skin by creating sink conditions for water on the outside of skin.[11]

Another way that solvents interact with the skin is by combining with or dissolving in the structures of substances making up the barrier. One such compound is dimethyl sulfoxide (DMSO). Much work has been done to understand its mechanism of action. One theory is that DMSO increases the permeability of the skin by displacing the bound water from the skin and causing structural changes in protein.[12-13] A second theory postulates that DMSO acts as a carrier.[14] Relatively high concentrations (over 50%) of DMSO are needed before a significant effect on penetration can be seen. In general, the aprotic solvents, e.g., dimethyl acetamide (DMA) and dimethyl formamide, cause the keratin to swell and leach out essential structural material from the stratum corneum. This results in decreased diffusional resistance of the barrier.[15] Substitution of the *n*-alkyl groups of DMA and the related aliphatic amides results in a decrease in the penetration enhancing capacity. This is related to the reduced tendency of the substituted compounds to accept protons, thus reducing their ability to interact with the skin.[16] Hydrophilic solvents like propylene glycol can also act as sorption promoters. However, their effectiveness is much lower compared to dipolar aprotic solvents.

In addition to proteins and water, lipids play an important role in the composition of the stratum corneum. Delipidization of the stratum corneum often destroys its barrier function.[17] Scheuplein showed this effect by delipidizing skin with various organic solvents.[18] However, the increase in permeability does not always relate to delipidization.[19] Ethanol and acetone react with the skin reversibly while chloroform-methanol and hexane cause irreversible damage to the skin.[20]

The pathological response to the solvent-skin interaction is generally limited to inflammation, even though on continuous exposure, sloughing and extensive damage can occur. The four cardinal signs of inflammation are redness, swelling, pain, and heat. It is characterized by localized cellular destruction, release of histamine, bradykinin, serotonin, and other enzymes from the mast cells, vasodilation with increased capillary permeability, and edema formation.[21]

Many of the penetration promoters also promote skin irritation. For example, the application of DMSO on human skin produces a burning sensation and localized irritation.

C. Cosolvent Effects on Percutaneous Absorption

Cosolvents have two types of effects on percutaneous absorption. First, they increase the solubility of the penetrating molecule in the vehicle. This increase in solubility changes the rate limiting step from dissolution control to barrier control, assuming that the thermodynamic activity is maintained in the presence of the cosolvent. These effects are discussed above. Cosolvents also interact with the skin and alter the permeability of the barrier membrane. Recently Barry et al.[22] compared the penetration of betamethasone 17-benzoate dissolved in several solvents. Only *N*-methyl-2-pyrrolidone and 2-pyrrolidone showed some penetration enhancement compared to a relatively noninteracting solvent, dimethyl isosorbide. Matheson et al.[23] determined the effect of the pretreatment of excised human skin with several other solvents on the transport of sarin. Except for methyl orthoformate, the pretreatment with solvents increased the sarin transport rate at least three times.

Essentially, the interaction of cosolvents with the skin alters either the hydration of the tissue or affects the protein or lipid layer. Except in the case of hygroscopic solvents, which dehydrate the skin, interaction between solvent and the skin generally promotes the penetration rate of the compound.

In in vitro penetration studies, cosolvents are sometimes used in the receptor solutions also.[24-25] The increase in solubility of the penetrating molecule in the receptor solution maintains sink conditions for the otherwise insoluble compound. Even though theoretically this manipulation is acceptable, one has to be careful with the amount and nature of the cosolvent used in the receptor medium. Figure 1[26] shows the cumulative amounts of an anti-inflammatory drug penetrated through human cadaver skin. In all cases, the drug was applied in excess on the donor side. The amount of the drug penetrated after 6 days dropped sharply when 20% polyethylene glycol 400 (PEG 400) was used in the receptor medium. A further increase in the concentration of PEG 400 does not seem to have any further effect. This is not expected because the drug is highly insoluble in water and has a very good solubility in PEG 400. Although, a sink condition is maintained more effectively with the increasing concentration of PEG 400 in the receptor, it appears that the penetration of the drug is adversely affected.

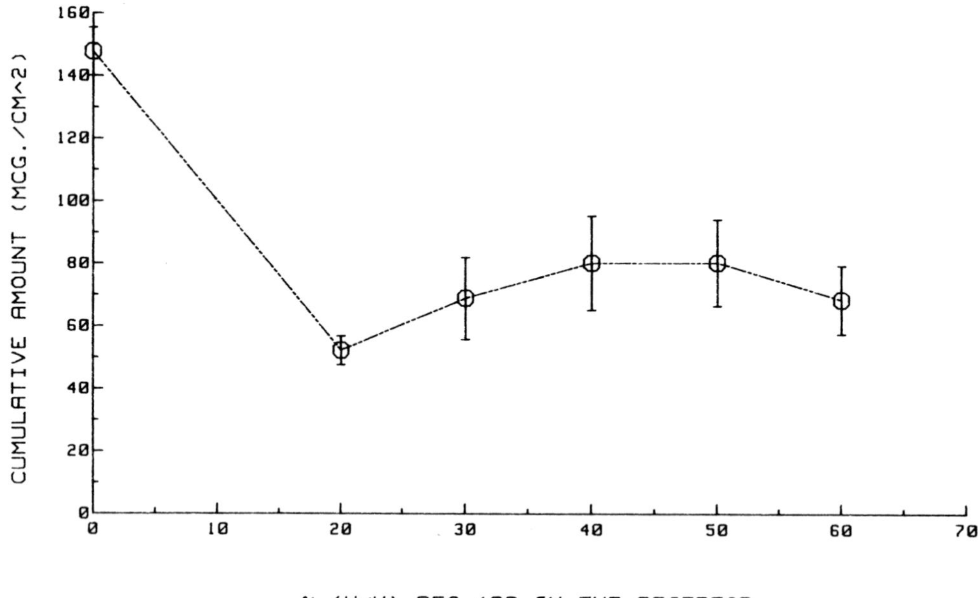

FIGURE 1. Cumulative amounts of oxaprozin penetrated through cadaver skin in 144 hr. Donor: 1% oxaprozin in methanol.

D. Measuring Solvent-Skin Interaction

In order to quantitate the interactive effects of solvents that influence percutaneous absorption, it is necessary to account for differences in escaping tendency. Roberts and Anderson[27] determined steady-state percutaneous absorption rates of phenol from different solvents using two membranes: rat skin and polyethylene film. In the absence of specific interactions with the skin membrane (in other words, if only escaping tendency controlled the penetration rate through each membrane), the ratio of permeability coefficients for each solvent should be the same. In fact, this turned out to be the case for light liquid paraffin, arachis oil, and glycerin. The skin-polyethylene permeability ratio was somewhat higher for water and ethanol, and considerably higher for dimethyl formamide and DMSO. The latter two compounds are known to enhance penetration by affecting skin properties.

Another approach to quantitation of skin-solvent interaction makes use of the fact that saturated solutions of a given drug in different solvents have the same escaping tendency. Therefore, in the absence of significant interactions with the membrane, the flux from solutions should be the same, independent of the solvent. Deviations are an indication of the extent of skin-solvent interaction. The flux from saturated solutions may be termed the maximal flux. It may be determined experimentally, or if this is not possible, it can be estimated from permeation data at lower drug concentrations. Data showing results for benzocaine penetration through two membranes are given in Table 3.[28]

The polypropylene membrane was chosen because of its inertness as a means of testing this method. Maximal flux values through this membrane (Table 3) differ by less than a factor of two despite the fact that the solubilities differ several hundredfold. This is not true for the maximal flux values through hairless mouse skin. While the maximal flux for water and propylene glycol are approximately the same, that for PEG 400 is about one-tenth the other values.

Because of the nature of the stratum corneum, there are probably very few (if any) solvents that are truly inert when placed in contact with this membrane. Water itself must be considered

Table 3
BENZOCAINE PERMEATION FROM VARIOUS SOLVENTS[28]

Solvent	Solubility at 30°C (mg/mℓ)	Js (maximum flux) (mg/cm ^{2}/hr) Polypropylene membrane	Hairless mouse skin
Water	1.26	0.089	0.10
Propylene glycol	146	0.16	0.094
Polyethylene glycol 400	435	0.13	0.010

interactive because the stratum corneum swells in the presence of water and the permeation rate of many substances is increased when the stratum corneum is hydrated. Consequently, comparisons of maximal flux should be thought of as indicating differences in the extent of interaction with skin which lead to changes in permeability.

The permeation of estradiol through excised human skin from solution in various non-volatile solvents was recently studied.[29] A constant concentration of estradiol was utilized so that the escaping tendency from the solutions varied considerably. Many of the solvents chosen appeared to influence penetration through interaction with the skin. Similar conclusions were obtained from comparison of maximum flux values estimated from data supplied in the paper.[30]

Irritation of the skin is an adverse reaction of the solvent-skin interaction. Primary skin irritation studies are usually done on animals. The American Society for Testing and Materials designates two tests; the first uses rabbit back (ASTM designation: F719-81) while the second uses guinea pigs (ASTM designation: F721-81). The Draize test[31] makes use of human volunteers to compare blanching effects. Several nondestructive methods are reviewed elsewhere[32] and are discussed in the chapter in this monograph.

Experimentally, solvent effects are evaluated either by in vitro or by in vivo techniques.

In vitro determination — Franz diffusion cells[33] or modifications of the original cell are commonly used in in vitro analysis. Excised skin of the hairless mouse, Swiss Webster mouse, rat, hairless dog, New Zealand rabbit, and guinea pig ears are some of the animal models. Use of excised human cadaver skin is becoming increasingly popular. The amount of intact drug which reaches the dermal side is detected by radioanalysis or any other suitable analytical technique.

In vivo determination — The analysis is based on the pharmacological response to the penetrating molecule or indirect analysis, e.g., urine analysis. Table 4 lists some of the techniques reported in literature.

IV. SURFACTANTS

Surfactants accumulate at interfaces and tend to be active at biological surfaces such as membranes. Many products applied to the skin contain surfactants which function as emulsifiers, wetting agents, solubilizers, etc. Whether they are included because of their effect on skin penetration or not, the possibility that they may interact with the skin and influence permeation should be kept in mind. A discussion of such interaction is also included in the chapter by Cooper and Berner.

Table 4
LIST OF TECHNIQUES USED IN IN VIVO DETERMINATION OF THE SOLVENT EFFECTS ON SKIN PENETRATION

Pharmacological response	Ref.
Vasoconstrictor assay	22, 34
T-lymphocytes count in peripheral blood	35
Urine analysis	36, 37
Electrical impedance	38, 39
Biopsy	40
Tissue distribution	41, 42
Morphological changes	43, 44
Immunofluorescence	45
Collagen content	46
Electron microscope autoradiography	47, 48
Breath analysis	49
Moisture analysis	50
Microautoradiography	51

A. Ionic Surfactants

Surfactant properties often depend on the nature of the polar head group. Ionic surfactants, particularly the anionics, may be somewhat irritating. Several anionic detergents reduce the water-holding capacity of the stratum corneum by leaching low molecular weight compounds. Another effect of interaction with the skin is the release of enzymes following contact with the skin. This was demonstrated by in vitro experiments on rat skin slices.[52]

Using an electrometric measuring technique, Dugard and Scheuplein[53] investigated changes in human epidermis brought about by contact with several ionic surfactants. Electrical conductance measurements were correlated with water permeation through the epidermal membranes. The magnitude of changes in conductance depended on the nature of the polar group as well as the hydrocarbon chain length of the surfactant. Maximum conductance values were obtained with surfactants containing 12 carbon atoms. It was suggested that proteins within the stratum corneum were the primary focus of surfactant activity.

Scheuplein and Ross[18] showed that the rate of water transport increased with time in the presence of sodium laurate and sodium lauryl sulfate. This was attributed to a denaturation of stratum corneum proteins by these detergents. The effect was reversible if the surfactants were washed out of the membranes after a short period of time.

Several studies have shown that drug permeation can be increased in the presence of anionic surfactants. The rate of penetration of chloramphenicol through hairless mouse skin was increased in the presence of sodium lauryl sulfate.[54] Naproxen flux through human abdominal skin from aqueous gels was increased by the addition of sodium lauryl sulfate.[55]

Many experiments which evaluate the effect of surfactants on skin penetration overlook the influence that surfactants may have on drug escaping tendency because of solubilization within the vehicle. If solubilization takes place, the bound drug is not available for partitioning into the skin surface and this would lead to a reduction in flux under certain conditions. The effect of solubilization must be accounted for if penetration of drugs from solutions containing surfactants is to be interpreted meaningfully.

B. Nonionic Surfactants

Nonionic surfactants are often used in pharmaceutical products applied to the skin because they are less irritating than ionic surfactants.

1. Wholly Aqueous Systems

Three nonionic surfactants (polysorbate 60, polyoxyethylene (5) nonylphenol, and polyoxyethylene (23) lauryl ether) had little effect on the a penetration of naproxen through excised human abdominal skin from aqueous gels.[55] In a recent study, the effect of members of a series of polyoxyethylene nonylphenols on the penetration of benzocaine through hairless mouse skin was reported.[56,57] In one series of experiments, aqueous solutions containing a fixed concentration (1.26 mg/mℓ) of benzocaine were employed. The inclusion of a nonionic surfactant resulted in a reduction in penetration flux. Flux was inversely related to surfactant concentration and also to polyoxyethylene chain length.[56] This was ascribed to benzocaine solubilization which reduced the escaping tendency of the permeant from the vehicle. The benzocaine concentration free to diffuse (not solubilized) was calculated from solubility studies. Flux was proportional to the free benzocaine concentration.

There were no statistically significant differences in benzocaine flux from aqueous suspentions containing the same nonionic surfactants.[57] Presumably, all of these suspensions contained the same concentration of diffusible drug, although the total benzocaine concentration varied. Consequently, these experiments provided evidence that the family of nonionic surfactants investigated had negligible influence on the integrity of the stratum corneum when applied in a purely aqueous medium.

2. Partially Aqueous Systems

Contrary to the aqueous systems, nonoinic surfactants do exert penetration enhancing effects when dissolved in a suitable partially aqueous system. Shahi and Zatz[6] noticed that polysorbate 80 increased hydrocortisone flux across hairless mouse skin from 2-propanol-water mixtures. Shen et al.[58] observed similar effects of the nonionic surfactants on the penetration of salicylic acid and sodium salicylate in the presence of DMSO. The stratum corneum is a heterogenous structure containing about 40% protein, 40% water, and 15 to 20% lipids. Mezei et al.[59-61] observed an increase in phospholipid turnover in the skin cells when rabbit skin was bathed in nonionic surfactant solutions. However, significant concentrations of nonionic surfactants are generally not present in the skin when dissolved in aqueous systems. This is probably due to the very low aqueous solubility of monomers as well as their low diffusivity. Solvents such as propylene glycol or 2-propanol suppress micelle formation, which results in an increased surfactant monomer concentration in the solution. This increase in the concentration gradient could sufficiently increase the surfactant concentration in the skin, which in turn could alter the permeability of the barrier membrane. Table 5[62] shows the effect of the presence of propylene glycol on the critical micelle concentration (CMC) of polysorbate 20 and polysorbate 60. The CMC of both surfactants increases in the presence of propylene glycol. A higher CMC value implies a higher effective concentration of diffusible surfactant monomers in the solution. This is expected to lead to an increased penetration of surfactant into the skin tissue, resulting in possible changes in the barrier properties. To determine the effect of the excess of free surfactant in the solution, penetration studies were carried out using hairless mouse skin in vitro. Lidocaine was used as a model drug and penetration studies were done using 1% w/w lidocaine solutions. An excess of each solution was applied on the surface of the skin under occlusion. The appearance of lidocaine in the receptor solution was monitored periodically. Figures 2 to 4 show the effect of these surfactants in the presence of 40, 60, and 80% propylene glycol, respectively. In all the solutions, the surfactants were dissolved so that their concentration was above the CMC. Opposite trends in the penetration of lidocaine are seen depending upon the concentration of propylene glycol. At the lower concentration of propylene glycol (Figure 2, 40% w/w of the solvent), the surfactants appear to have decreased the penetration of lidocaine. This effect also appears to be concentration dependent. At 80% propylene glycol concentrations (Figure 3), the surfactants increased the penetration of lidocaine threefold, while at

Table 5
CRITICAL MICELLE CONCENTRATIONS OF NONIONIC SURFACTANTS[62]

Surfactant	Solvent	Critical micelle concentration % w/v
Polysorbate 20	Water	0.0044[a]
Polysorbate 20	Propylene glycol/water 40/60	0.016
Polysorbate 20	Prop. G/Water 60/40	0.049
Polysorbate 20	Prop. G/Water 80/20	0.33
Polysorbate 60	Water	0.0026[a]
Polysorbate 60	Prop. G/Water 40/60	0.024

[a] Values obtained from ICI Americas Inc.; Private communications.

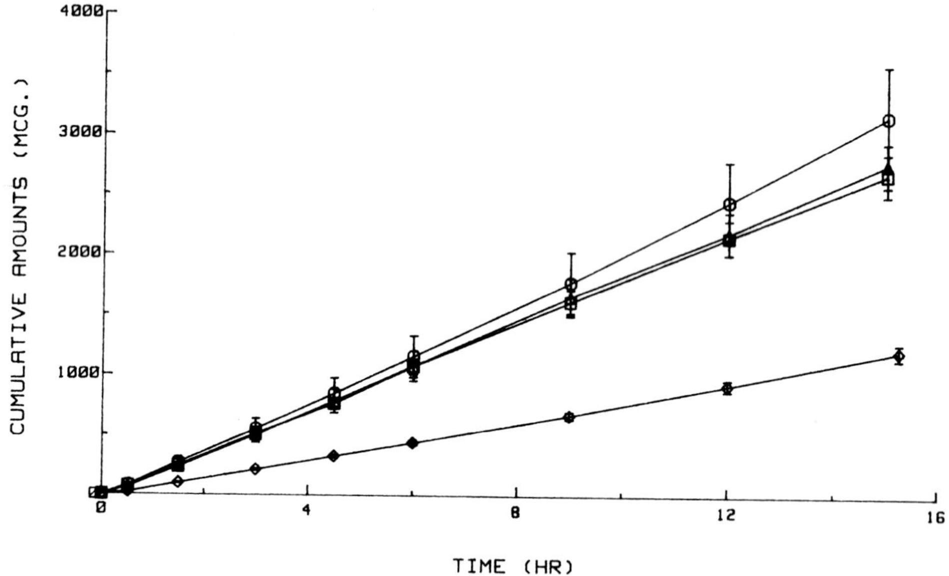

FIGURE 2. Effect of surfactant concentration on skin penetration of 1% lidocaine solutions. All solutions contain 40% propylene glycol. (○——○) No surfactant; (△——△) 1% Polysorbate 20; (□——□) 1% Polysorbate 60; (♦——♦) 3% Polysorbate 60.

60% propylene glycol concentration (Figure 4), the surfactants have little or no effect. Surfactants are causing two opposing effects simultaneously. They are solubilizing the drug which results in the lowering of the thermodynamic activity of the drug in the solution. At the same time, free surfactant monomer is penetrating the skin, altering the barrier permeability. The first effect (solubilization) appears to be more prominent at lower propylene glycol concentrations when the concentration of free surfactant monomer is still relatively low. However, at 80% propylene glycol, the concentration of the surfactant monomer appears to alter the skin permeability enough to counter the solubilization effect. At 60% propylene glycol concentration, these effects appear to balance each other. If surfactants alter the permeability of the barrier, there must be some effect of the surfactants on the skin permeability in 40% propylene glycol solutions (even though it is over shadowed by the drop in

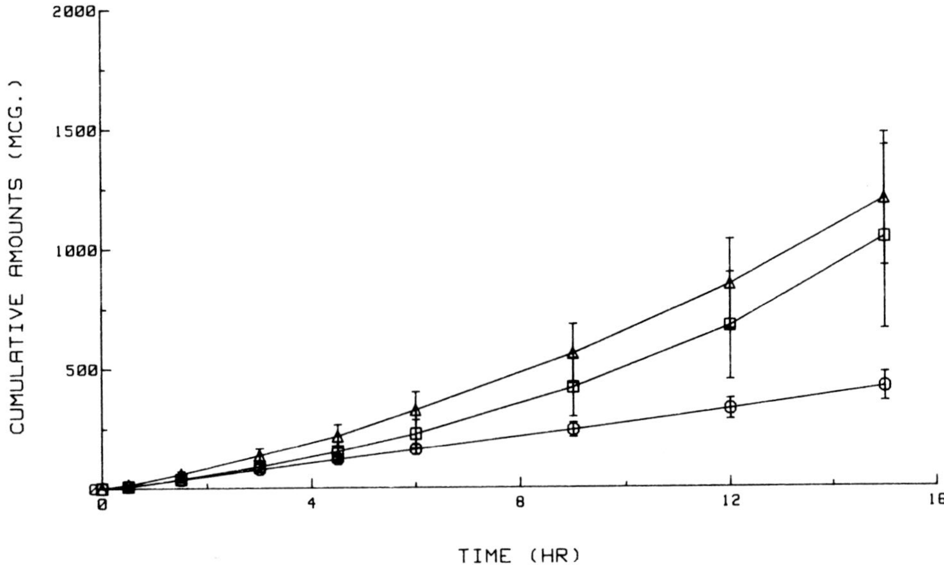

FIGURE 3. Effect of nonionic surfactants on skin penetration of 1% lidocaine solutions. All solutions contain 80% propylene glycol. (○——○) No surfactant; (□——□) 1% Polysorbate 20; (△——△) 1% Polysorbate 60.

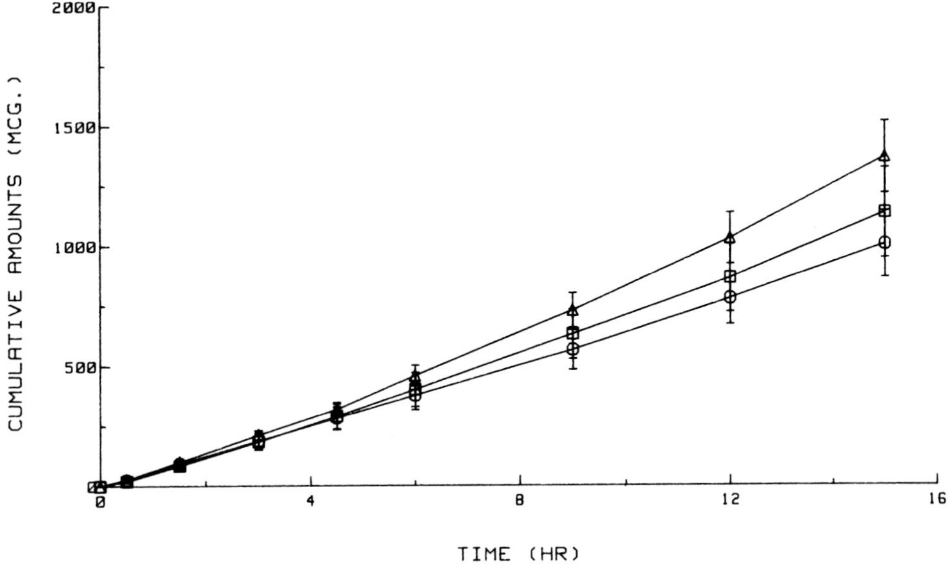

FIGURE 4. Effect of nonionic surfactants on skin penetration of 1% lidocaine solutions. All solutions contain 60% propylene glycol. (○——○) No surfactant; (□——□) 1% Polysorbate 20; (△——△) 1% Polysorbate 60

the thermodynamic activity of the drug). Figure 5 shows penetration when saturated solutions of lidocaine were used. Again, propylene glycol constitutes 40% w/w of the solvent. A slight but significant increase in the penetration of lidocaine is observed in the presence of surfactants. This is contrary to the effect observed by Dalvi and Zatz[56] for purely aqueous systems and confirms the action of surfactants on the permeability of the barrier, provided that sufficient quantities of the surfactant could be transported into the skin tissue. Similar results were also noted for hydrocortisone and for lidocaine, applied as a thin layer of solution on the surface of the skin in an open system.[62,63]

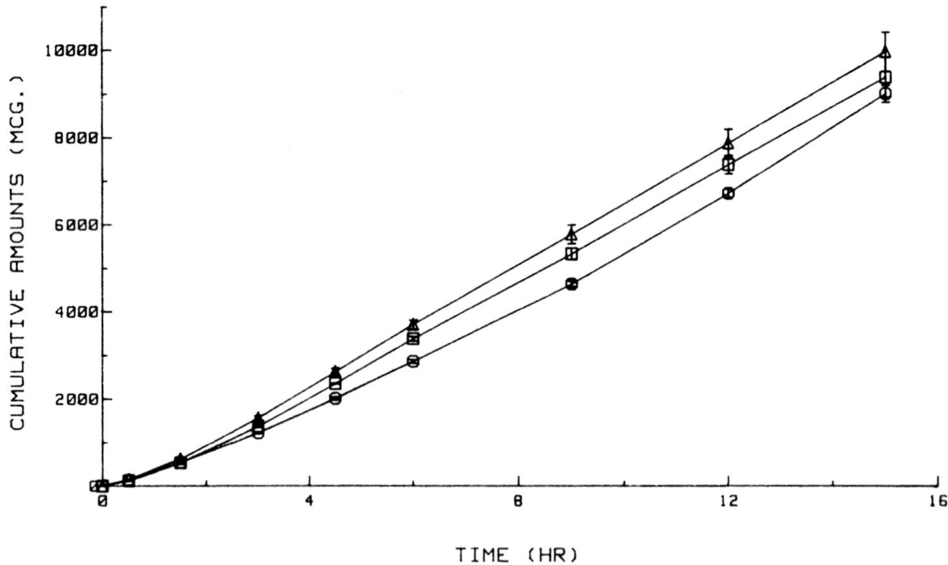

FIGURE 5. Effect of nonionic surfactants on skin penetration of saturated lidocaine solutions. All solutions contain 40% propylene glycol. (○——○) No surfactant; (□——□) 1% Polysorbate 20; (△——△) 1% Polysorbate 60.

REFERENCES

1. **Michaels, A. S., Chandrashekharan, S. K., and Shaw, J. S.,** Drug permeation through human skin: theory and in-vitro experimental measurement, *A.I.Ch.E.J.*, 21, 985, 1975.
2. **Wallace, S. M., Runikis, J. D., and Stewart, W. D.,** The effect of pH on in-vitro percutaneous penetration of methotrexate: correlation with solubility and partition coefficient, *Can. J. Pharm. Sci.*, 13, 66, 1978.
3. **Liron, Z. and Cohen, S.,** Percutaneous absorption of alkanoic acids. II. Application of regular solution theory, *J. Pharm. Sci.*, 73, 538, 1984.
4. **Turi, J. S., Danielson, D., and Woltersom, J. W.,** Effects of polyoxypropylene 15 stearyl ether and propylene glycol on percutaneous penetration rate of diflorasone diacetate, *J. Pharm. Sci.*, 68, 275, 1979.
5. **Komatsu, H. and Suzuki, M.,** Percutaneous absorption of butylparaben through guinea pig skin in-vitro, *J. Pharm. Sci.*, 68, 596, 1979.
6. **Shahi, V. and Zatz, J. L.,** Effect of formulation factors on penetration of hydrocortisone through mouse skin, *J. Pharm. Sci.*, 67, 789, 1978.
7. **Scheuplein, R. J. and Blank, I. H.,** Permeability of the skin, *Physiol. Rev.*, 51, 702, 1971.
8. **Scheuplein, R. J. and Ross, L. W.,** Mechanism of percutaneous absorption. V. Percutaneous absorption of solvent deposited solids, *J. Invest. Dermatol.*, 62, 353, 1974.
9. **Blank, I. H., Scheuplein, R. J., and McFarlane, D. J.,** Mechanism of percutaneous absorption. III. The effect of temperature on the transport of nonelectrolytes across the skin, *J. Invest. Dermatol.*, 49, 582, 1967.
10. **Stoughton, R. B.,** Penetration of drugs through the skin, *Dermatologica*, 152(Suppl. 1), 27, 1976.
11. **Barry, B. W.,** Properties that influence percutaneous absorption, in *Dermatological Formulations*, Vol. 18, Swarbrick, J., Ed., Marcel Dekker, New York, 1983, 155.
12. **Scheuplein, R. J.,** Site variations in diffusion and permeability, in *The Physiology and Pathophysiology of the Skin*, Vol. 5, Jarrett, A., Ed., Academic Press, New York, 1978, 1743.
13. **Weiner, N. D., Lu, M. Y., and Rosoff, M.,** Interactions of dimethyl sufoxide with lipid and protein monolayers, *J. Pharm. Sci.*, 61, 1098, 1972.
14. **Chandrashekharan, S. K., Campbell, P. S., and Michaels, A. S.,** Effect of dimethyl sulfoxide on drug permeation through human skin, *A.I.Ch.E.J.*, 23, 810, 1977.
15. **Idson, B.,** Percutaneous absorption, *J. Pharm. Sci.*, 64, 901, 1975.

16. **Akerman, B., Haegerstam, G., Pring, B. G., and Sandberg, R.,** Penetration enhancers and other factors governing percutaneous local anesthesia with lidocaine, *Acta Pharmacol. Toxicol.,* 45, 58, 1979.
17. **Matoltsy, A. G.,** Keratinization, *J. Invest. Dermatol.,* 67, 20, 1976.
18. **Scheuplein, R. J. and Ross, L. W.,** Effects of surfactants and solvents on the permeability of epidermis, *J. Soc. Cosmet. Chem.,* 21, 853, 1970.
19. **Sweeney, T. M. and Downing, D. T.,** The role of lipids in the epidermal barrier to water diffusion, *J. Invest. Dermatol.,* 55, 135, 1970.
20. **Komatsu, H. and Suzuki, M.,** Prevention of adverse skin reaction to cosmetics via percutaneous absorption control, *Cosmet. Toilet.,* 93, 39, 1978.
21. **Katz, M. and Poulsen, B. J.,** Adsorption of drugs through the skin, in *Handbook of Experimental Pharmacology,* Vol. 28, Brodie, B. B. and Gillette, J., Eds., Springer Verlag, New York, 1971, 103.
22. **Barry, B. W., Southwell, D., and Woodford, R.,** Optimization of bioavailability of topical steroids: penetration enhancers under occlusion, *J. Invest. Dermatol.,* 82, 49, 1984.
23. **Matheson, L. E., Wurster, D. E., and Ostrenga, J. A.,** Sarin transport across excised human skin. II. Effect of solvent pretreatment on permeability, *J. Pharm. Sci.,* 68, 1410, 1979.
24. **Chien, Y. W., Keshary, P. R., Huang, Y. C., and Sarpotdar, P. P.,** Comparative controlled skin penetration of nitroglycerin from marketed transdermal delivery systems, *J. Pharm. Sci.,* 72, 968, 1983.
25. **Akhtar, S. A. and Barry, B. W.,** Classification of penetration enhancers for human skin: effect on mannitol and octanol absorption, *J. Pharm. Pharmacol. Suppl.,* 35, 28, 1983.
26. **Sarpotdar, P. P., Gaskill, J. L., and Giannini, R. P.,** *J. Pharm. Sci.,* 75, 26, 1986.
27. **Roberts, M. S. and Anderson, R. A.,** The percutaneous absorption of phenolic compounds: the effect of vehicles on the penetration of phenol, *J. Pharm. Pharmacol.,* 27, 599, 1975.
28. **Zatz, J. L. and Dalvi, U. G.,** Evaluation of solvent-skin interaction in percutaneous absorption, *J. Soc. Cosmet. Chem.,* 34, 327, 1983.
29. **Mollgaard, B. and Hoelgaard, A.,** Permeation of estradiol through the skin-effect of vehicles, *Int. J. Pharm.,* 15, 185, 1983.
30. **Zatz, J. L. and Twist, J. N.,** personal communication.
31. **Draize, J. H., Woodard, G., and Calvery, H. O.,** Methods for the study of irritation and toxicity of substances applied topically to the skin and mucous membranes, *J. Pharmacol. Exp. Ther.,* 82, 377, 1944.
32. **Pittz, E. P.,** Non-destructive methods for evaluation of cutaneous irritancy, *Cosmet. Toilet.,* 98, 51, 1983.
33. **Franz, T. J.,** Percutaneous absorption: on the relavence of in-vitro data, *J. Invest. Dermatol.,* 64, 190, 1975.
34. **Haigh, J. M. and Kanfer, I.,** Assessment of topical corticosteroid preparations: the human skin blanching assay, *Int. J. Pharm.,* 19, 245, 1984.
35. **Moszczynski, P.,** Cytochemical and immunological examinations of workers exposed to organic solvents of paints and varnishes. III. Results of the E rosette test and skin reactions against tuburculin and distreptase, *Med. Press,* 33, 21, 1982.
36. **Maibach, H. I. and Anjo, D. M.,** Percutaneous penetration of benzene and benzene contained in solvents used in the rubber industry, *Arch. Environ. Health,* 36, 256, 1981.
37. **Schulte, E., Schulte, G. and Mrongovius, R. I.,** Percutaneous absorption of 3H-pethidine in the rat, *Arzneim. Forsch.,* 30, 267, 1980.
38. **Kiss, G.,** Study of the irritative effect of some organic solvents, *Munkavedelem,* 27, 25, 1981.
39. **Allenby, A. C., Fletcher, J., Schock, C., and Tees, T. F. S.,** Effect of heat, pH, and organic solvents on the electrical impedance and permeability of excised human skin, *Br. J. Dermatol. Suppl.,* 81, 31, 1969.
40. **Kronevi, T., Wahlberg, J. E., and Holmberg, B.,** Skin pathology following epicutaneous exposure to seven organic solvents, *Int. J. Tissue React.,* 3, 21, 1981.
41. **Poiger, H. and Schlatter, C.,** Influence of solvents and adsorbents on dermal and intestinal absorption of TCDD, *Food Cosmet. Toxicol.,* 18, 477, 1980.
42. **Nakaue, H. S. and Buhler, D. R.,** Percutaneous absorption of hexachlorophene in the rat, *Toxicol. Appl. Pharmacol.,* 35, 381, 1976.
43. **Sul'zhenko, A. I.,** Changes in the morphological structure of guinea pig skin after repeated applications of polymer compounds, *Vestn. Dermatol. Venerol.,* 11, 20, 1979.
44. **El-Shimi, A. F. and Princen, H. M.,** Some aspects of the stratum corneum-organic solvent system, *J. Soc. Cosmet. Chem.,* 28, 243, 1977.
45. **Nakagawa, S. and Tanioku, K.,** Study on the in vivo and in vitro reactivity of guinea pig skin with dinitrobenzene compounds, *Kawasaki Med. J.,* 3, 29, 1977.
46. **Mazzucco, K.,** Effect of some solvents (benzene, toulene, acetone) used for carcenogens on the collagen content of mouse dorsal skin, *Oesterr. Z. Onkol.,* 2, 49, 1975.
47. **Lupulescu, A. P. and Birmingham, D. J.,** Effect of lipid solvents on protein, DNA, and collagen synthesis in human skin. Electron microscopic autoradiographic study, *J. Invest. Dermatol.,* 65, 419, 1975.

48. **Dotenwill, W., Christoforis, A., Wiebecke, B., and Feaux de la Croix, P.,** Comparative autoradiographic investigations of the action of carcinogens, cigaret smoke condensates, and solvents on mouse skin, *Z. Krebsforsch.*, 66, 466, 1965.
49. **Guillemin, M., Murset, J. C., Lob, M., and Riquez, J.,** Simple method to determine efficiency of a cream used for skin protection against solvents, *Br. J. Ind. Med.*, 31, 310, 1974.
50. **Rietschel, R. L.,** A method to evaluate skin moisturizers in vivo, *J. Invest. Dermatol.*, 70, 152, 1978.
51. **Franz, J. M., Gaillard, A., Maibach, H. I., and Schweitzer, A.,** Percutaneous absorption of griseofulvin and proquazone in the rat and in isolated human skin, *Arch. Dermatol.Res.*, 271, 275, 1981.
52. **Gibson, W. T. and Teall, M. R.,** Interactions of C12 surfactants with the skin: studies on enzyme release and percutaneous absorption in vitro, *Food Chem. Toxicol.*, 21, 581, 1983.
53. **Dugard, P. H. and Scheuplein, R. J.,** Effects of ionic surfactants on the permeability of human epidermis: an electrometric study, *J. Invest. Dermatol.*, 60, 263, 1973.
54. **Aguiar, A. J. and Weiner, M. A.,** Percutaneous absorption studies of chloramphenicol solutions, *J. Pharm. Sci.*, 58, 210, 1969.
55. **Chowhan, Z. T. and Pritchard, R.,** Effect of surfactants on percutaneous absorption of naproxen. I. Comparison of rabbit, rat, and human excised skin, *J. Pharm. Sci.*, 67, 1272, 1978.
56. **Dalvi, U. G. and Zatz, J. L.,** Effect of nonionic surfactants on penetration of dissolved benzocaine through hairless mouse skin, *J. Soc. Cosmet. Chem.*, 32, 87, 1981.
57. **Dalvi, U. G. and Zatz, J. L.,** Effect of skin binding on percutaneous transport of benzocaine from aqueous suspentions and solutions, *J. Pharm. Sci.*, 71, 824, 1982.
58. **Shen, W., Danti, A. G., and Bruscato, F. N.,** Effect of nonionic surfactants on percutaneous absorption of salicylic acid and sodium salicylate in the presence of dimethyl sulfoxide, *J. Pharm. Sci.*, 67, 1780, 1976.
59. **Mezei, M., Sager, R. W., Stewart, W. D., and Deruyter, A. L.,** Dermatitic effect of nonionic surfactants. I. Gross, microscopic, and metabolic changes in rabbit skin treated with nonionic surface-active agents, *J. Pharm. Sci.*, 55, 584, 1966.
60. **Mezei, M. and Sager, R. W.,** Dermatitic effect of nonionic surfactants. II. Changes in phospholipid and in deoxyribonucleic acid content of rabbit epidermis in vivo, *J. Pharm. Sci.*, 56, 1604, 1967.
61. **Mezei, M. and White, G. N.,** Dermatitic effect of nonionic surfactants.III. Incorporation of 32P into phospholipids and acid soluble material of normal and surfactant-treated rabbit skin in vitro, *J. Pharm. Sci.*, 58, 1209, 1969.
62. **Sarpotdar, P. P. and Zatz, J. L.,** Evaluation of penetration enhancement of lidocaine by nonionics surfactants through hairless mouse skin in vitro, *J. Pharm. Sci.*, 75, 176, 1986.
63. **Sarpotdar, P. P. and Zatz, J. L.,** Percutaneous absorption enhancement by monionic surfactants, *Drug Dev. Ind. Pharm.*, in press, 1986.

Chapter 7

TRANSDERMAL DELIVERY SYSTEMS CUTANEOUS TOXICOLOGY

James J. Leyden and Gary L. Grove

TABLE OF CONTENTS

I. OVERVIEW

The development of transdermal delivery systems which achieve sustained blood levels of pharmacologically active agents such as nitroglycerin and scopolamine heralds a new era in pharmaceutical science. In the past, systemic effects from topically applied agents were viewed in terms of their toxicological significance, e.g., central nervous system damage in infants who had excessive quantities of hexachlorophene applied to their skin.[1] It is now quite clear that controlled delivery of a drug via the skin is achievable and that former concepts that the skin acts as a "barrier" to externally applied agents must be refined. It should be stressed that all chemicals penetrate skin. The rate of penetration and the amount finding its way through the outer membrane — the stratum corneum — and the underlying viable epithelial layer (epidermis) into the dermis where clearance by blood vessels occurs depend on a variety of physical chemical factors discussed elsewhere in this monograph.

While a great deal has been learned about the principles affecting percutaneous absorption which is used to advantage in designing transdermal systems, significant individual variations in the structure and function of skin exist which can have important consequences both from the standpoint of therapeutic efficacies and cutaneous side effects. For example, the thickness of the outer stratum corneum membrane can show wide variation from patient to patient, e.g., the stratum corneum of the forearm varies from 12 to 25 cell layers.[2] Individuals with chronic inflammatory disorders, e.g., atopic dermatitis, an extremely prevalent condition in which the barrier properties of the stratum corneum are severely compromised, will have greater absorption of chemicals. Individuals with atopic dermatitis also will frequently be more vulnerable to contact irritation. Individuals with "dry skin", an extremely common disorder in those over age 50, frequently have a stratum corneum which is structurally defective in that abnormal desquamation with fissuring occurs.[3] These individuals also will be at greater risk for adverse cutaneous reactions. The enormous range of structural and functional capacity of skin from one individual to another compounds the difficulty in assessing the potential adverse effects a transdermal system may have on skin.

In this chapter, we will review the major cutaneous toxicological reactions which can be associated with transdermal delivery systems and how one screens new systems for cutaneous toxicological properties.

II. CONTACT DERMATITIS

Contact dermatitis can be broadly divided into two major categories, contact irritant and contact allergic dermatitis.

A. Contact Irritant Dermatitis

Contact irritation is far more common than allergic dermatitis and is a major consideration for any new transdermal system. This is particularly true for systems in which various agents such as propylene glycol and other glycols and alcohols are used to enhance percutaneous absorption. Absorption enhancers all too frequently pay the price of increased cutaneous irritation. In our experience, contact dermatitis of the irritant type has been a major stumbling block for many agents deemed promising on the basis of in vitro studies. We strongly advocate *early testing in humans* to assess the potential of any new system.

Contact irritant dermatitis results from direct toxic injury to cell membranes, cytoplasms, or nuclei. While this type of injury does not involve host immunological reactivity such as occurs in contact allergic dermatitis, a host inflammatory reaction of vasodilatation and an influx of polymorphonuclear leukocytes with cutaneous erythema and itching can be incited by toxic injury to the stratum corneum, epidermis, and dermis. With transdermal delivery systems, contact irritant dermatitis can occur not only from the drug and its vehicle but also from the adhesive used to secure the system. Another complicating feature of contact irritant dermatitis is the existence of a significant population of individuals who have been labeled "sensitive skinned" because of a history of frequent adverse reactions to topically applied drugs, cosmetics, and toiletries. Identification of such individuals and a suitable methodology for determining whether or not an adverse reaction may occur in such a population, while being used safely by others, has not yet been achieved.

Despite the realization that contact irritation is the most frequent form of contact dermatitis and is responsible for enormous loss of man hours in many industries, methodologies for evaluating the potential for contact irritation are relatively crude in comparison to testing for contact allergy. The methodological failings are in large part due to the enormous variation in the structure and function, and cutaneous reactivity from individual to individual.

Testing must be done in humans. Pretesting in animals, particularly rabbits and guinea pigs, is useful only to detect very serious irritants. Minimal irritation or even absence of irritation in animals does not guarantee safe use on human skin.

1. Testing for Contact Irritation in Humans

Two types of protocols have evolved which are widely used and provide useful information on the irritant potential of an agent. Both involve repeated application under an occlusive dressing in human volunteers. In the case of transdermal delivery systems, the system itself is used rather than various chambers and tapes used for testing agents not designed for use in a clinical system.

a. Ten-Day Primary Irritation Test

A panel of ten subjects has the test agent applied daily Monday through Friday for 2 weeks (Table 1). The transdermal system should be applied to the site to be used in clinical situations in order to avoid differences in stratum corneum thickness for different body areas which can influence irritant reaction. The test agent is left in place over the weekend between the first and second 5 days of repeated application. Adverse reactions consist of erythema and scaling which are generally graded on 0 to 3 scale of none, mild, moderate, and severe, or a 0 to 6 scale to permit some discrimination. These grades are made daily prior to reapplication of the test agent. Because of the obvious crudeness of such a grading system, it is useful to include controls of agents with an established profile of safety and adverse reactions when possible. In the case of transdermal delivery systems, there are only a few agents in the market place and use of controls is difficult. Use of controls is particularly desirable to avoid seasonal variations, such as muting of irritant readings caused by increased sweating in the summer.

Interpretation of results from a 10-day irritation study must be done carefully. An agent which results in no erythema or scaling in any of the 10 panelists is unlikely to result in contact irritation when used in clinical settings. Most transdermal delivery systems are changed every few days and are not intended to be worn in exactly the same site with each change. Materials which fail to induce erythema or scaling after 10 applications to the same site are extremely unlikely to induce contact irritation. Materials which induce marked irritations, e.g., +2 or +3 erythema, are likely to be associated with significant contact irritation during clinical use. The difficult judgment comes with agents which produce mild to moderate erythema (+1, +2) in several, but not all, subjects. Will such an agent produce clinically significant irritant reactions? The power of this test then needs to be enhanced by increasing the number of subjects and the time of application unless control agents with a known profile of safety are included or can be included by a cross-over design in which the panelists are tested with the agent of a known irritancy profile subsequent to testing with the new agent. In most cases, increasing the number of subjects and the time of application is the tactic preferred.

Table 1
TEN-DAY IRRITATION PROTOCOL

N = 10	M	T	W	T	F	S	S	M	T	W	T	F
Test agent applied under occlusive dressing	X	X	X	X	X	X	X	X	X	X	X	X
Material reapplied	X	X	X	X	X			X	X	X	X	X
Clinical grades	X	X	X	X	X			X	X	X	X	X

b. Twenty-One-Day Irritation Test

A panel of 25 volunteers has the test agent applied daily, 5 days a week with the Friday application left in place until Monday morning under an occlusive dressing for 21 days (Table 2). In the case of a transdermal system, no additional occlusive devices are applied. Daily scores for erythema and scaling are made as described above. Again, interpretation of results must be carefully done. No erythema or scaling or only an occasional mild reaction indicates an agent which is unlikely to induce contact irritant dermatitis while agents which induce +2 and +3 reactions, particularly agents which show +1 reactions after the first few applications with progression to +2 and +3 reactions, are very likely to induce clinically significant reactions. Agents which have a profile between those two polar extremes deserve very careful scrutiny during early clinical trials. The clinical investigator will usually not be a dermatologist and some provision for observation by a dermatologist during clinical trials is preferred.

2. Newer Methodologies for Evaluating Cutaneous Drugs

Current methodologies for evaluation of the irritant potential of a material such as a transdermal delivery system involve relatively a crude assessment of dermatitis. It is well known that long before the clinical eye can appreciate erythema or scaling, histological evidence of damage is present. Biopsies would add valuable information but are obviously very problematic for human volunteers.

Recently, several laboratories including our own have begun exploring various methodologies for in vivo measurement of skin function by noninvasive procedures.[4] Among the two most promising for cutaneous toxicological assessment are (1) laser Doppler measurements of cutaneous microcirculation and (2) evaporative water loss for stratum corneum barrier integrity.

a. Laser Doppler

The Periflux Laser Doppler Flowmeter is based on the fact that as a laser light beam passes through a specimen, it is scattered when it impinges upon either static structures or moving objects, they will undergo a frequency shift according to the Doppler effect, while light beams scattered in static tissue will remain unshifted. By illuminating the skin with a monochromatic laser light and electronically processing the frequency mix of the backscattered light collected by a photodetector system at the skin surface, we can obtain a continuous measure of the red cell flux in the microvascular bed. In Figure 1, we illustrate how this technique can be used to demonstrate that occlusion of the skin surface can lead to increased integumental reactivity of a topically applied vasoactive substance such as trafuril. Since contact irritation invariably causes an increase in cutaneous blood flow, this device offers a convenient and highly objective approach to assess the severity of this type of response.

b. Evaporative Water Loss Measurements

Contact irritation also disrupts the stratum corneum barrier and causes an excessive water

Table 2
TWENTY-ONE DAY IRRITATION PROTOCOL

N = 25	M	T	W	T	F	S	S	M	T	W	T	F	S	S	M	T	W	T	F
Test agent applied under occlusive dressing	X	X	X	X	X	X	X	X	X	X	X	X	X	X	X	X	X	X	X
Material reapplied	X	X	X	X	X			X	X	X	X	X			X	X	X	X	X
Clinical grades	X	X	X	X	X			X	X	X	X	X			X	X	X	X	X

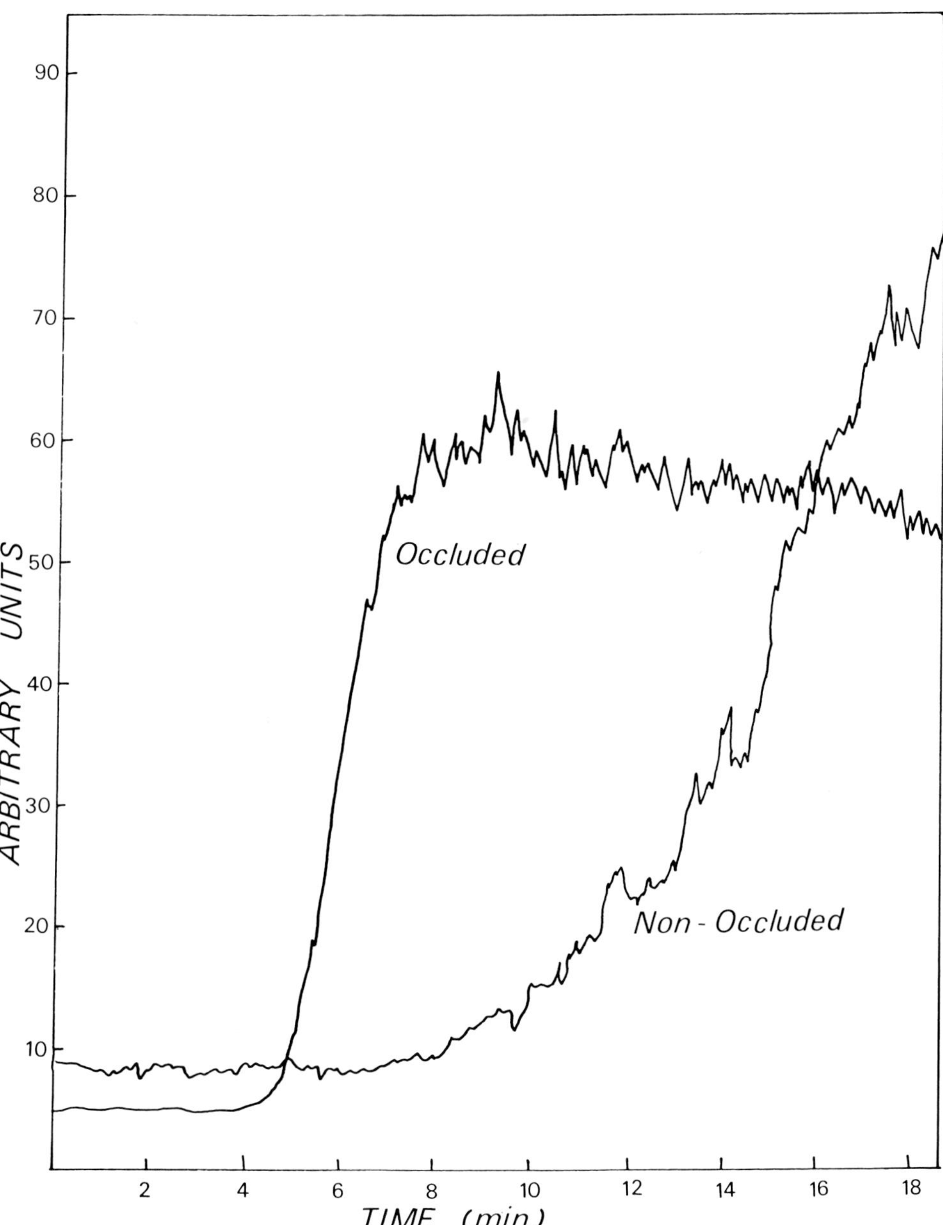

FIGURE 1. Dynamic monitoring by the laser Doppler velocimeter of the microcirculatory blood flow following topical applications of a 0.125% aqueous solution of Trafuril.

loss from that damaged surface that can be objectively measured by means of evaporimetry.[5,6] The ServoMed® Evaporimeter probe consists of an open cylinder that protects the skin surface from disturbing drafts. At each of two different fixed distances above the skin surface, there are a pair of transducers which can sense both the local temperature and relative humidity. From the signals generated by these transducers, the instrument first computes the partial pressure of the water vapor at each fixed point, then the gradient which exists between them, and finally, the evaporative water rate from the skin surface required to maintain this gradient.

Figure 2 illustrates how this approach has been used to assess the degree of damage incurred upon removal of an adhesive device. Please note that two of these eight panelists were exquisitely sensitive to this type of injury. This type of measurement is also very sensitive when subclinical damage is present. With severe erythema and heavy scaling, measurement of evaporative water loss can sometimes fail to directly correlate with clinical scores due to alterations in the composition and configuration of the evaporative surface and thermal influences brought about by the associated inflammation.

B. Contact Allergic Dermatitis

Contact allergic dermatitis involves a host immunological reactions to an antigen. Classically, the antigen is viewed to be a complex between an externally applied compound and skin proteins. Antigens processed by epidermal monocyte-macrophage cells, called Langerhans cells, present antigens to regional lymph nodes where a specific clone of *t*-cells is induced. On re-exposure to the antigen, *t*-cells hone in on antigens present in epidermal Langerhans cells and produce a cytological reaction resulting in acute inflammation with an oozing, vesicular, or papulovesicular, highly pruritic reaction. This type of reaction is clinically quite easily distinguished from contact irritation types of reactions.

Despite the fact that contact allergy is far less common that contact irritation, our knowledge of the mechanisms by which this reaction is induced and methodologies for screening for this potential are far more complete. Very valuable animal models exist with the so-called guinea pig maximization test, the most widely accepted and useful test.[7] In this test, intracutaneous injections with Freund's adjuvant are used to induce immune reactivity. Two protocols have evolved which are widely employed and produce useful information on the allergenic potential of a material in humans. One procedure is known as the Kligman maximization test in which a panel of 25 volunteers have a low grade dermatitis induced by occlusive application of 1 to 5% sodium lauryl sulfate (concentration varies with season and individual subjects reactivity) to enhance penetration and maximize any allergenic potential. Five applications in a 2-week induction period are followed by a 10-day rest period and then a challenge, closed patch test (Table 3). In the other procedure, repeated applications are made to the skin of 75 to 200 volunteers under occlusive patch tests for five applications. The test agent is applied for 24 hr followed by a 24-hr rest (Draize procedure) or applied for successive 48-hr periods without rest (Jordan modification). After a 7- to 10-day rest period, challenge is done by closed patch testing. Both procedures have been used successfully to determine the allergenic potential of agents designed for use on skin.

Interpretation of results requires careful weighing of the benefits vs. the risk of a relatively minor event such as a localized contact dermatitis. Agents which show an allergenic potential may still be used by millions of patients without adverse effects and agents should not be too hastily rejected because of an allergenic potential.

III. GROWTH OF MICROORGANISMS UNDER TRANSDERMAL SYSTEMS

A. Localized Superficial Infections

Bacteria, yeast, and fungi will proliferate under occlusive dressings.[8] The increased tem-

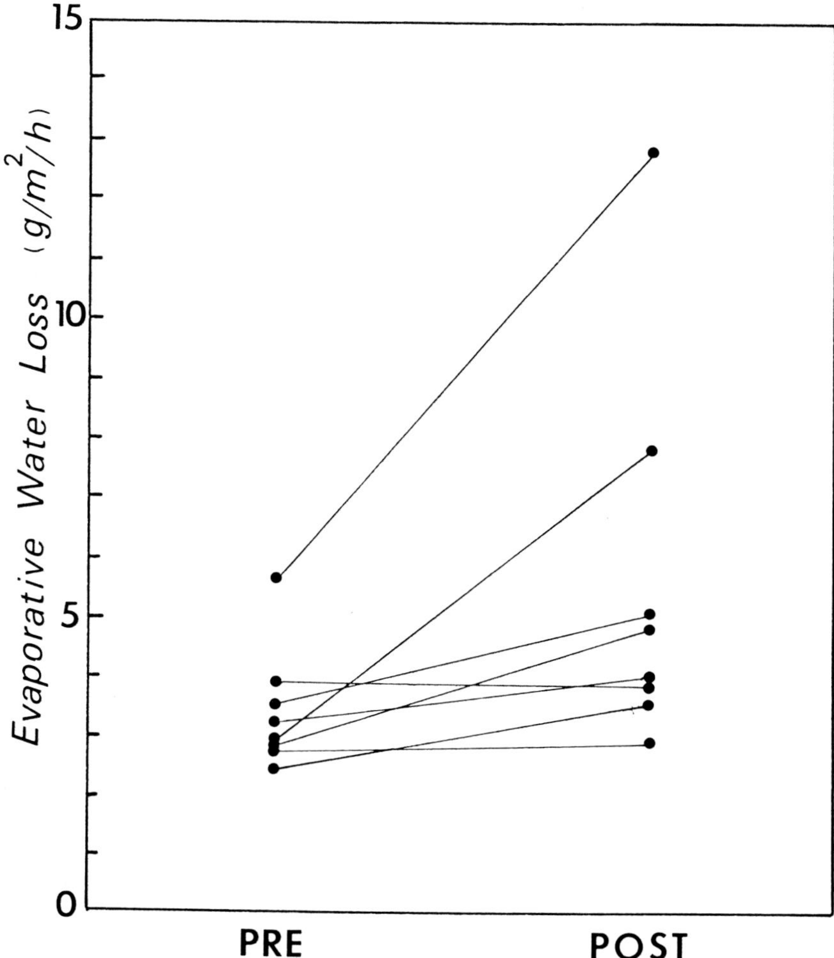

FIGURE 2. Evaporative water loss measurements obtained before and after removal of an adhesive device from the volar forearms of eight test subjects.

Table 3
MAXIMIZATION TEST FOR CONTACT ALLERGY

	M	T	W	T	F	S	S	M	T	W	T	F	S	S	M	T	W	T	10-day rest period	Challenge
S.L.S.	X			X				X			X				X					
Material applied under occlusive dressing		X			X				X			X				X				
Clinical grades				X				X			X				X			X		X

perature, hydration, and other changes such as increased CO_2 pressure and pH changes provide suitable environmental factors for microbial growth. Localized superficial infections from *Staphylococcus aureus* or *Candida albicans* can develop under transdermal occlusion patches. Patients with chronic skin disease frequently harbor *S. aureus* without overt signs of infection both on lesional and clinically normal skin. Proliferation of *S. aureus* can result in superficial pustules. Likewise, growth of *C. albicans* with invasion of skin and localized highly inflamed papulopustules can develop under an occlusive dressing. In the case of *C. albicans*, it is worth noting that very small inocula of that yeast can result in proliferation and localized infection.

Growth of microorganisms and development of superficial infection is not likely to be more than a rare event but should be considered in the evaluation of any adverse reaction with a transdermal system.

One can easily evaluate the potential for promoting growth of microorganisms by quantitative bacteriological cultures of skin sites before and after use of a transdermal system. Quantitative cultures can be obtained with nonionic detergents such as Triton®-X-100 or Tween®-80.[9] Cultures taken before and after repeated application, e.g., before and after a 10- or 21-day irritation study, will determine the potential for growth of the resident flora under a transdermal system. These results can be topically extended to give a reasonable estimate of the potential growth of pathogens such as *S. aureus* or *C. albicans*. If the resident flora show a significant increase under a transdermal system, then it may be wise to test deliberately whether *S. aureus* or other pathogens also proliferate under that system by inoculating *S. aureus* and covering with the test agent in human volunteers. This can be safely done without risk of serious infection.

B. Miliaria

Miliaria (prickly heat) can develop under occlusive dressings when there is a strong thermal stimulus for sweating. Resident bacteria proliferate under an occlusive dressing and produce toxin(s) which damage sweat duct epithelium. A P.A.S. positive necrotic coagulum of damaged sweat duct epithelium develops which interferes with delivery of sweat to the skin surface. If a sufficient thermal stimulus to sweating is present, the distal sweat gland produces sweat which cannot reach the skin surface because of the sweat duct obstruction. Sweat duct dilatation develops between the gland and the ductal obstruction. Rupture of sweat duct epithelium then occurs if sweating continues and then extravasated sweat induces an inflammatory reaction. The usual clinical reaction is that of a discrete pruritic inflammatory papule (miliaria rubra).

Miliaria is not likely to occur with transdermal systems applied for relatively brief time periods since several days are usually required for sufficient proliferation of cutaneous bacteria and sweat duct occlusion to develop. However, the future undoubtedly will bring transdermal systems designed for prolonged applications, e.g., 7 days or more and this potential toxicological reaction will become more prevalent.

REFERENCES

1. **Curley, A., Hawk, R. E., Kimbrough, R. D., Nathenson, G., and Finbey, L.,** Dermal absorption of hexachlorophene in infants, *Lancet*, 2, 296, 1971.
2. **Frosh, P. and Kligman, A. M.,** Rapid blister formation in human skin with ammonium hydroxide, *Br. J. Dermatol.*, 96, 461, 1977.
3. **Kligman, A. M., Lavker, R. M., Grove, G. L., and Stoudemayer, T.,** Some aspects of dry skin and its treatment, in *Safety and Efficacy of Topical Drugs and Cosmetics*, Kligman, A. M. and Leyden, J. J. Eds., Grune and Stratton, New York, 1982.
4. **Grove, G. L., Lavker, R. M., Hoelzle, E., and Kligman, A. M.,** Use of nonintrusive tests to monitor age-associated changes in human skin, *J. Soc. Cos. Chem.*, 32, 15, 1981.
5. **Nilsson, G. E.,** Measurement of water exchange through skin, *Med. Biol. Eng. Comput.*, 15, 209, 1977.
6. **van der Valk, P. G. M., Nater, J. P., and Bleumink, E.,** Skin irritancy of surfactants as assessed by water vapor loss measurements, *J. Invest. Dermatol.*, 82, 291, 1984.
7. **Magnusson, B. and Kligman, A. M.,** Identification of contact allergens by animal assay — the guinea pig maximization test, *J. Invest. Dermatol.*, 52, 268, 1969.

8. **Kligman, A. M. and Epstein, W.,** Updating the maximization test for identifying contact allergens, *Contact Dermatitis,* 1, 231, 1975.
9. **Leyden, J. J,** Cutaneous microbiology, in *Biochemistry and Physiology of Skin,* Goldsmith, L. A., Ed., Oxford University Press, New York, 1983.

Chapter 8

INFLUENCE OF AGE ON PERCUTANEOUS ABSORPTION OF DRUG SUBSTANCES

Charanjit R. Behl, Nancy H. Bellantone, and Gordon L. Flynn

TABLE OF CONTENTS

I. INTRODUCTION

With the current interest in using skin as an alternate route of administration of drug substances for their systemic availability, more attention is being given to the understanding of percutaneous absorption processes. Various factors which affect the skin permeability have been and are being studied in detail. A survey of the literature indicates that the area which is least explored is the study of influences of aging on the skin permeability. There are no published reports which describe any systematically designed studies to determine how aging alters chemical penetration through the skin over the entire life span of human or animal. This is true for in vivo as well as for in vitro studies. There are several reasons for this deficiency. It is very difficult to obtain "normal" human skin specimens for in vitro studies or to have access to human for in vivo studies covering desired age groups. Rather large intersubject and site-to-site variabilities have been experienced. Lack of suitable methods to study percutaneous absorption and difficulties in the interpretation of experimental data have also contributed to the problem.

The biological and the physiological changes associated with aging have, however, been studied in detail. Extensive reports are available in the literature which deals with the effects of aging on the stratum corneum, the epidermis, the dermis, hair-follicles, melanocytes, nerve endings, activities of the sweat and the eccrine glands, etc. Several reports also present possible theories of aging and factors which can affect the aging process. All these changes can influence the manner in which aging influences the skin permeability. Changes in the cutaneous enzymes can affect the absorption of prodrugs and other substances prone to metabolism. Skin from different sites may age differently and thus, may undergo site-related aging influences. It is generally believed and has been reasonably shown that the stratum corneum is the major flux controlling barrier to penetration; therefore, the change in this layer will influence the permeability of most substances. These changes may relate to cell turnover times, state of hydration, composition of the cells, size of the cells, and the compaction and the thickness of the whole stratum. The skin of males and females may age differently as the result of sex related variabilities in the aging process. Skin from humans of different races may age differently and therefore, race might greatly affect the degree and kind of observed aging influences. All these factors need to be investigated in depth.

In this chapter, brief reference will be made to literature reports on in vivo and in vitro aging effects of some substances. A greater emphasis will, however, be given to the recently systematically carried out in vitro studies in hairless mice.

II. IN VIVO PERCUTANEOUS ABSORPTION STUDIES

A survey of the literature reveals that the first indication of age-related differences in percutaneous absorption might be traced as early as 1886 when Rayner reported a sudden onset of significant cyanosis in infants which was attributed to freshly stamped diapers. The cases of this type were reported by several other investigators where the cause of poisoning could have been due to absorption through the infant skin.[32,33,36,51,57,60,62,69] There were more than 60 cases reported in these publications. It has been suggested in many of these reports that the observed toxicities might be due to the unusually high permeability of the infant skin, especially that of preterm infants. Cases of pentachlorophenol poisoning in nurseries for newborn infants have been reported.[1,54] These results are consistent with those referred to earlier in this section of the chapter.

Clinicopathologic studies in infants who were washed in hexachlorophene and rinsed off by immersing in water revealed substantial brain damage attributed to this agent. The level of the brain damage was about five times higher in babies who were only 8-months gestation than in full-term babies.[58] Since hexachlorophene has been shown to be well absorbed

Table 1
PERCUTANEOUS ABSORPTION OF TESTOSTERONE[21]

Young			Aged		
Subject	Age	% Absorbed (24 hr)	Subject	Age	% Absorbed (24 hr)
1	22	30.4	1	76	10.0
2	26	62.9	2	76	11.8
3	22	50.1	3	71	13.2
4	23	33.2	4	82	14.7
5	26	38.2	5	76	1.1
6	27	26.8	6	71	22.7
7	26	44.1	7	80	7.0
8	19	40.5	8	75	12.1
9	22	35.8	9	72	8.0
10	30	17.1	10	72	25.2
Av	24	37.9	Av	75	12.6
±S. D.	±3	±12.7	±S. D.	±4	±7.1

dermally, the systemic availability of the chemical can be a factor in the observed brain damage. This was followed by similar studies performed in rhesus monkey.[45] The newborn monkeys washed with hexachlorophene developed brain effects whereas 4- to 7-year-old monkeys did not.

Perhaps the first controlled study to assess the effect of age on skin permeability was reported by Nachman and Esterly.[59] They studied the percutaneous absorption of Neosynephrine®·HCl in infants of gestation ages ranging from 28 through 42 weeks. The extent of absorption was determined by measuring the time of blanching. They found that the skins at about 7 months were substantially more permeable than at full term.

Wester et al.[63] studied the percutaneous absorption of testosterone in newborn and adult rhesus monkeys. They normalized the absorption data with respect to the body weight to account for differences in the systemic accumulations. When accounting for the surface area to body weight differences, the systemic absorption in the newborn was found to be three times that of the adult.

A more recent study[35] has shown that the skins of preterm 27-week gestation infants can be very susceptible to simple alcohol because of the high skin permeability at this age. Some more direct approaches have been taken by other researchers. Christophers and Kligman[21] studied the percutaneous absorption of testosterone through the dorsal skins of two age groups, old and young. The method of Malkinson[40] was used in these studies. A suitable volume of radiolabeled drug in ethylene glycol-monomethyl ether was placed on a 1.8-cm^2 section of the dorsum and the extent of absorption was assessed by monitoring the residual drug in 24 hr. The results (Table 1) indicated rather large intersubject variability in the aged group. The absorption in the young subjects (average was 24 years) was about 38% compared to about 13% absorption in the older subjects (average was 75 years). These results were noted to be in contradiction to their earlier in vitro studies. Similarly, Malkinson and Ferguson[39] studied the percutaneous absorption of carbon-14-labeled hydrocortisone in two age groups, in this case ages of 41 and of 58 years. The drug was applied in the form of an ointment (2.5% in petrolatum) and the absorption was assessed by monitoring hydrocortisone appearance in the urine. They found that only 1 to 2% of the dose was absorbed and there was no age related difference in these skin populations. About a decade later, Feinblatt et al.[29] studied the percutaneous absorption of hydrocortisone in young subjects ranging from 2 to 22 months in age. The carbon-14-labeled drug was applied in the form of a 1% water soluble cream. Their results indicated about 22% absorption as estimated

Table 2
TRANSEPIDERMAL WATER LOSS DATA

Age	Site	Water loss (mg/cm²/hr) ±SD	Ref.
Newborn	Upper back	0.18 ± 0.06	64
Newborn	Rump	0.17 ± 0.04	64
Adult	Upper back	0.27 ± 0.04	64
19—26 years	Leg (lateral)	0.05 ± 0.03	37
	forearm (dorsal)	0.16 ± 0.06	37
66—81 years	Leg (lateral)	0.12 ± 0.06	37
	forearm (dorsal)	0.10 ± 0.03	37

from the urine samples. Although the two studies were carried out about a decade apart with different methodologies, the results were revealing. There is a strong indication that the skin of infants is more permeable than that of adults. Similar interpretations can be implicated in other case reports which have suggested that topical corticosteroids are more dangerous to use on children than in adults.[14,28,30,49]

Studies by Wildnauer and Kennedy[64] indicated a slower transepidermal water loss in newborns than in adults (Table 2). A similar observation has been reported by Kligman[37] where he studied the rate of transdermal water loss in young (19 to 26 years old) and in old (66 to 81 years old) subjects using the lateral leg and the dorsal forearm sites (Table 2). The rate was found to be about 2.5 times higher in the leg site of old subjects compared to the young subjects. A reverse trend was observed in the case of the forearm site. These results do not provide a clear age dependence of water permeability through the skin but they do show that differences exist. In an interesting study, Hammarlund and Sedin[34] determined the transepidermal water loss in newborn infants and related it with the age of gestation. They found that at between 25- and 39-weeks gestational age, the rate of transepidermal water loss declined exponentially with the age of gestation (Figure 1A). Actually, one should be careful in using the measurement of transepidermal water loss as a criterion to determine the effect of aging on the skin permeability unless other factors such as age-altered eccrine activity, which plays an important role in the loss of water, are ruled out.

Behavior similar to that observed for water has been seen in the emission rates of carbon dioxide in newborns and adults. Wilson and Maibach[65] found that the rate of carbon dioxide emission was not different from the back and forearm skins of neonates and adults. Since carbon dioxide loss can also be affected by sweating, it may also be inappropriate to reflect aging influences on the skin permeability to other chemicals unless sweating is absent.

III. IN VITRO SKIN PERMEATION STUDIES

A. General

It is widely believed that the permeation of chemicals through the skin follows, for the most part, physical diffusional laws. Since the early 1960s it has been recognized that the major resistance to skin permeation resides in the stratum corneum.[44,45] The stratum corneum maintains its characteristic barrier properties after it is fully formed from the underlying epidermal cells. This is true despite the fact that the horny layer continuously undergoes the process of cyclic turnover. The stratum corneum is composed of biologically dead and keratinized cells, which undergo little change upon isolation from the body. Therefore, the in vitro and in vivo permeation rates are of the same order of magnitude under comparable circumstances. According to Christophers and Kligman[21] once having crossed the horny

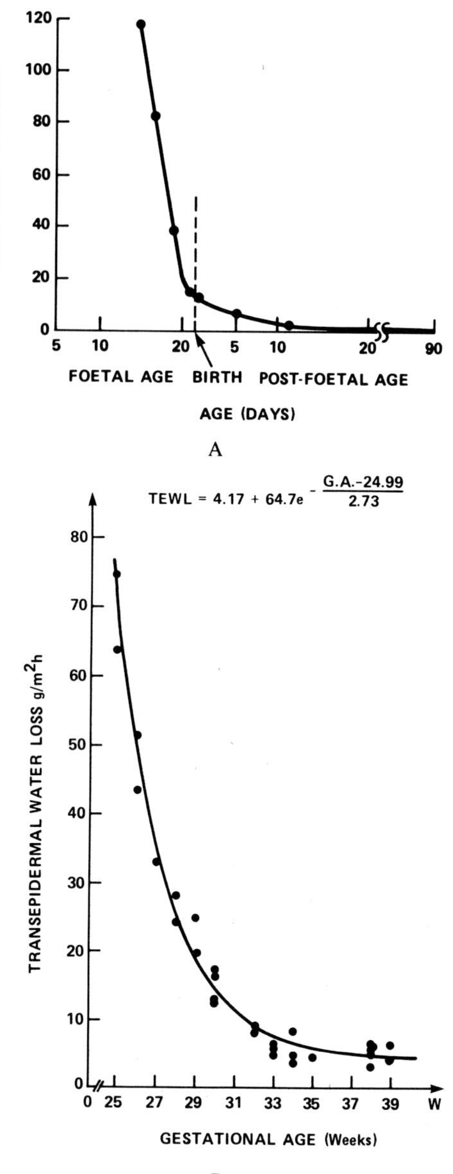

FIGURE 1. (A) Transepidermal water loss (TEWL) as a function of gestation age (GA); w = completed weeks of gestation.[34] (B) Plot of skin permeability to triethyl phosphate as a function of age.[61]

layer barrier, a permeant finds no important obstacle to its inward diffusion to the circulation through the epidermis, basement membrane, and superficial dermis. Therefore, penetration in vitro should be a valid measurement of the permeability characteristics of the horny layer in vivo. While this has been accepted as true for most part, the issue of in vitro/in vivo correlation needs further investigation. Studies are presently underway to examine this aspect in detail, using test permeants and the hairless mouse and fuzzy rat as the model systems.[5,7-9]

Using excised skin samples, Marzulli[45] determined the steady-state penetration rates of tri-*n*-propyl phosphate (TNPP) through various anatomical sites of humans of ages ranging

Table 3
STEADY-STATE RATES OF PENETRATION OF TNPP[a] THROUGH SKIN AND ITS COMPONENTS AT 10 TO 20 HR AFTER APPLICATION OF 2 MG TO 0.2 CM² SURFACE[44]

Age (Years)	Site	Full skin	Stripped skin	Dermis	Epidermis	S. c. c.[b]
3	Chest, midline	4.70	2.41	4.30	2.13	0.83
3	Chest, side	3.15	2.80	3.62	0.60	1.90
Adult	Chest, side	0.30	1.50	1.80	0.27	0.40
Adult	Chest, side	1.83	2.84	2.57	0.41	0.37
34	Chest, midline	3.50	4.04	5.15	4.01	0.70
57	Leg above ankle (outer)	0.98	3.55	2.43	0.89	1.40
57	Leg above ankle (inner)	2.40	3.85	3.25	0.90	0.65
57	Foot, dorsum	0.91	2.49	4.05	0.18	0.78
57	Ankle, inner	1.70	1.82	3.82	0.30	0.47
57	Abdomen, midline	2.15	1.64	3.45	0.23	0.50
	Mean rates	2.16	2.69	3.44	0.99	0.80

Note; Rates are μg/cm²/mℓ.

[a] TNPP = tri-*n*-propyl phosphate.
[b] S. c. c. = Stratum corneum conjuctum.

from 3 to 57 years. While the sample size was too small to draw any firm quantitative conclusions, the data showed a general trend of decreasing skin permeability with increasing age. For example, the average penetration rate in 57-year-old full thickness skin (regardless of the anatomical site) is 1.6 μg/cm²/min compared to 3.9 μg/cm²/min in 3-year-old skins (see Table 3). The table also shows data from the sectioned skins.

The effect of two age groups, young, and aged, on the permeation of water through the skin was investigated by Christophers and Kligman.[21] They used diffusion chambers and procedures similar to those used by Blank.[16] Briefly, the epidermis was sealed over water in diffusion chambers and was maintained at 37°C in a desiccator. The water permeation was determined by weight loss over a 6-day period. The observed average permeation rates were 0.74 mg/hr/cm² for the aged skin and 0.82 mg/hr/cm² for the young skin, indicating that there was no significant effect of age on in vitro water transport (Table 4). Lack of definite correlation between in vivo transdermal water loss and age was also reported elsewhere.[64] This reaffirms our earlier statement that perhaps the skin permeability to water does not reflect age differences.

Using a modified diffusion apparatus (two-compartment permeation cell), Christophers and Kligman[21] extended their efforts to study of Na-fluorescein permeation as a function of age. The results indicate that aged skin is about seven times more permeable than young skin (Table 5). As can be noted, the data for aged skin are highly variable, an observation consistent with the variable histology of aged skin. These data suggest that water and chemical permeation through the skin may follow different mechanisms.

Permeation of ethanol, benzyl alcohol, decanol, and cetyl alcohol through neonatal and adult skins was studied by McCormack et al.[38] The neonatal skins were more permeable than either the full term or the adult skins. When the studies were repeated with fatty acids such as caprylic acid, oleic acid, stearic acid, and lauric acid, the data did not reveal any age related differences. The information in these reports is insufficient to define the reasons behind this different behavior.

Tregear[61] studied the skin permeability of triethyl phosphate by using excised skin samples

Table 4
TRANSEPIDERMAL WATER LOSS DATA[21]

Aged			Young		
Subject	Age	Water loss (mg/hr/cm^2)	Subject	Age	Water loss (mg/hr/cm^2)
1	77	0.67	1	22	0.82
2	74	0.76	2	28	1.05
3	73	0.59	3	23	0.60
4	73	0.62	4	27	0.83
5	69	1.63	5	26	1.03
6	68	0.50	6	24	0.68
7	68	1.07	7	25	0.90
8	75	0.40	8	22	0.47
9	76	0.51	9	25	0.81
10	82	0.73	10	21	0.79
11	74	0.77	11	23	1.00
12	75	0.59			
Av ± SD	74 ± 4	0.74 ± 0.33	Av ± SD	24 ± 2	0.82 ± 0.18

Table 5
IN VITRO PENETRATION OF SODIUM FLUORESCEIN[21]

Young			Aged		
Subject	Age	Penetration (μg/hr/cm^2)	Subject	Age	Penetration (μg/hr/cm^2)
1	29	1.17	1	72	7.3
2	24	1.10	2	69	10.3
3	26	0.23	3	70	22.1
4	25	0.88	4	68	6.3
5	26	1.76	5	72	3.9
6	24	0.68	6	71	3.8
7	21	0.82	7	67	1.1
			8	78	1.9
			9	74	4.4
Av ± SD	25 ± 2	0.95 ± 0.47	Av ± SD	71 ± 3	6.79 ± 6.39

of rats with ages ranging from several weeks preterm to about 3 months postbirth. As shown in Figure 1B the permeability sharply falls from ~15 days of fetal age to birth, then drops more gradually up to ~3 months postbirth. These results can be compared with those of Hammarlund and Sedin[34] in Figure 1A. Although the two studies are not identical, the similarity in the initial rapid declines in the rate of transepidermal water loss in human (Figure 1A) and the in vitro skin permeability of rat fetus (Figure 1B) shoud not be overlooked.

B. Skin Permeation Studies Using Hairless Mouse

The permeability characteristics of the hairless mouse skin to *n*-alkanols[4,27,31] have been shown to be comparable to those of the human skin.[65] Both skins have been demonstrated to offer three major mechanisms for the in vitro permeation of *n*-alkanols. These include (1) an aqueous pore type pathway which may occur through the appendages or microchannels in the stratum corneum (Region I of Figure 2), (2) partitioning through the lipoidal com-

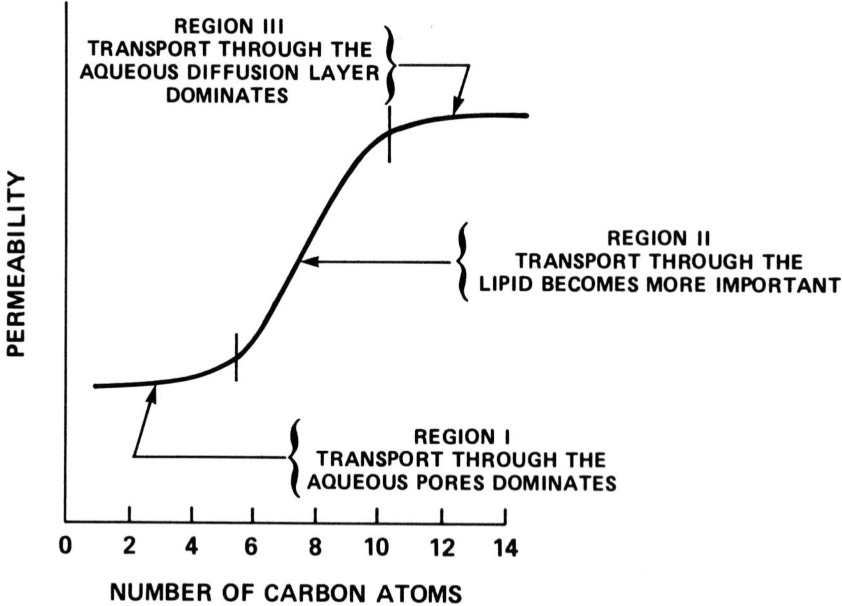

FIGURE 2. Schematic representation of biological membrane permeability as a function of the alkyl chain length of *n*-alkanols.[2]

ponents of the stratum corneum (Region II of Figure 2), and (3) diffusion through the aqueous strata, viable epidermis and dermis (Region III of Figure 2). On a relative scale polar, moderately nonpolar, and nonpolar solutes follow Region I, II, III, respectively.

Recent studies were carried out to investigate the influence of age on the in vitro permeability of test compounds, water, methanol, ethanol, butanol, hexanol, and octanol through the abdominal and the dorsal skins of the hairless mice, both male and female.[10,13] The homologous series of alcohols were chosen because they are simple, straight chain neutral molecules and represent an approximate 100-fold spread in lipophilicity. The hairless mouse was selected as the animal model because its skin permeability characteristics appear similar to those of the human skin, it is readily available, and its whole life span is relatively short (about 1.5 years). The methods used in these studies were those reported earlier.[4,27] Briefly, the skin samples were excised from the abdominal or the dorsal sites of freshly sacrificed animals and were sandwiched between the cell-halves of the two-compartment permeation cells. the permeation was studied from saline solution (0.9% NaCl) at 37°C by monitoring the permeant concentration in the receiving chamber as a function of time. Permeability coefficients were calculated from steady-state fluxes.

1. Anatomical and Histological Changes In Hairless Mouse with Age

The visual and histological changes in the skin as a function of age can be of great value in explaining the age-permeation data. Such properties of laboratory animals have been extensively studied by a number of researchers.[18,20,22,24-26,41,42,48,52,66,68] At birth, the mice are glabrous but the follicular appendages rapidly develop. The skin is taut, smooth, pinkish, and delicate, characteristics also seen in the skin of the newborn human. The skin of the mouse is rapidly covered with a dense white fur by about 2 weeks of age. Excepting the human scalp, this is an obvious and exaggerated departure from the development of the human integument. Starting in the third week, the animal begins to lose hair caudally and by the beginning of the fourth week, it appears fully hairless. Before this hair loss begins, the hairless mouse is visually indistinguishable from mice strains such as the Swiss mouse.

Young adult hairless mice have smooth, pinkish skins, with a visual resemblance to the skin of the human preadolescent. Histologically, this mouse skin is punctuated with cystic follicular appendages. These cysts become more prominent and more numerous with further aging. Usually, there is a sparse distribution of prominent hairs, most notably about 2 months after birth, which represent a highly incomplete secondary cycle of hair. Of great importance, the gross anatomical construction of the hairless mouse skin past the initial hair cycle is similar to the human skin (hairy regions excluded) in aspects which relate to the chemical barrier properties of the skin. Specifically, there is follicular presence but no prominent hair. Exact dimensions aside, the compositions of the epidermises are similar; each is overlayed by tightly compacted layers of horny cells. Even the kinetics of turnover of the epidermises are similar if viewed in proportion to the masses of the respective tissues. Furthermore, blemishing, wrinkling, and textural changes occur with aging in both hairless mouse and man, albeit though, the root causes may be substantially different. In the mouse skin, the increasingly stippled appearance of the skin during aging is the result of increased prominency of the follicular cysts. An additional observation, reported here, is that the animal's weight increases to an asymptote of 36 to 38 g at about the age of 140 days, approximately 1/3 to 1/4 of the mean animal life span. When put in terms of fractional age, even attainment of full adult size and weight is comparable to the human.

2. Skin Thickness vs. Age And Hair Cycle

In some cases, the follicular cycles have been related to changes in the dimensions of the skin. For instance, Chase et al.[20] have reported precise data on thickness of the whole skin and the individual strata of the skin (epidermis, dermis, and adipose layers) during the first hair cycle of the Swiss mouse. The overall skin thickness expands to its maximum during the anagen phase of follicle growth, there is contraction during the catagen phase, and a minimum is reached in skin width during the telogen phase. The decrease in full skin thickness during the telogen phase is concurrent with thickening of the epidermis.

The general development of hairless mouse skin in terms of its full thickness during the early hair cycle is substantially the same as reported for the Swiss strain.[20] The skin thickness of the abdominal and the dorsal skins of hairless mice were measured over the first year of age. An excised piece of skin several square centimeters in area was sandwiched between glass microscope slides. Using a micrometer, the thickness of the sandwich was measured with and without skin, the difference being the net thickness of the skin. The measurements were made in triplicate and were found to be not affected by varying pressure of the micrometer on the glass plates.

The data displayed in Figure 3 shows the dorsal skin thickness to be greater than that of the abdomen at all ages. However, the complex patterns of change in thickness over the age span are qualitatively the same between the two sites. There are marked increases in thickness associated with the development of hair, approximately extending to 10 days. Loss of hair and atrophy of the follicles is accompanied by a sharp decline in skin thickness. The thickness reaches a minimum value for either site by the 25th day of age which occurs approximately when the mouse becomes hairless. Past this age, the skin systematically thickens, a process which is relatively rapid up to 45 days and gradual thereafter. This measured thickening may be due to the continued development of the follicular cysts which form layers beneath the skin surface. These age-thickness profiles are in contradiction to what is known in the human skin. It has been reported that the human skin actually thins with age.[15,46,48,59]

The results of one such study[59] are shown in Figure 4.

The data reported in Figure 3 are the thicknesses of the whole skins. The individual stratum thicknesses were not measured. Since the thicknesses of the epidermis of adult hairless mouse[67] is about 40 μ, it can be safely assumed that the variations in thickness of the whole

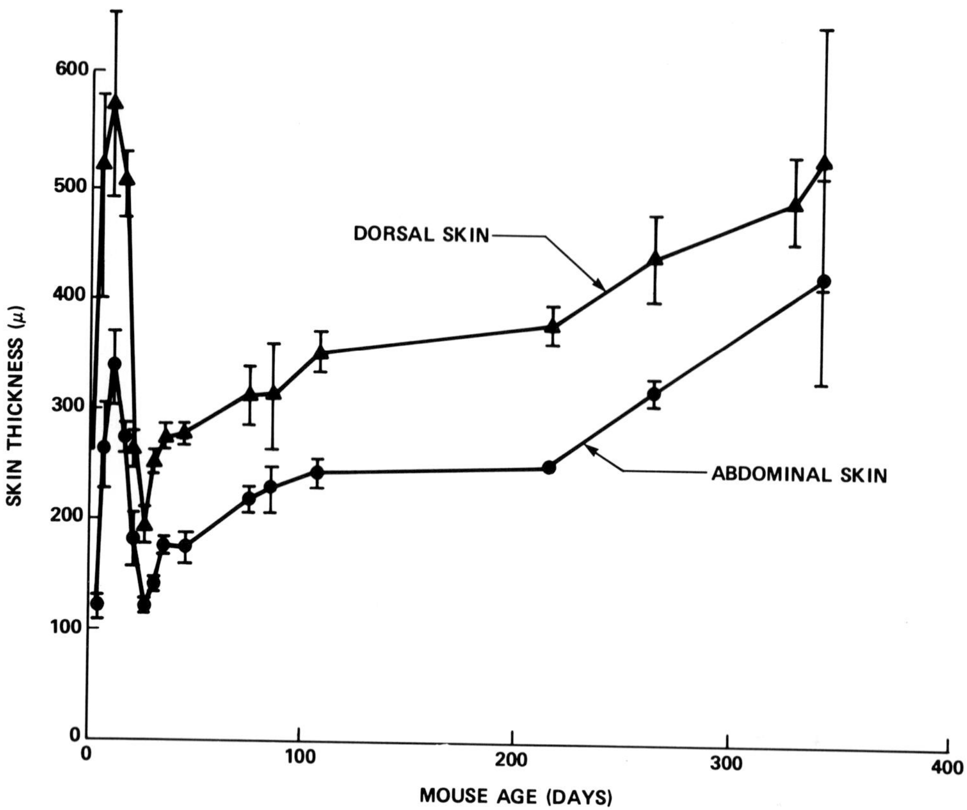

FIGURE 3. Plots of average skin thickness of male hairless mouse as a function of age.[10]

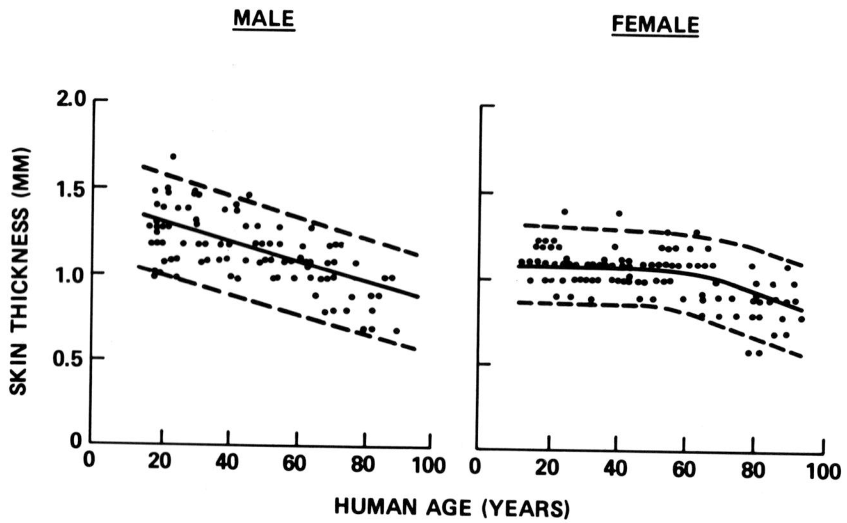

FIGURE 4. Plots of human skin thickness as a function of age.[59]

skin are far too large to be strictly epidermal in origin and must therefore represent changes occurring in the dermal layer. This is in agreement with the observations made by Chase and Montagna.[19]

3. Permeability vs. Age

Figure 5 contains age-permeability profiles for water, methanol, ethanol, butanol, hexanol, and octanol. All these plots show a general pattern. The skin permeability increases to reach a maximum value around 25 days, then declines rather sharply up to ~60 days of age and remains more or less invariant thereafter. During the hair cycle, there seems to be a three- to fivefold change in the permeability coefficients. For all these compounds, the dorsal skins are more permeable than the abdominal skins. It is important to note that the dorsal skins are more permeable only up to about 60 days and the permeabilities of the two sites converge thereafter. Octanol data show exception to this observation. Its permeation rates are about the same through either site throughout the age studied. Note that the dorsal skins are consistently thicker than the abdominal skins (Figure 3). These results are understandable since for water and polar alkanols, the rate controlling mechanism has been shown to be permeation through the stratum corneum.[31,47]

In separate studies the effects of aging on the permeabilities of hairless mouse skin to hydrocortisone and phenol were investigated.[11,12]

The observed age-permeability profiles are qualitatively similar to those of water and *n*-alkanols (Figures 6 and 7).

4. Alkyl Chain Length Influences Vs. Age

The permeability coefficients are plotted semilogarithmically as a function of the alkyl chain length for ages 4, 5, 20, 25, 53, 210, 270, and 360 days (Figure 8). All these plots demonstrate a sigmoidal shape showing the three regions discussed earlier (Figure 2); these are the lower plateau, exponentially increasing middle region, and the second plateau. The data for the two sites are qualitatively comparable. The middle exponentially linear portion is due to the alkyl chain length partitioning dependency of the permeability coefficients. The slope of this portion is called methylene group sensitivity and is designated as π. The π-values were determined and are plotted as a function of age separately for the abdominal and the dorsal sites (Figure 9). The π-values are constant between the ages of 53 and 360 days, indicating that the alkyl chain-length sensitivities and the underlying transport mechanisms for these ages are uniform. However, there appears to be a slight irregularity in the π-values during the hair cycle with a minimum value observed at 25 days. Recall that the permeability vs. age profiles indicated a maximum value at 25 days (Figure 5), the skin thickness vs. age profile had shown a minimum at the same age (Figure 3), and the animals were observed to become fully hairless around 25 days of age. All the available anatomical and histological observations indicate that the hairless mouse skin contains a maximum number of fully developed and active hair follicles around this age. In view of all this information, it is difficult not to attach at least some significance to the possibility that the contribution of the transfollicular pathway varies with age during the hair cycle and may be partly responsible for the observed minimum in the π vs. age plot.

5. Normalization of the Permeability Data

Wester et al.[63] reported that the body surface area to body weight ratio changes with age and has a significant effect on the systemic accumulation of topically applied chemicals. The method recommended by these investigators to demonstrate the increased risk to younger animals is to normalize the permeabilities to body weight. Using this approach, our data on alkanols[10] were normalized and the resulting profiles are presented in Figure 10 for water, methanol, ethanol, butanol, hexanol, and octanol; all for both the abdominal and the dorsal

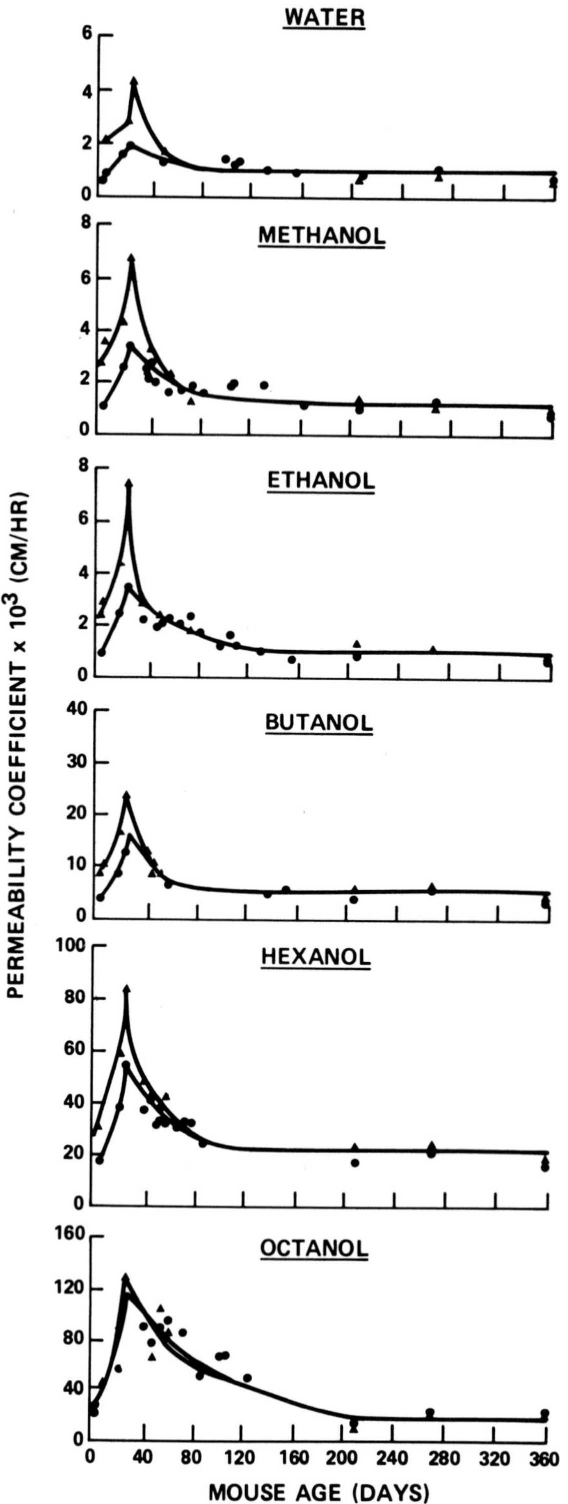

FIGURE 5. Plots of permeability coefficients of male hairless mouse skin as a function of age. Data are graphed for water, methanol, ethanol, butanol, hexanol, and octanol. Symbols: ▲ = dorsal skin and ● = abdominal skin.[10]

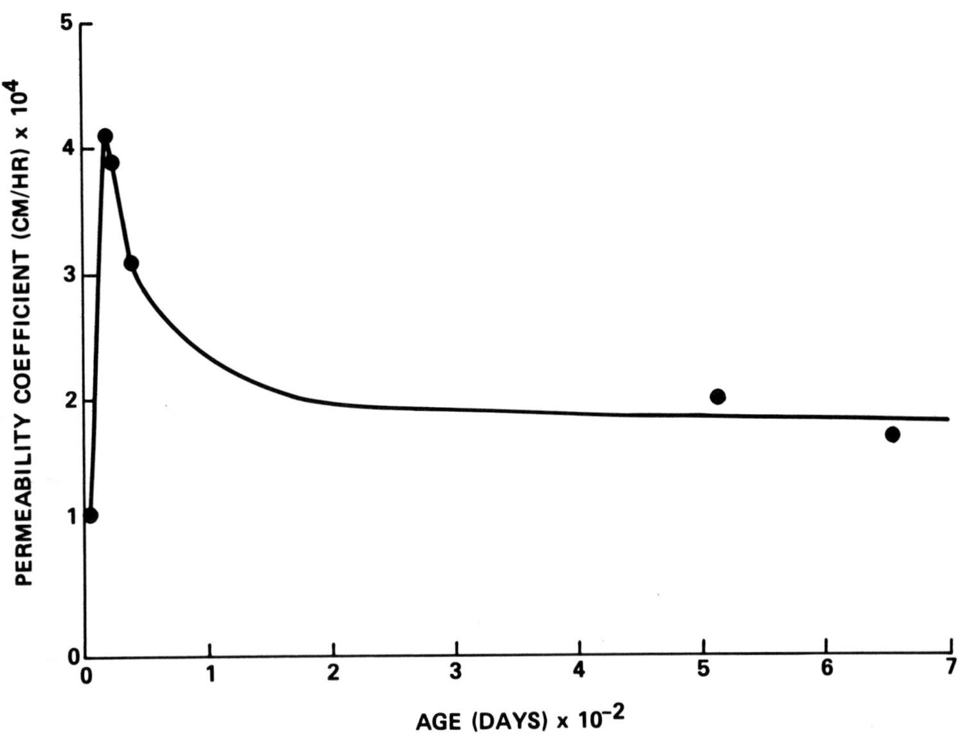

FIGURE 6. Plot of permeability coefficients of hydrocortisone through male hairless mouse skin as a function of age.[11]

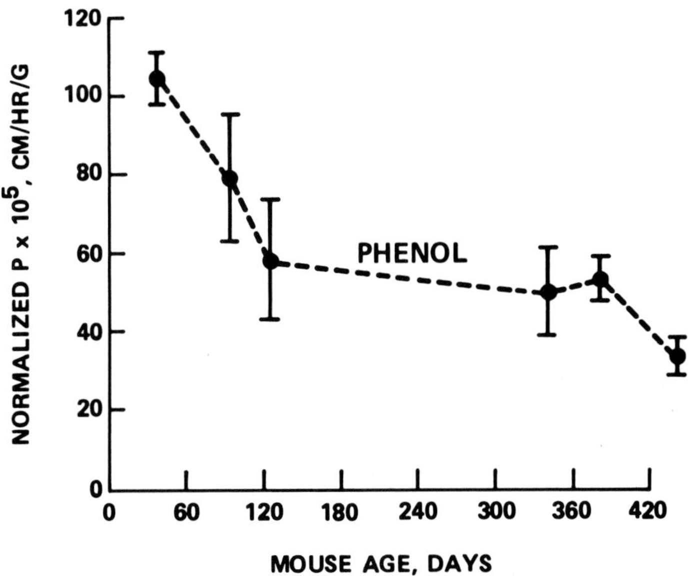

FIGURE 7. Plot of normalized permeability coefficients of phenol through male hairless mouse skin as a function of age.[12]

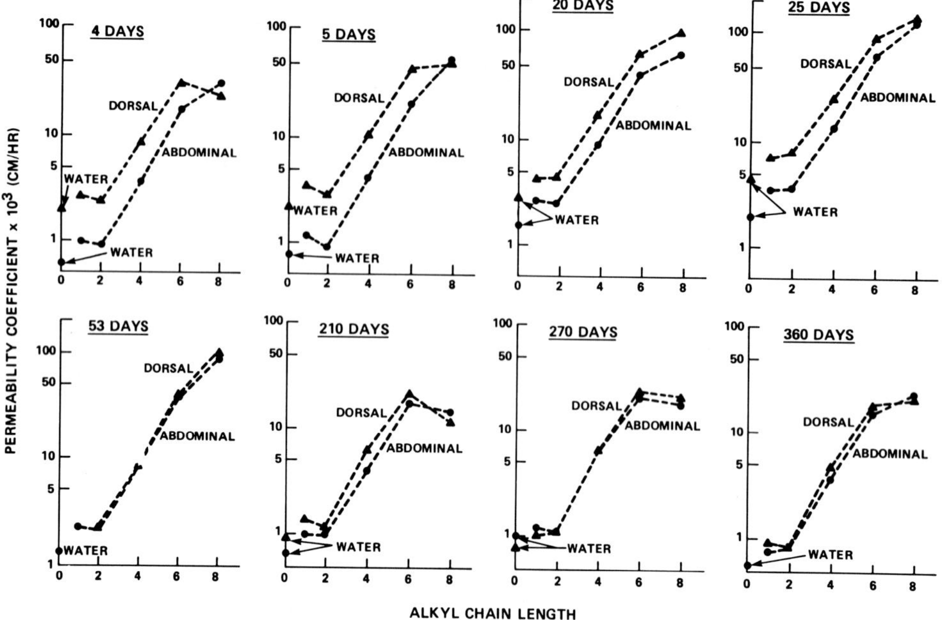

FIGURE 8. Semilogarithmic plots of permeability coefficients of *n*-alkanols through the abdominal and the dorsal skins of male hairless mice of different ages as a function of the alkyl chain length.[13]

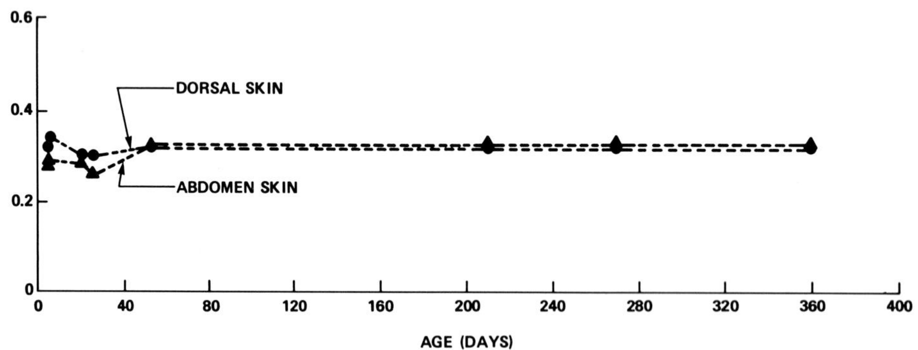

FIGURE 9. Plot of π - values vs. age of male hairless mouse.[10]

skin sites. The normalized permeabilities are large in the beginning and fall rather rapidly until about 60 days of age to remain invariant thereafter. Even in the absence of any real age related permeability differences these profiles indicate that young animals will systemically accumulate topically applied chemicals about ten times faster than adults. The comparable weight differences seen between human infants and adults suggest that one must be careful when treating infants to limit the area of treatment application.

6. Effect of Sex on Age-Thickness and Age-Permeability Profiles

The results reported thus far pertain to the skins of the male hairless mice. The entire study was repeated in female hairless mouse skins to determine the effect of sex on the skin thickness and the skin permeability as a function of age, using skins from both the abdominal and the dorsal sites and alkanols as test permeants.[13]

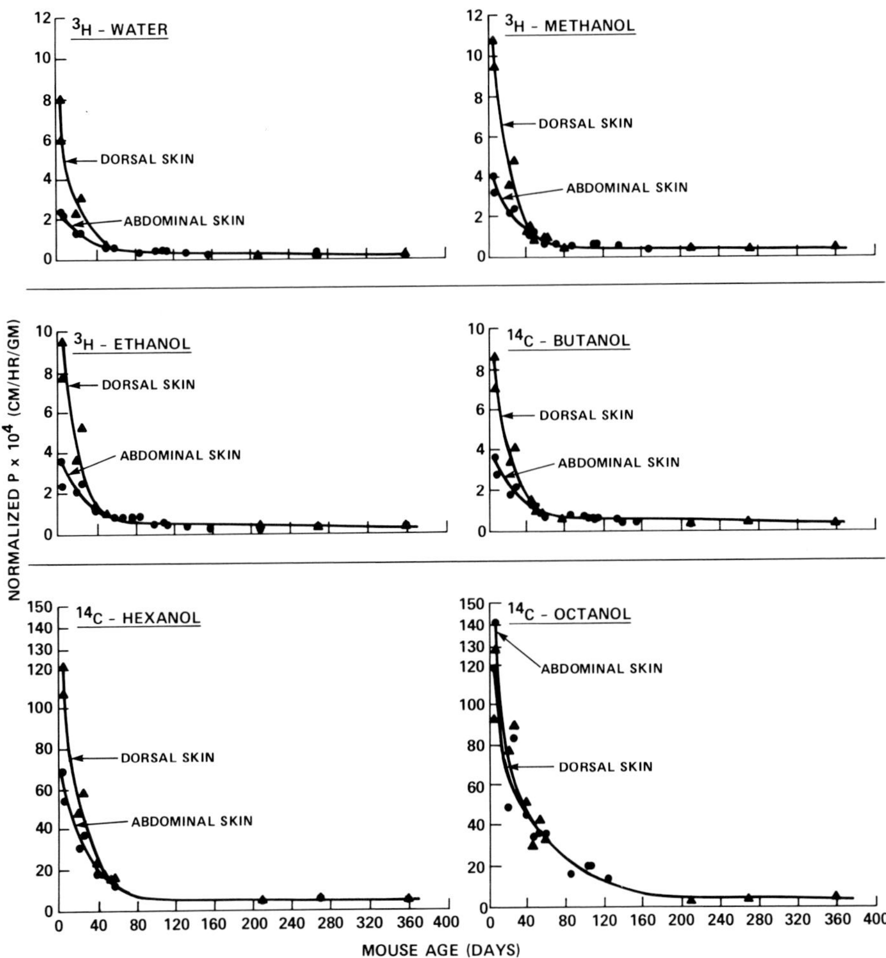

FIGURE 10. Plots of weight normalized permeability coefficients of the abdominal and the dorsal skins of male hairless mouse as a function of age. Data are graphed for water, methanol, ethanol, butanol, hexanol, and octanol.[10]

The results indicated that there are *no* substantial sex-related differences in the aging influences on skin thickness vs. age profiles (compare Figure 11 with Figure 3), skin permeability vs. age profiles (compare Figure 12 with Figure 5), the alkyl chain length effects as a function of age (compare Figure 13 with Figure 8; Figure 14 with Figure 9), or normalized permeability vs. age profile (compare Figure 15 with Figure 10).

7. *Significance of the Hairless Mouse Study*

As mentioned earlier, the hairless mouse skin undergoes dramatic visual and histological changes especially during the first 60 days of age. Some of these changes are schematically depicted in Figure 16. These changes make this animal a unique model to make some mechanistic interpretations.

The question can be posed whether the increase in permeation rates during the metamorphosis of the skin is directly due to the increased follicular presence. Additionally, can

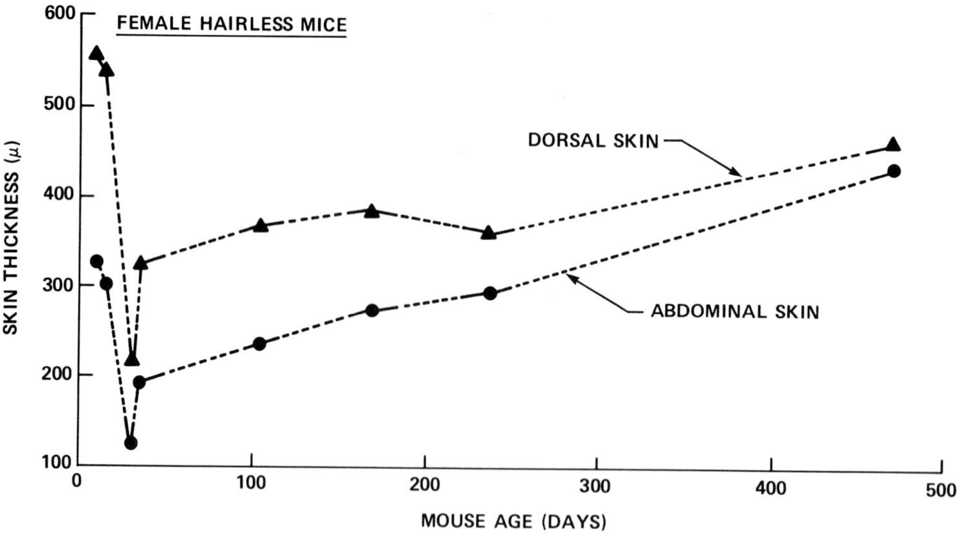

FIGURE 11. Plots of average thickness of female hairless mouse skin as a function of age.[13]

the lower plateau in the semilogarithmic plot of permeability vs. alkyl chain length be explained in terms of the follicular pathway? Certainly the follicles enlarge and the opportunity for transfollicular passage is expanded. A three- to fivefold rise in rates is not entirely unreasonable. In this hypothesis, the aqueous shunt route consists of the follicular pores filled with a heterogenous medium of lipid and water. It should be noted that the follicle orifice is the only histologically demonstrated pore portal of entry through the skin.

An alternate hypothesis is that there are concurrent changes in the stratum corneum accompanying the follicular developments which may cause it to be either thinner or of diminished barrier competency. Lipogenesis by the keratinocytes might be depressed, for instance, during the period when the tissue becomes involved in the formation of hair, with a general loss in integrity of the horny tissue. As in the previous follicular case, both lipoidal and aqueous pathways would have to be similarly affected considering that the increases in permeability are similar for polar and nonpolar solutes. Under the circumstances that the passage is transepidermal, the nature of the shunt route remains ill-defined.

Unfortunately, not enough is known concerning the biology of the hairless mouse skin and how it changes during the hair cycle to unequivocally assign the observed phenomena to one or another of the mechanisms or to accept some combination of the two. Perhaps the favored hypothesis,[4,10,16,31,55] the transepidermal explanation for the middle chain-length homologs where the partitioning dependence, is evident. The origin of the shunt route, however, needs further study. On-going studies may also provide additional insight into the issue.

The more gradual decline with age in the permeability coefficient for octanol (possibly to a lesser extent for hexanol as well) would seem to be related to changes in tissue other than the stratum corneum. It has already been pointed out that the permeability of the octanol is not strictly stratum corneum controlled and that the thickness of the full skin gradually increases throughout the life of a mouse, excepting, of course, the first 25 days of age. Increased thickness of the dermis (Figure 3) and increased filamentation of the dermis together would cause decreases in the π-values which are sensitive to mass transfer across strata beneath the horny layer.

Irrespective of mechanism, human infants have increased liability to systemic toxicity by the topical route. When the permeability coefficients are normalized with respect to body

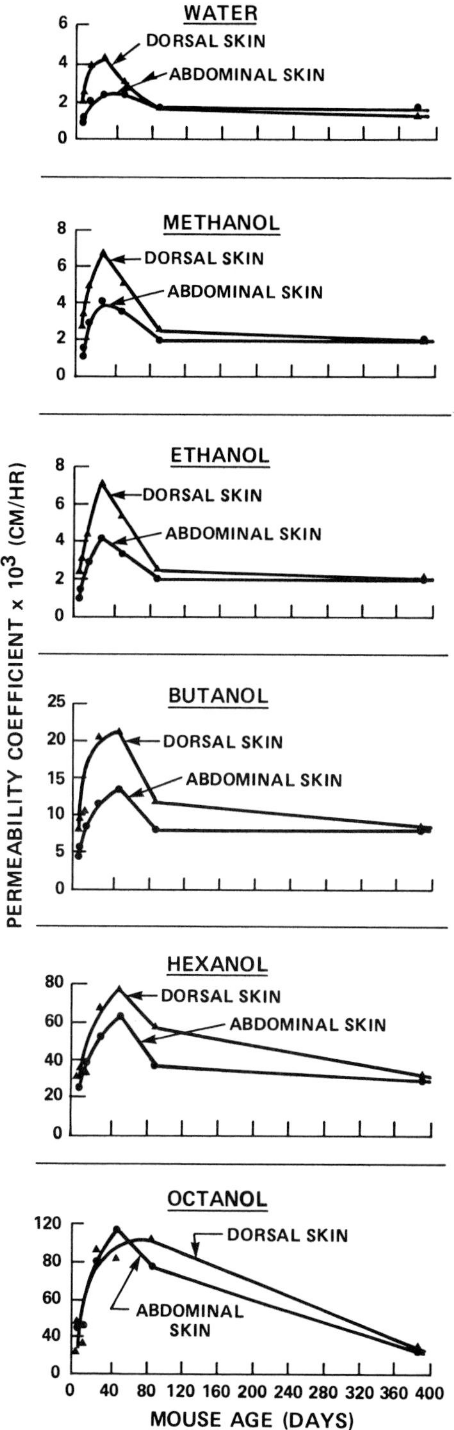

FIGURE 12. Plots of permeability coefficients of female hairless mouse skin as a function of age. Data are graphed for water, methanol, ethanol, butanol, hexanol, and octanol.[13]

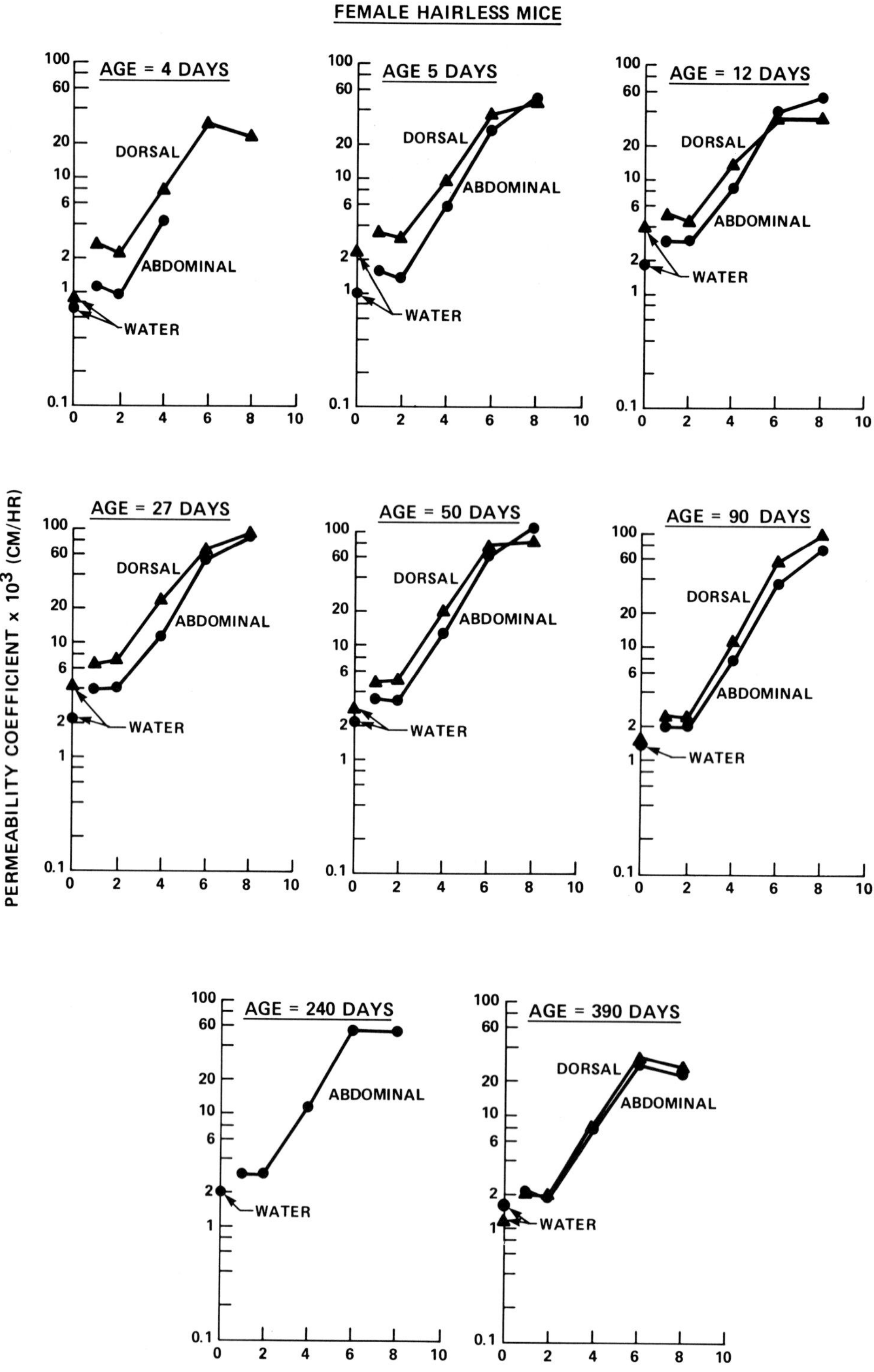

FIGURE 13. Semilogarithmic plots of permeability coefficients of *n*-alkanols through the abdominal and the dorsal skins of female hairless mice of different ages as a function of the alkyl chain length.[13]

FIGURE 14. Plot of π-values vs. age of female hairless mouse. Data are graphed for the abdominal and the dorsal skin sites.[13]

weight, young animals are seen to be substantially more subject to systemic accumulation than the adults. This factor is over and above considerations of the shifting permeability patterns and offers significant clinical implications.

Finally, there are certain observations which are important for the use of the hairless mouse to study percutaneous absorption. The skin of the young hairless mouse undergoes a rapid transformation in its permeability properties and, based on the alkanol data, it is not until about 100 days of age that these effects are essentially stabilized. Moreover, up to about 60 days, the dorsal skin is more permeable than the abdominal skin. It appears, then, that investigators must be careful to fix the age of the animals used in their studies and to excise skin sections from clearly defined sites to minimize variability. A general technique where the dorsal surface is traumatized and the abdominal surface is used as the control for permeation studies has been developed.[4,6]

In this case, it is important to wait to an age of about 60 days where the permeability coefficients of the two sites tend to converge to make comparisons of the normal and treated surfaces.

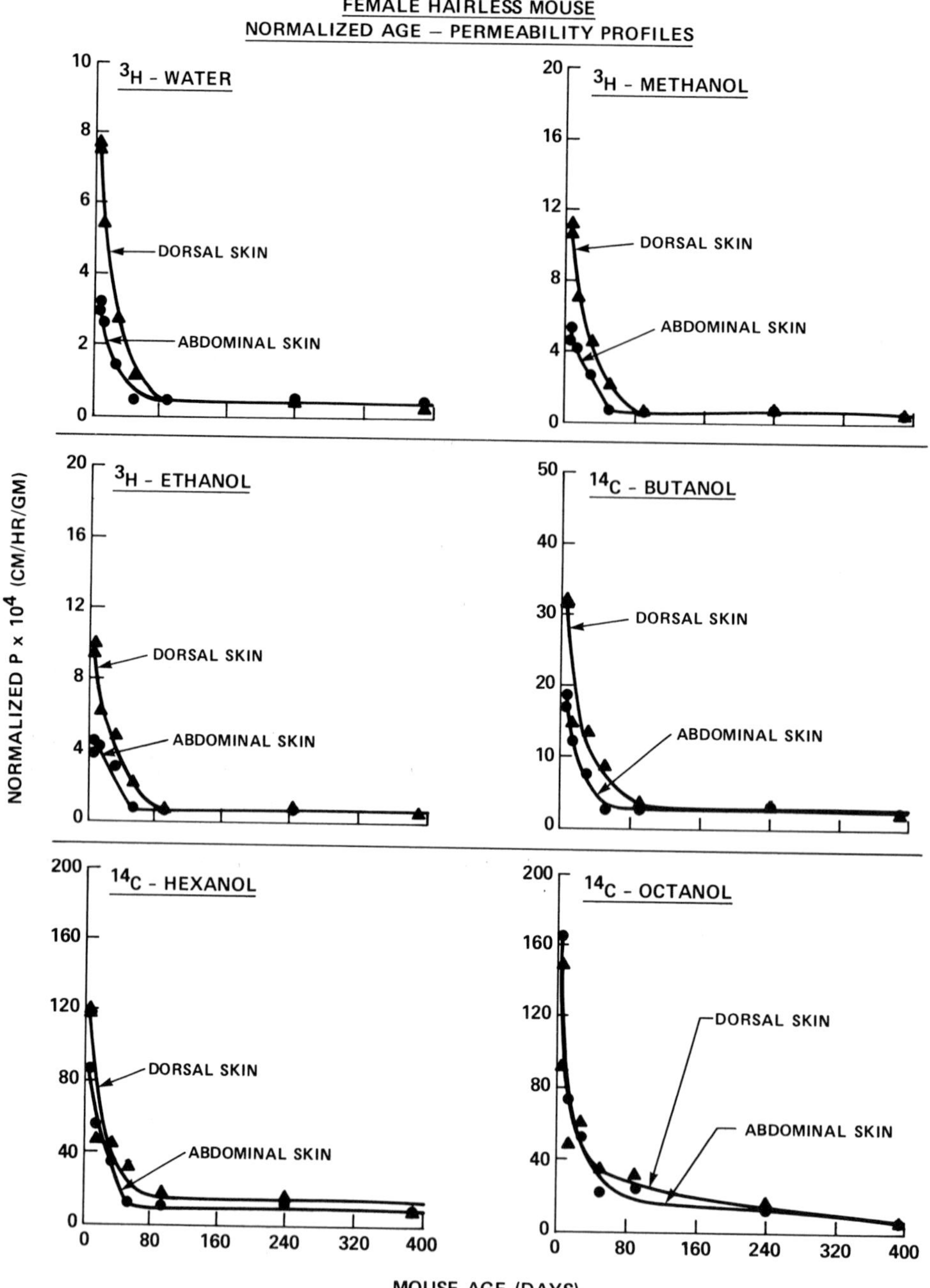

FIGURE 15. Plots of weight normalized permeability coefficients of the abdominal and the dorsal skins of female hairless mice as a function of age. Data are graphed for water, methanol, ethanol, butanol, hexanol, and octanol.[13]

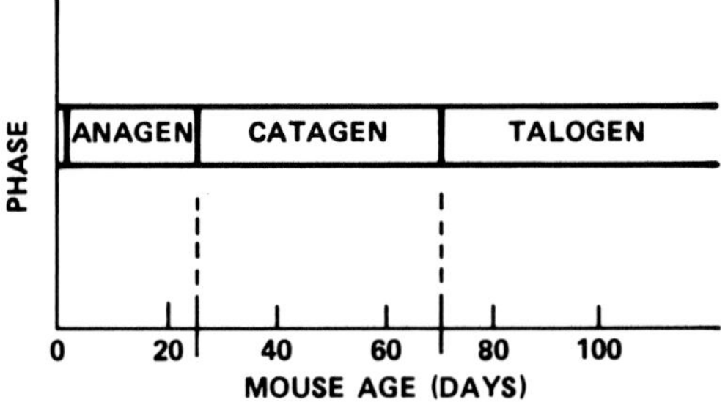

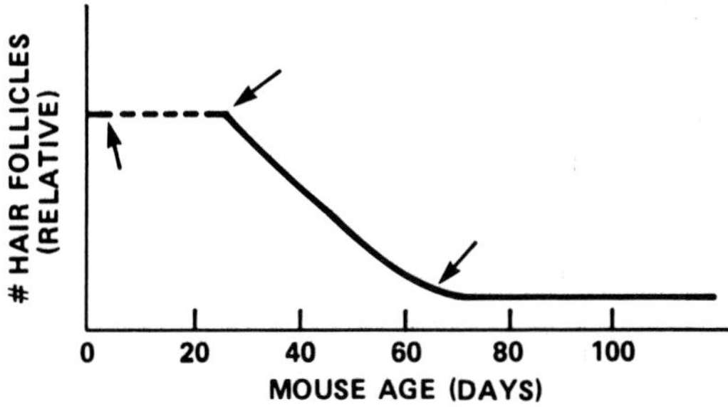

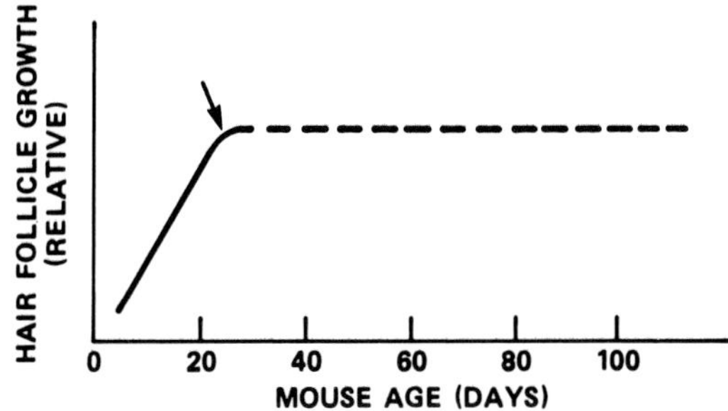

FIGURE 16. Schematic representation of certain anatomical and histological changes in the hairless mouse skins as a function of age. Graphs are made for the three phases (plot A), # of hair follicles (plot B), and hair follicle growth (plot C).

REFERENCES

1. **Armstrong, R. W., Eichner, E. R., Klein, D. E., Barthel, W. F., Bennett, J. V., Johnson, V., Bruce, H. and Loveless, L. E.,** Pentachlorophenol poisoning in a nursery for newborn infants. II. Epidermiologic and toxicologic studies, *J. Pediatr.*, 75, 317, 1969.
2. **Behl, C. R.,** Systems Approach to the Study of Vaginal Drug Absorption in the Rhesus Monkey, Ph.D. thesis, University of Michigan, Ann Arbor, 1979.
3. **Behl, C. R., Flynn, G. L., Kurihara, T., Smith, W. M., Gatmaitan, O., Higuchi, W. I., Ho, N. F. H., and Pierson, C. L.,** Permeability of thermally damaged skin. I. Immediate influences of scalding on hairless mouse skin, *J. Invest. Dermatol.*, 75, 340, 1980.
4. **Behl, C. R., Flynn, G. L., Kurihara, T., Harper, N., Smith, W. M., Higuchi, W. I., Ho, N. F. H., and Pierson, C. L.,** Hydration and percutaneous absorption. I. Influence of hydration on alkanol permeation through hairless mouse skin, *J. Invest. Dermatol.*, 75, 346, 1980.

5. **Behl, C. R., Meyer, R., and Flynn, G. L.,** Percutaneous Absorption by the Living Mouse — Uptake of Water and *N*-Alkanols Across Normal and Stripped Skins, presented at the 128th Annu. American Pharmaceutical Assoc., St. Louis, Mo, April, 1981, Basic Pharmaceutics Abstract 22, 1981.
6. **Behl, C. R., Flynn, G. L., Barrett, M., Walters, K. A., Linn, E. E., Mohamed, Z., Kurihara, T., Pierson, C. L.,** Permeability of thermally damaged skin. II. Immediate influences of branding at 60°C on hairless mouse skin permeability, *Burns,* 7, 389, 1981.
7. **Behl, C. R., Pei, J., Bellantone, N. H., and Matluck, M.,** Correlation of *In Vitro* and *In Vivo* Permeation of Propranolol Through Hairless Mouse Skin. Comparisons with Swiss Mouse and Silastic Data, presented at the 130th Annu. American Pharmaceutical Assoc., New Orleans, La. April, 1983, Basic Pharmaceutics Abstract 10, 1983.
8. **Behl, C. R., Bellantone, N. H., and Pei, J.,** Effects of the Alkyl Chain Length and Anatomical Site on the Alkanol Permeation Through Fuzzy Rat Skins, presented at the 130th Annu. Meet. American Pharmaceutical Assoc., New Orleans, La. April, 1983, Basic Pharmaceutics Abstract 32, 1983.
9. **Behl, C. R. and Bellantone, N. H.,** Influence of the Alkyl Chain Length on the *In-Situ* Permeation of N-Alkanols Through Fuzzy Rat Skins and Comparison with the *In Vitro* Data, presented at the 31st Nat. Meet. of the Acad. Pharma. Sci., Miami, Fla., November, 1983, Basic Pharmaceutics Abstract 38, 1983.
10. **Behl, C. R., Flynn, G. L., Kurihara, T., Smith, W. M., Bellantone, N. H., Gatmaitan, O., Pierson, C. L., Higuchi, W. I., and Ho, N. F. H.,** Age and anatomical site influences on permeation of skin of male hairless mouse. *J. Soc. Cosmet. Chem.,* 35, 237, 1984, submitted 1983.
11. **Behl, C. R., Flynn, G. L., Linn, E. E., and Smith, W. M.,** Percutaneous absorption of corticosteroids: age, site, and skin sectioning influences on rates of permeation of hydrocortisone through hairless mouse skins, *J. Pharm. Sci.,* 73, 1287, 1984, submitted 1983.
12. **Behl, C. R., Linn, E. E., Flynn, G. L., and Pierson, C. L.,** Permeation of skin and eschar by antiseeptics. I. Baseline studies with phenol, *J. Pharm. Sci.,* 72, 391, 1983.
13. **Behl, C. R., Flynn, G. L., Kurihara, T., Smith, W. M., Bellantone, N. H., Gatmaitan, O., Pierson, C. L., Higuchi, W. I., and Ho, N. F. H.,** Aging and Anatomical Site Influences on the Permeation of Water and *A*-Alkanols Through Female Hairless Mouse Skin, presented at the 131st Annual Meeting of American Pharmaceutical Association, May 1984, Montreal Basic Pharmaceutics Abstract 2, 1984.
14. **Benson, P. F. and Pharoah, P. O. D.,** Benign intracranial hypertension due to adrenal steroid therapy, *Guys Hosp. Rep.,* 109, 212, 1960.
15. **Black, M. M.,** A modified radiographic method for measuring skin thickness, *Br. J. Dermatol.,* 81, 661, 1969.
16. **Blank, I. H.,** Factors which influence the water content of the stratum corneum, *J. Invest. Dermatol.,* 18, 433, 1952.
17. **Blank, I. H.,** Penetration of low molecular-weight alcohols into skin. I. Effect of concentration of alcohol and type of vehicle, *J. Invest. Dermatol.,* 43, 415, 1963.
18. **Brooke, H.,** Hairless mice, *J. Hered.,* 17, 173, 1926.
19. **Chase, H. B. and Montagna, W.,** Relation of hair proliferation to damage induced in the mouse skin, *Proc. Soc. Exp. Biol. Med.,* 76, 35, 1951.
20. **Chase, H. B., Montagna, W., and Malone, J. D.,** Changes in the skin in relation to the hair growth cycle, *Anat. Rec.,* 116, 75, 1953.
21. **Christophers, E. and Kligman, A. M.,** Percutaneous absorption in aged skin in, *Advances in Biology of Skin,* Vol. 6. Montagna, W., Ed., Pergamon Press, New York, 1964, 163.
22. **Crew, F. A. F. and Mirskaia, L.,** The character *hairless* in the mouse, *J. Genet.,* 25, 17, 1931.
23. **Curley, A., Hawk, R. E., Kimbrough, R. D., and Finberg, L.,** Dermal absorption of hexachlorophene in infants, *Lancet,* 2, 296, 1971.
24. **David, L. T.,** The external expression and comparative dermal histology of hereditary hairless in mammals, *Z. Zellforsh. Mikrosk. Anat.,* 14, 616, 1932.
25. **David, L. T.,** Modification of hair direction and slope on mice and rats (mus musculus and mus norvegicus albinus), *J. Exp. Zool.,* 68, 519, 1934.
26. **Dry, F. W.,** The coat of the mouse, mus musculur, *J. Genet.,* 16, 286, 1926.
27. **Durrheim, H., Flynn, G. L., Higuchi, W. I., and Behl, C. R.,** Permeation of hairless mouse skin. I. Experimental methods and comparisons with human epidermis by alkanols, *J. Pharm. Sci.,* 69, 781, 1981.
28. **Fanconi, V. G.,** Inhibition of growth in an infant by excessive use of a 1% hydrocortisone ointment." *Helv. Paediatr. Acta,* 17, 267, 1962.
29. **Feinblatt, B. I., Aceto, T., Beckhorn, G., and Bruck, E.,** Percutaneous absorption of hydrocortisone in children, *Am. J. Dis. Child.,* 112, 218, 1966.
30. **Feiwel, M., James, V. H. T., and Barnet, E. S.,** Percutaneous absorption of topical steroids in children, *Lancet,* 1, 485, 1969.
31. **Flynn, G. L., Durrheim, H., and Higuchi, W. I.,** Permeation of hairless mouse skin. II: Membrane sectioning techniques and influences on alkanol permeabilities, *J. Pharm. Sci.,* 70, 52, 1980.

32. **Gottschall, R. Y. and Burney, W. E.,** The effect of age on the spread of dye in the skin of normal, antigenically stimulated, and tuberculous guinea pigs, *J. Immunol.*, 38, 345, 1940.
33. **Graubarth, M., Bloom, C. J., Coleman, F. C., and Solomon, H. N.,** Dye poisoning in the nursery. A review of seventy cases, *JAMA*, 128, 1155, 1945.
34. **Hammarlund, K. and Sedin, G.,** Transdermal water loss in newborn infants, *Acta Paediatr. Scand.*, 68, 795, 1979.
35. **Harpin, V. and Ratter, N.,** Percutaneous alcohol absorption and skin necrosis in pre-term infants, *Arch. Dis. Child.*, 57, 477, 1982.
36. **Kagan, B. M., Mirman, B., Calvin, J., and Lunden, E.,** Cyanosis in premature infants due to aniline dye intoxication, *J. Pediatr.*, 34, 574, 1949.
37. **Kligman, A. M.,** Perspectives and problems in cutaneous gerontology, *J. Invest. Dermatol.*, 73, 39, 1979.
38. **McCormack, J., Biosits, E. K., and Fisher, L. B.,** An *In-Vitro* Comparison of the Permeability of Adult Versus Neonatal Skin, in, *Neonatal Skin, Structure, and Function,* Maibach, H. I. and Boisits, E. K., Eds., Marcel Dekker, New York, 1982, 149.
39. **Malkinson, F. D. and Ferguson, E. H.,** Preliminary and short report: percutaneous absorption of hydrocortisone in human subjects, *J. Invest. Dermatol.*, 25, 281, 1955.
40. **Malkinson, F. D.,** Studies on the percutaneous absorption of ^{14}C labeled steroids by used of the gas-flow cells, *J. Invest. Dermatol.*, 31, 29, 1958.
41. **Mann, S. J. and Straile, W. E.,** New observations on hair loss in the hairless mouse, *Anat. Rec.*, 140, 97, 1961.
42. **Mann, S. J.,** Hair loss and cyst formation in hairless and rhino mutant mice, *Anat. Rec.*, 170, 485, 1971.
43. **Marzulli, F. N. and Maibach, H. I.,** Relevance of animal models: the hexachlorophene story in, *Animal Models in Dermatology,* Maibach, H. I. Ed., Churchill-Livingstone, New York, 1975, 156.
44. **Marzulli, F. N. and Tregear, R. T.,** Identification of a barrier layer in the skin, *J. Physiol.*, 157, 52, 1961.
45. **Marzulli, F. N.,** Barriers to Skin Penetration, *J. Invest. Dermatol.*, 39, 387, 1962.
46. **Meema, H. E., Sheppard, R. H., and Rapopart, A.,** Roentgenographic visualization and measurement of skin thickness and its diagnostic application in acromegaly radiology, *Radiology*, 82, 411, 1964.
47. **Meyer, R., Behl, C. R., and Flynn, G. L.,** Influences of anatomical site on the permeabilities of water and *N*-alkanols through stripped skins on hairless mice, *J. Pharm. Sci.*, submitted, 1981.
48. **Montagna, W., Chase, H. B., and Melaragno, H. P.,** The skin of hairless mice. I. The formation of cysts and the distribution of lipids, *J. Invest. Dermatol.*, 19, 83, 1952.
49. **Munro, D. D.,** The relationship between percutaneous absorption and stratum corneum retention, *Br. J. Dermatol.*, 94, 67, 1976.
50. **Nachman, R. and Esterly, N. B.,** Increased skin permeability in pre-term infants, *J. Pediatr.*, 79, 628, 1971.
51. **Neuland, W.,** Poisoning of infants and children by methemoglobin producing substances, *Med. Klin. (Munich),* 17, 906, 1921.
52. **Orwin, D. F. G., Chase, M. B., and Silver, A. F.,** Catagen in hairless house mouse, *Am. J. Anat.*, 121, 489, 1967.
53. **Raynar, W.,** Cyanosis in newly born children caused by aniline marking ink, *Br. Med. J.*, 1, 294, 1886.
54. **Robson, A. M., Kissane, J. M., Elvick, N. H., and Pundavela, L.,** Pentachlorophenol poisoning in a nursery for newborn infants clinical features and treatment, *J. Pediatr.*, 75, 309, 1969.
55. **Scheuplein, R. J. and Blank, I. H.,** Permeability of the skin, *Physiol. Rev.*, 51, 702, 1971.
56. **Scheuplein, R. J. and Blank, I. H.,** Mechanisms of percutaneous absorption. IV. Penetration of nonelectrolytes (alcohols) from aqueous solutions and from pure liquids, *J. Invest. Dermatol.*, 60, 286, 1973.
57. **Scott, E. P., Prince, G. E., and Rotondo, C. C.,** Dye poisoning in infancy, *J. Pediatr.*, 28, 713, 1946.
58. **Shuman, R. M., Leech, R. W., and Alvord, E. C.,** Neurotoxicity of hexachlorophene in humans, a clinopathological study of the premature infants, *Arch. Neurol. (Chicago),* 32, 320, 1975.
59. **Shuster, S., Black, M. M., and Mevitie, E.,** The influence of age and sex on skin thickness, skin collagen, and density, *Br. J. Dermatol.*, 93, 639, 1975.
60. **Stevens, A. N.,** Infant Skin Poisoning, *JAMA,* 90, 116, 1928.
61. **Tregear, R. T.,** Molecular movement. The permeability of skin, in *Theoretical and Experimental Biology — Physical Functions of Skin, Vol. 5,* Academic Press, New York, 1966, 13.
62. **Weimberg, A. A.,** Aniline poisoning in the newborn, with a report of thirteen cases, *Am. J. Obstet. Gynecol.*, 21, 104, 1931.
63. **Wester, R. C., Noonan, P. K., Cole, M. P., and Maibach, H. I.,** Percutaneous absorption of testosterone in the newborn rhesus monkey: comparison to the adult, *Pediatr. Res.*, 11, 737, 1977.
64. **Wildnauer, R. H. and Kennedy, R.,** Transdermal water loss of human newborn, *J. Invest. Dermatol.*, 54, 483, 1970.
65. **Wilson, D. and Maibach, H. I.,** Carbon dioxide emission rate in the newborn in *Neonatal Skin, Structure, and Function,* Maibach, H. I. and Boisits, E. K., Eds., Marcel Dekker, New York, 1982, 111.

66. **Wolbach, S. B.,** The hair cycle of the mouse and its importance in the study of sequence of experimental carcinogenesis, *Ann. N.Y. Acad. Sci.*, 53, 517, 1951.
67. **Yu, Chen-der,** Prodrug Based Topical Delivery: Simultaneous Skin Transport and Bioconversion, Ph.D. thesis, University of Michigan, Ann Arbor, 1978.
68. **Yun, J. S. and Montagna, W.,** The skin of hairless mice. III. The distribution of alkaline phosphatase, *Anat. Rec.*, 140, 77, 1961.
69. **Zeligs, M.,** Aniline and nitrobenzene poisoning in infants, *Arch. Pediatr.*, 46, 502.

Chapter 9

PHARMACOKINETICS OF SKIN PENETRATION

Bret Berner

TABLE OF CONTENTS

I. INTRODUCTION

While there is growing enthusiasm for transdermal drug delivery, the pharmacokinetics of transdermal drug delivery remains largely unexplored. In this chapter, rules are developed to interpret the four basic types of transdermal pharmacokinetics experiments: (1) infinite dose, (2) finite dose, (3) patch removal, and (4) multiple dosing. A simple model combining pharmacokinetics and skin diffusion is used for this analysis. A critique and summary of the predictions of this model conclude the chapter. To guide the reader solely interested in the general behavior of pharmacokinetics experiments, a summary section precedes the detailed discussion of each of the four types of experiments.

II. THE PHARMACOKINETIC MODEL FOR TRANSDERMAL DELIVERY

In transdermal drug delivery, a dose of a drug is applied to an area of skin, A, and the concentration of drug in the blood or urine is measured as a function of time. If a linear single compartment model is assumed for the pharmacokinetics,[1] then S, the total amount of drug in the compartment is[2]

$$\frac{dS}{dt} = -kS + A\,J \tag{1}$$

where k is the sum of the elimination rate constants and J is the flux of drug across the skin.

A typical transdermal device with a reservoir is modeled in Figure 1. Such membrane devices include three layers: an impermeable backing, a drug reservoir, and a patch membrane. To understand the pharmacokinetics, we assume that:

1. The reservoir is well-stirred (compared to the patch membrane or skin) at constant drug concentration $P_R C_o$
2. At time, $t = 0$, the membrane layer of the patch is at drug concentration, PC_o (Figure 1)
3. Diffusion in both the patch and the stratum corneum is ideal and both phases are homogeneous
4. There is good contact between the patch and the skin
5. The stratum corneum is the rate-limiting barrier to skin transport[3]

For two series membranes (the stratum corneum and the patch), the steady-state flux, J_{ss}, is

$$J_{ss} = C_0/(\ell/PD + \ell_s/P_sD_s) \tag{2}$$

Here P_i, D_i, and ℓ_i indicate the partition coefficient, diffusion constant, and membrane thickness for the ith phase. The subscript R (not shown), no subscript, and the subscript s refer to the reservoir, patch membrane, and stratum corneum layers, respectively.

III. THE INFINITE DOSE EXPERIMENT

A. A Summary

The simplest method to interpret in vivo transdermal experiments is to analyze the cumulative urinary output of drug analogously to a diffusion experiment in terms of a steady-state slope and a pharmacokinetic time lag. When most of the drug is excreted unmetabolized,

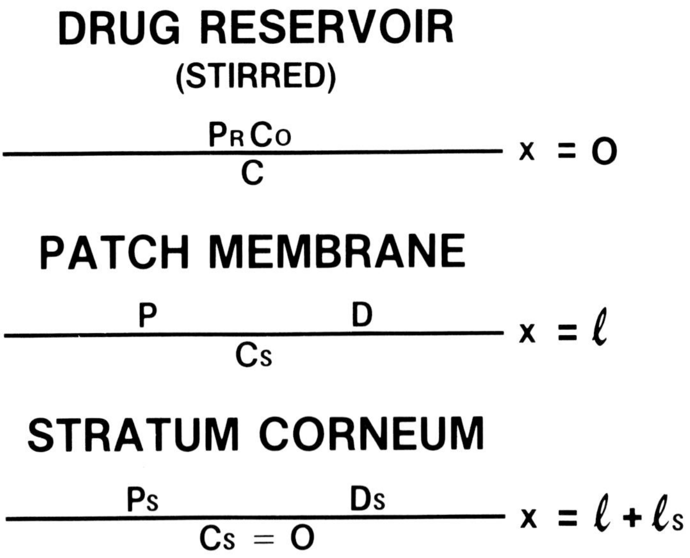

DRUG RESERVOIR
(STIRRED)

$P_R C_O$
C — $x = 0$

PATCH MEMBRANE

P D
C_S — $x = \ell$

STRATUM CORNEUM

P_S D_S
$C_S = 0$ — $x = \ell + \ell_S$

FIGURE 1. The model for a membrane transdermal device and skin. A ''well-stirred'' drug reservoir of concentration, C_o, is at equilibrium with the patch membrane at $x = 0$. At $x = \ell$, the membrane is at equilibrium with the stratum corneum. Sink conditions are assumed at $x = \ell + \ell_s$.

the steady-state slope of the cumulative urinary output is a direct measure of the skin permeation. On the other hand, the steady-state plasma level of drug is the skin permeation divided by the total clearance.

Transdermal experiments are often designed to compare either different drug structures or different vehicles. To compare the permeation of the same drug from different vehicles, minimal data are required while more detailed data are required to compare different drug structures.

A measure of the time for steady state to obtain is the pharmacokinetic time lag. The pharmacokinetic time lag is a sum of (1) the time to fill the body compartment and (2) the time to reach steady-state diffusion across the skin-patch multilaminate. When the skin (and not the patch) is the rate-limiting barrier to skin permeation, the patch usually will increase the pharmacokinetic time lag. On the other hand, when the patch is the rate-limiting membrane, the patch membrane ''burst effect'' (the initial emptying of a controlled-release membrane device equilibrated in its package) can be used to shorten the pharmacokinetic time lag.

B. The Theory

The simplest transdermal delivery experiment to understand is the delivery of a drug from an infinite reservoir or dose. It is easiest to interpret the results of such an experiment in terms of M^D, the total amount of drug excreted in the urine vs. time,

$$M^D(t) = k_u \int_0^t dt'S \tag{3}$$

where k_u is the excretion rate constant for the drug. This cumulative excretion approach allows us to analyze pharmacokinetics analogously to diffusion experiments in terms of a steady-state slope and time lag. To derive this approach, we integrate Equation 1, take the asymptotic limit, and find that

$$M_A^D(t) = \frac{k_u A J_{ss}}{k} (t - t_L^D - 1/k) \tag{4}$$

where t_L^D and J_{ss} are the diffusional time lag and steady-state flux, respectively, for the appropriate skin permeation problem. The subscript A indicates the long-time asymptotic limit of M^D. To obtain Equation 4, we used (1) the linearity of the long-time asymptote[4] of Equations 1 and 3 and (2) the steady-state blood concentration, C_b, where

$$C_b = \frac{S}{V_D} = \frac{AJ_{ss}}{kV_D} \tag{5}$$

Here V_D is the effective volume of distribution of the drug. A similar result may be obtained for the area under the curve of the plasma levels (Equation 5).

The key to analyzing infinite dose transdermal pharmacokinetic experiments is to relate (1) the slope of M_D^A to the flux of drug through the skin and (2) the intercept to the pharmacokinetic time lag, t_L.

We first study the slope. The simplest interpretation of transdermal pharmacokinetics is given in terms of the cumulative urinary output and not the plasma levels. The steady-state slope of M_A^D is

$$\text{Slope} = k_u AJ_{ss}/k \tag{6}$$

where J_{ss} is given by Equation 2. That is, the steady-state slope or urinary excretion rate equals the product of (1) the steady-state skin permeation and (2) the fraction of drug excreted in the urine k_u/k. When most of the drug is excreted unmetabolized, the slope of the urinary output directly measures the skin permeation of the drug. If metabolism is significant, one may still obtain AJ_{ss}. By measuring the amount of drug remaining in the patch at the end of an experiment, and excreted, one may approximate the fraction of drug excreted in the urine.

The steady-state skin permeation may also be determined by the plasma levels or C_b (Equation 5). Note that the extraction of AJ_{ss} from C_b is complicated by the clearance or kV_D. Thus, additional pharmacokinetic data may be required to extract skin permeation data from C_b as compared to urinary data.

The purpose of the in vivo experiment determines the quality of M^D data required. Pharmacokinetics experiments may be designed either to compare permeation of different drug structures or the same drug in different vehicles. To compare relative skin permeation of the same drug in different vehicles, the slope of M_A^D is sufficient, because k_u/k is a constant for the same drug (Equation 6). When different drugs are compared, however, k_u/k may vary, and consequently, more detailed pharmacokinetic data are required to separate the variation of k_u/k and AJ_{ss}. Thus, minimal urinary pharmacokinetic data will suffice to understand vehicle effects, but more detailed data are required to compare the permeation of different drugs.

The second parameter in the infinite dose experiment is the pharmacokinetic time lag, t_L, the intercept of M_A^D with the time axis. From Equation 4

$$t_L = 1/k + t_L^D \tag{7}$$

The $1/k$ term on the right-hand side of the equation is the time to fill the body compartment, and t_L^D is the time for steady-state diffusion to obtain through the combined patch membrane and stratum corneum system.

Using the extended method of Frisch to solve for t_L^D[5,6] we find that:

$$t_L = 1/k + \left[\frac{\ell_s^3}{6P_sD_s^2} - \frac{\ell^3}{3PD^2} + \frac{\ell\ell_s}{2DD_sP}\right] \Big/ \left[\frac{\ell_s}{P_sD_s} + \frac{\ell}{PD}\right] \tag{8}$$

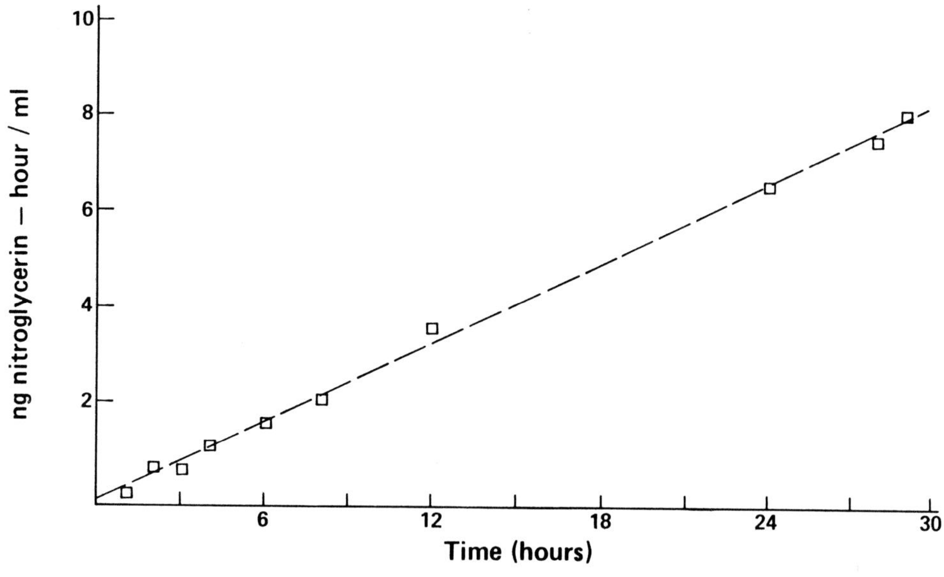

FIGURE 2. The transdermal delivery of nitroglycerin is demonstrated by plotting the AUC plasma levels vs. time.[9]

Let us study the two limits of Equation 8. In the skin-controlled limit where $(\ell_s/P_sD_s)/(\ell/PD) >> 1$, the stratum corneum is the rate-limiting barrier; in the patch-controlled limit where $(\ell_s/P_sD_s)/(\ell/PD) << 1$, the membrane layer of the patch is rate-limiting. Note the minus sign in one term of Equation 8. The origin of this minus sign is the initial "burst effect" from the patch membrane. This "burst effect" refers to the initial emptying of drug (until steady state obtains) from a controlled-release device which has equilibrated in its package. Such "burst effects" may be important in the patch-controlled limit.

C. The Skin-Controlled Limit

Typically, the skin is the rate-limiting barrier to permeation, and

$$t_L = 1/k + \ell_s^2/6D_s + (\ell_s^2/2D_s - \ell^2/3D)/(PD\ell_s/P_sD_s\ell) \quad (9)$$

The third term, is usually negligible, and

$$t_L = 1/k + \ell_s^2/6D_s \quad (10)$$

When the stratum corneum is rate-limiting, the pharmacokinetic time lag consists of a pharmacokinetic contribution and the time lag for diffusion across the stratum corneum. This result is identical to that for skin permeation alone.[2] Provided the skin is rate-limiting, the membrane "burst effect" seldom shortens the time lag. Usually, the patch can increase the time lag in this limit.

An example of the skin-controlled limit[7] is the transdermal delivery of nitroglycerin (Figure 2). Due to the rapid half-life (3 min) of nitroglycerin,[8] only blood level data can be analyzed. The observed and theoretical time lags ($k = 14$/hr and $t_L^D = 0.25$ hr) are -0.1 and 0.3 hr, respectively. Considering the experimental difficulty in the measurement of t_L, the agreement is excellent. On the other hand, the observed and theoretical steady-state nitroglycerin concentrations in the blood (clearance equals 3×10^6 mℓ/hr[8]) are 0.28 and 0.1 ng/mℓ, respectively. This discrepancy is probably due to difficulties in measuring k and V_D and site-to-site variation in the measurement of nitroglycerin blood levels.[9] Experimental agreement for drugs with longer half-lives is generally better.

D. The Patch-Controlled Limit

When the patch-membrane is rate-limiting,

$$t_L = 1/k + \ell_s^2/2D_s - \ell^2/3D \tag{11}$$

The three terms are due to elimination, skin diffusion, and the patch membrane "burst effect", respectively.

Compared to the skin-controlled limit, the patch-controlled limit has two new features, (1) the time lag contribution from the stratum corneum is three times longer than normal and (2) a negative contribution due to the "burst effect". For the patch-controlled limit, the initial burst of drug from the patch membrane shortens the time lag. To employ the "burst effect" effectively to shorten the time lag, one must overcome this increased stratum corneum contribution with a sufficiently large patch membrane burst. That is, the time lag for the patch membrane must be greater than 1.5 times the time lag for the stratum corneum to dramatically reduce the pharmacokinetic time lag. One can enhance the "burst effect" by selecting an outer patch coating (against the skin) which is a poor barrier and has a large partition coefficient for the drug. In practice, however, one minimizes "bursts" to prevent adhesion problems.

Unfortunately for transdermal drug delivery, the stratum corneum is an excellent barrier and the patch-controlled limit seldom occurs. In the literature, one example of the patch-controlled limit may be the transdermal delivery of scopolamine.[10] An analysis of these scopolamine data in the context of this discussion is presented in Figure 3 ($\ell^2/3D$ equals H/Gh as defined in Reference 11). There is excellent agreement between the experimental value of J_{ss} and the theoretical value predicted for the patch membrane alone (Figure 3). On the other hand, the experimental and theoretical values of t_L are 2.5 and 1.6 hr, respectively. Due to the difficulties involved in the time lag measurements with skin, the agreement is as good as can be expected. However, the interpretation of these data is complex because the predicted time lag for percutaneous absorption of scopolamine in the skin-controlled limit is 2.6 hr.

IV. THE FINITE DOSE PROBLEM

Infinite dose in vivo skin penetration experiments from large volumes of vehicles are often difficult to perform as a result of spreading and rubbing off of the vehicle. Consequently, small, finite doses are often used in vivo. For these finite dose experiments, the urinary excretion initially increases, reaches a maximum, and then decays with time. The interpretation of the pharmacokinetics is more complex than for infinite dose experiments. In fact, depending on the dose, one may measure either a property of the skin or of drug elimination. Another important reason to study the finite dose problem is to define a useful device lifetime after which drug is delivered to the body at too slow a rate to be effective. After the summary, we study a model of delivery from a finite monolithic device and then discuss the pharmacokinetics.

A. A Summary

While finite dose experiments may be easier to perform, the interpretation of the data is difficult and depends not only on the skin permeation, but also on the pharmacokinetics. The maximum urinary excretion rate only reflects skin permeation for quite large doses. In

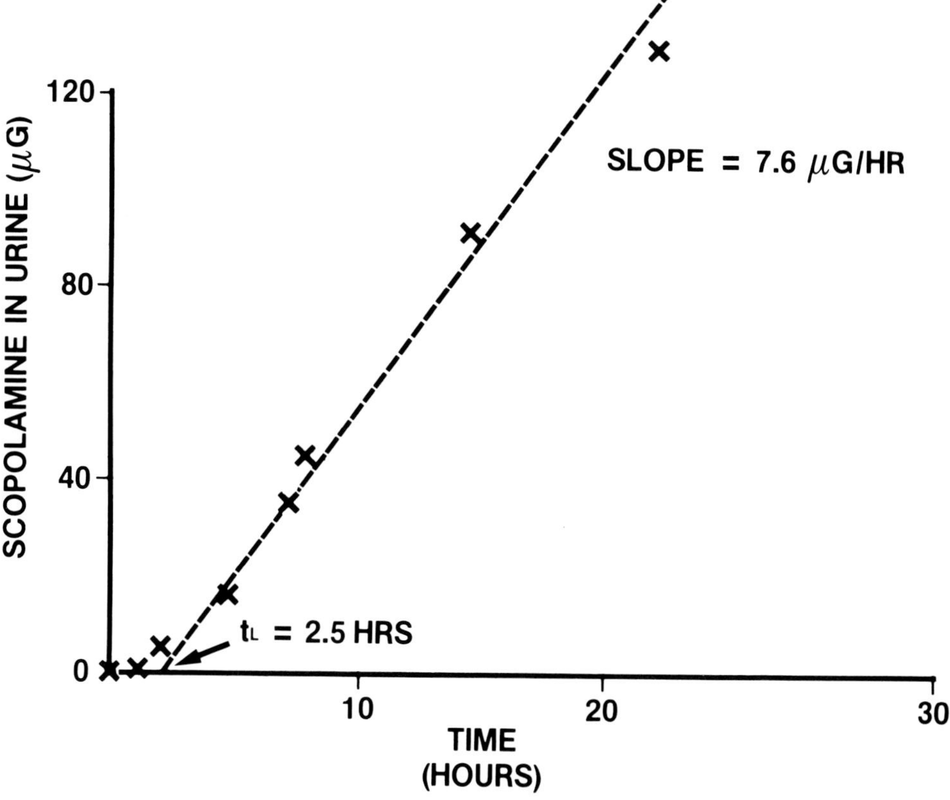

FIGURE 3. The cumulative urinary output of scopolamine delivered transdermally. A slope of 7.6 μg/hr and time lag of 2.5 hr were observed.[10]

principle, study of the dose dependence of the final slope of a plot of ln (urinary excretion rate) vs. time can provide information about skin permeation and pharmacokinetics.

The finite dose problem can be employed to determine how long a transdermal device is useful. This useful lifetime depends on the time lag for the stratum corneum, the size of the dose, and the logarithm of the useful therapeutic range.

B. The Model for a Finite Dose

For simplicity, we consider a monolithic device. Let us assume that (1) the stratum corneum is the rate-limiting barrier for diffusion, (2) the device acts like a well-stirred layer, (3) the stratum corneum is homogeneous, and (4) diffusion in the stratum corneum is ideal. The monolithic device of volume, V_R, and area, A, is shown in Figure 4.

For this finite dose problem, the urinary excretion rate is[5,11,12]

$$\frac{dM^D}{dt} = \frac{2k_u BAD_sC_o}{\ell_s} \sum_{n=1}^{\infty} \frac{\alpha\, n(e^{-\alpha_n^2 D_s t/\ell_s^2} - e^{-kt})}{\sin \alpha_n (B + B^2 + \alpha_n^2)\left(k - \frac{D_s\alpha_n^2}{\ell_s^2}\right)} \tag{12}$$

where the α_n's are the solution of

$$\alpha_n \tan \alpha_n = B \tag{13}$$

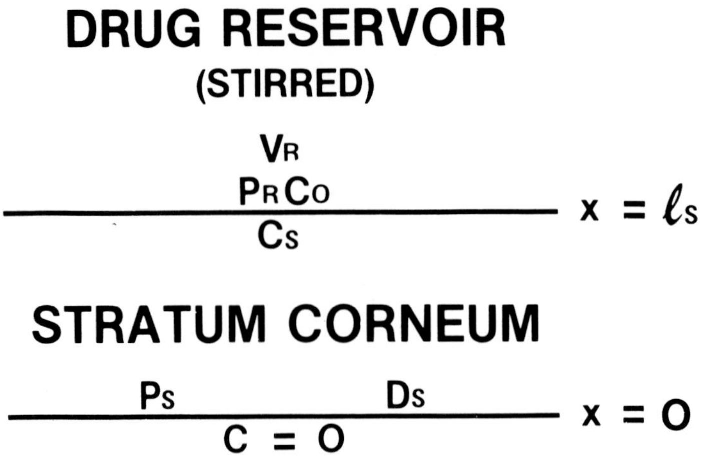

FIGURE 4. A model for a monolithic transdermal device. A "well-stirred" drug reservoir of concentration, C_o, and volume, V_R, is at equilibrium with the stratum corneum at $x = \ell_s$. Sink conditions are assumed at $x = 0$.

and B (the reciprocal dose parameter) is defined as

$$B = \frac{A\ell_s P_s}{P_R V_R} \tag{14}$$

B is the ratio of the amounts of drug that can partition into the skin to the patch.

When $B << 1$, or the large dose limit, the monolithic device acts like an infinite reservoir. In this limit for short times, Equation 12 is identical to the skin-controlled limit of the result for the infinite dose problem, and thus, the method of data analysis for an infinite dose may be applied.

At longer times, the finite dose aspects of the problem dominate. From these finite dose aspects, one may determine how long a zero-order transdermal delivery system releases the drug at a value acceptably close to the steady-state flux; that is, how long the device is useful. This useful device lifetime, t_u, equals the time to reach steady state (t_L) plus the time for the flux to decay to some specified fraction of J_{ss}. An estimate of the useful lifetime of a monolithic device is

$$t_u = t_L - \ell n(\gamma)\ell_s^2/D_s\alpha_1^2 \tag{15}$$

where t_u is defined as the time until the excretion rate has decayed to γ times its maximum value and α_1 is defined by Equation 13. Note that the useful device lifetime is determined by the pharmacokinetic time lag, the time lag for skin diffusion, and the size of the dose (through α_1). For example, let us consider a patch for which (1) $B = 0.01$ ($\alpha_1 = 0.0998$), i.e., the patch holds 100 times as much drug as the skin, and (2) the pharmacokinetic and diffusional time lags are 1 and 4 hr, respectively. If one is willing to accept $\gamma = 0.9$, then $t_u = 67$ hr. On the other hand, if one will tolerate $\gamma = 0.8$, then $t_u = 133$ hr. Thus, one can achieve sizeable increases in t_u by either increasing the dose or redefining the useful therapeutic range.

C. The Pharmacokinetics of the Finite Dose

Finite dose pharmacokinetics are much more complex than infinite dose pharmacokinetics. To interpret finite dose pharmacokinetics easily, it is useful to define the dimensionless quantities,

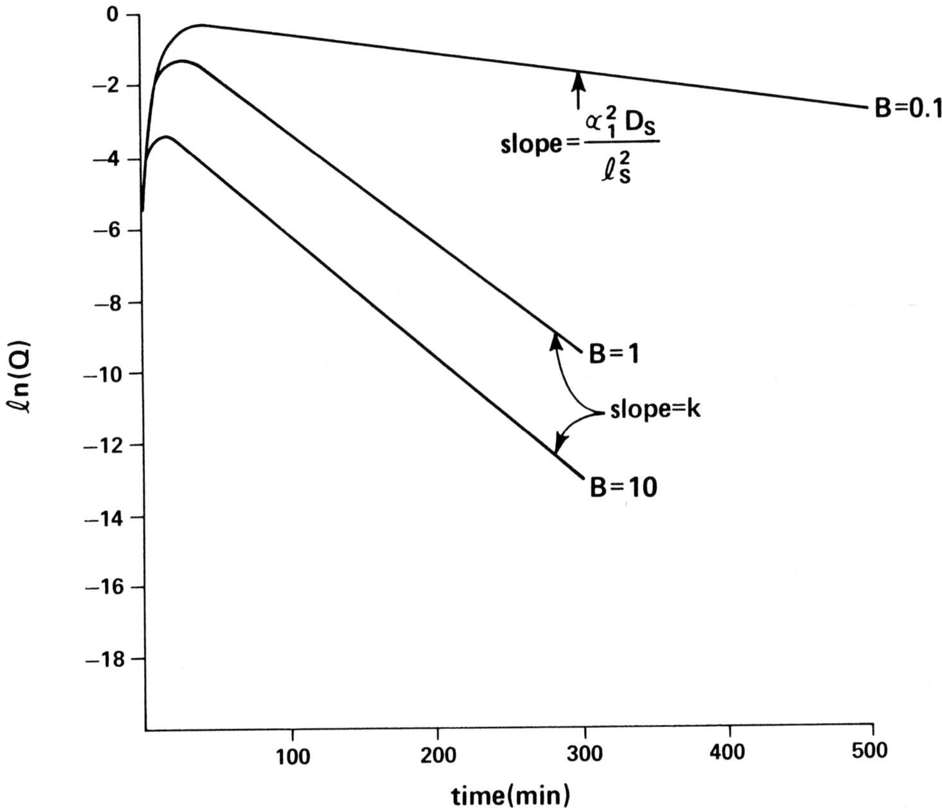

FIGURE 5. The finite dose behavior as exhibited in a ln (Q) vs. t plot. Note the decrease in the maximum with increasing B and the change in the dependence of the slope with changing B.

$$Q = S/S_{ss}$$

$$R = kt_L^D \tag{16}$$

Q equals unity at steady state and deviations in Q from unity will reflect the decay of the blood levels due to the depletion of drug. When $R << 1$, diffusion is rapid compared to drug elimination and conversely for $R >> 1$.

Time plots vs. ln (Q) for several B are shown in Figure 5 for $k = 0.36$/min and $t_L^D = 2.8$ min ($R = 0.1$). From such plots it is evident that there are two important features to measure in a finite dose experiment, the maximum urinary excretion rate and the decay time of the excretion rate from its maximum.

The more important feature is the maximum urinary excretion rate. When $R << 1$ and $B \leq 0.1$ (very large dose), Q_{max}, the maximum in Q (Figure 5) is close to unity, and consequently, the maximum urinary excretion rate is an excellent approximation to the steady-state flux. However, for the case, shown where $R << 1$ and $B >> 0.1$, Q_{max} may be orders of magnitude smaller than unity, and therefore, this maximum does not reflect skin permeation. Q_{max} only provides information about skin permeation for quite large doses. Q_{max} may be used as a lower bound to the steady-state skin permeation, but this lower bound may be orders of magnitude too small.

To determine when Q_{max} reflects skin permeability, Q_{max} is plotted vs. log (B) for several R in Figure 6. Given prior knowledge of R one can use this graph to select B such that the dose is sufficient for the maximum urinary excretion rate to approximate the steady-state skin permeation ($Q_{max} = 1$).

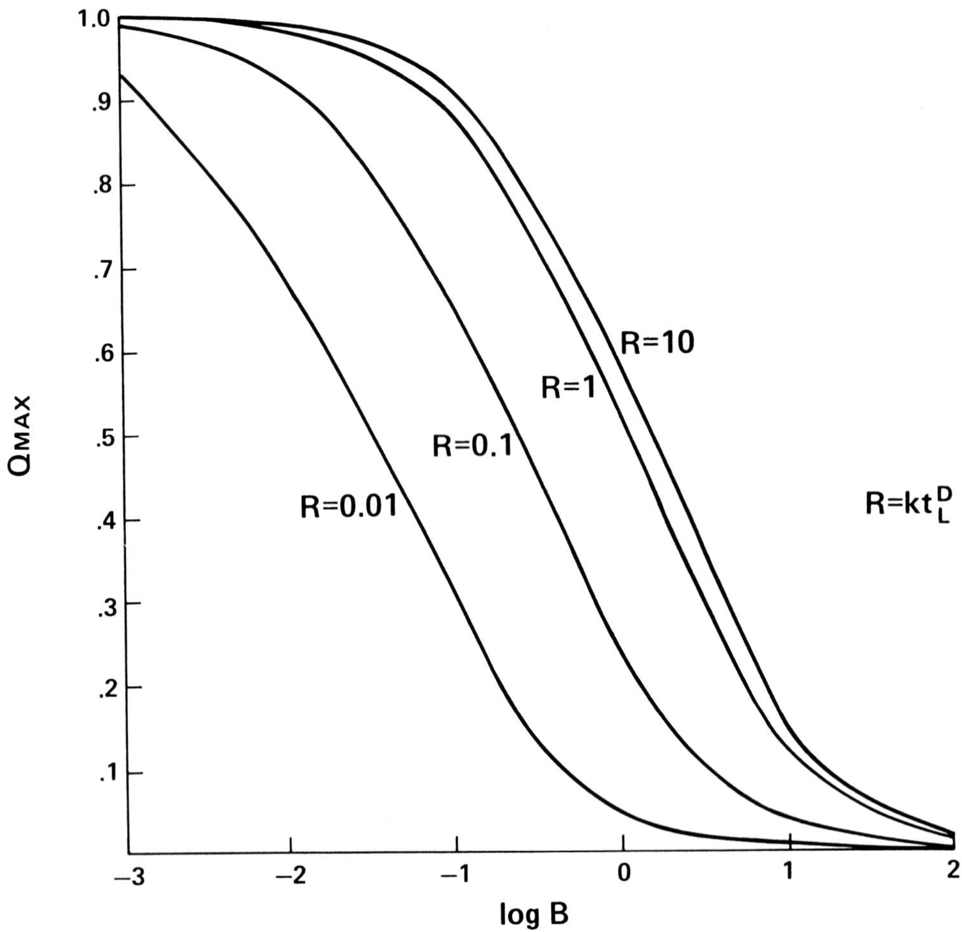

FIGURE 6. The maximum urinary excretion rate, Q_{max}, vs. log B. This figure may be used to calculate the dose required to approximate steady-state skin permeation.

The second parameter in finite dose pharmacokinetics is the final slope of a ln (Q) vs. time plot. When $R \ll 1$ and $B \leqslant 0.1$ (Figure 5), the final slope depends on t_L^D and the size of the dose. However, for the cases when $R \ll 1$ and $B \gg 0.1$, the final slope depends on k and not on skin permeation. Thus, for $R \ll 1$ one can in principle measure the dose dependence of the final slope to determine both t_L^D and k. On the other hand, for $R \geqslant 15$, the final slope always equals $-\alpha_1^2/6t_L^D$. Interpretation of the final slope varies considerably with B and R and should be approached with some caution.

V. THE REMOVAL OF A TRANSDERMAL PATCH

A. A Summary

When a transdermal patch is removed, the skin and the body compartment form two drug reservoirs. If most of the drug is in the body compartment, the plasma levels decay mainly due to pharmacokinetic elimination. In this case, transdermal delivery is terminated as rapidly as an intravenous injection. However, when most of the drug remains in the stratum corneum, the plasma levels decay as 2.4 times the time lag for diffusion through the stratum corneum. Depending on the length of the time lag, termination of transdermal delivery in such cases may be quite slow.

B. The Theory

One hypothesized advantage of transdermal drug delivery is the ability to terminate abruptly drug delivery to the body by removing the drug reservoir. To test this hypothesis, we consider a model for removal of a transdermal device. A transdermal patch of area, A, is applied to the skin for $t > t_L$. We assume that (1) the stratum corneum and not the device nor other layers of skin is rate-limiting, (2) a linear single compartment pharmacokinetic model is adequate, (3) the device is an infinite well-stirred reservoir, and (4) the stratum corneum acts like an ideal membrane and is homogeneous. When the patch is removed at time zero, steady-state concentrations and fluxes obtain. That is

$$J_{ss} = P_s D C_o / P\ell$$

$$C_{ss}(x) = P_s C_o (1 - x/\ell)/P$$

$$S_{ss} = AJ_{ss}/k \tag{17}$$

To characterize the removal problem, we again introduce the dimensionless variables, Q and R (Equation 16). The decrease in Q from unity represents the decay in the plasma levels from steady-state; R, the removal parameter, is a measure of whether diffusion or pharmacokinetic elimination is the rate-limiting step.

To gain insight into the patch removal problem, we recall that the pharmacokinetic model includes two processes, pharmacokinetic elimination in the body and diffusion in the skin and patch. When the patch is removed, two reservoirs of drug remain, the skin and the body compartment. It may be shown that L, the ratio of the size of the reservoir of the drug in the skin to the body compartment equals[13]

$$L = 3R = 3k\,t_L^D \tag{18}$$

R and L measure whether there is more drug in the skin or in the body. That is, for small L and R, pharmacokinetic elimination from the body reservoir dominates; for large L and R, diffusion from the skin reservoir dominates.

This intuitive model is borne out in the more rigorous analysis of the behavior of Q. When $R << 0.4$, pharmacokinetic elimination and not skin diffusion is rate-limiting,

$$Q \approx \exp[-kt] \tag{19}$$

Thus, for $R >> 0.4$, the slope of a plot of ln (Q) vs. t equals $-k$ (Figure 7). In this limit, transdermal delivery is terminated as rapidly as an intravenous injection.

On the other hand, when diffusion through the stratum corneum is the slower process ($R >> 0.4$), the slope of a plot of ln (Q) vs. t yields $1/t_L^D$ (Figure 7), because

$$Q \approx (4/\pi)\exp[-t/2.4t_L^D] \tag{20}$$

Note that the time to empty the stratum corneum of drug is a factor of 2.4 larger than the time to fill it.

The rapidity of termination of transdermal delivery in the diffusion-controlled ($R >> 0.4$) limit depends on the value of t_L^D. When t_L^D is short, transdermal delivery is terminated rapidly because the decay time for Q is 2.4 t_L^D. This is the case for nitroglycerin ($k = 0.23$/min and $t_L^D = 10$ min[8] or $R = kt_L^D = 2.3$), where the characteristic time for the termination of transdermal delivery is a few minutes. For scopolamine ($t_L^D = 2$ hr and $k = 0.62$/hr or $R = kt_L^D = 1.2$)[10] delivery is terminated in some 5 hr, which is longer than for an intravenous bolus.

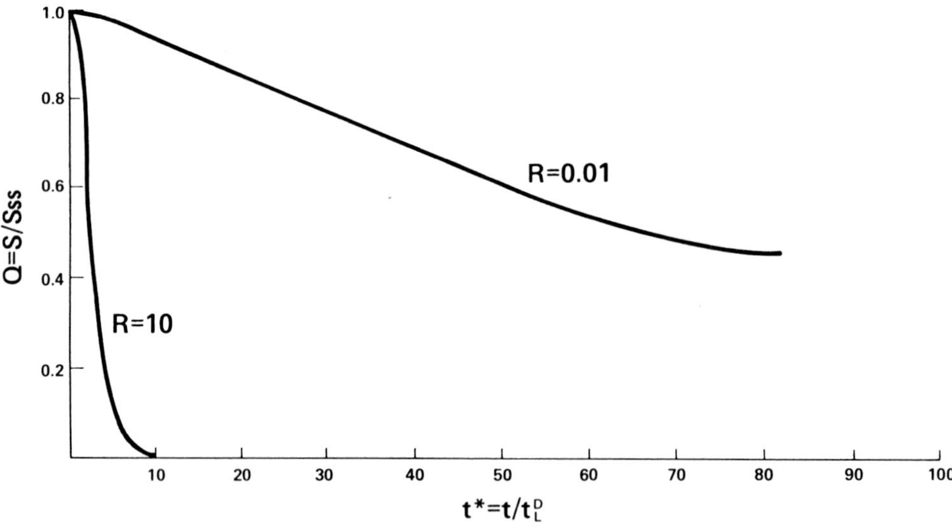

FIGURE 7. Dimensionless blood levels and time after removal of a transdermal device. Note the change in the dependence of the slopes with changing R.

On the other hand, when R >> 0.4 and t_L^D is long, transdermal delivery may be terminated very slowly compared to other dosage forms. For example, for hydrocortisone (k = 0.4/hr[14] and t_L = 16 hr^3 or R = 6.4), the predicted decay time for transdermal delivery is 38 hr. Thus, transdermal delivery is terminated rapidly compared to other dosage forms except when R >> 0.4 and t_L^D is long.

In the small and large R limits, the analysis of patch removal experiments by ln (Q) vs. t plots can provide information about either pharmacokinetics or skin diffusion, respectively (Figure 7). However, in analyzing patch removal experiments, one generally does not know the value of R, and consequently, one is ignorant whether the slope of a ln (Q) plot represents k or t_L^D. As will be demonstrated in the next section, patch reapplication experiments may provide the necessary information about R to interpret the pharmacokinetics of patch removal.

VI. MULTIPLE DOSING

A. A Summary

When a depleted transdermal device is removed, a fresh device is applied to a second skin site to avoid skin irritation. One might expect large deviations from the steady-state plasma levels during this reapplication process. However, provided the skin is rate controlling, the plasma levels never exceed their steady-state value by more than 50%. During this process, the plasma levels remain remarkably constant.

For patch-controlled transdermal delivery, the deviations of the plasma levels from steady state may be larger.

B. The Theory

For a given transdermal patch, drug delivery approximates zero order. However, when a used (depleted) transdermal device is removed and a fresh device is applied, there is a period during which the constant rate of drug delivery may be interrupted. Provided the fresh device is applied to the same skin location, there is no interruption of zero-order delivery because steady state already has been obtained. To avoid skin irritation, however, one may rotate the device application site to a second, but equivalent skin location. For a period after the fresh patch is applied to the second site, the concentration of drug in the blood might fall

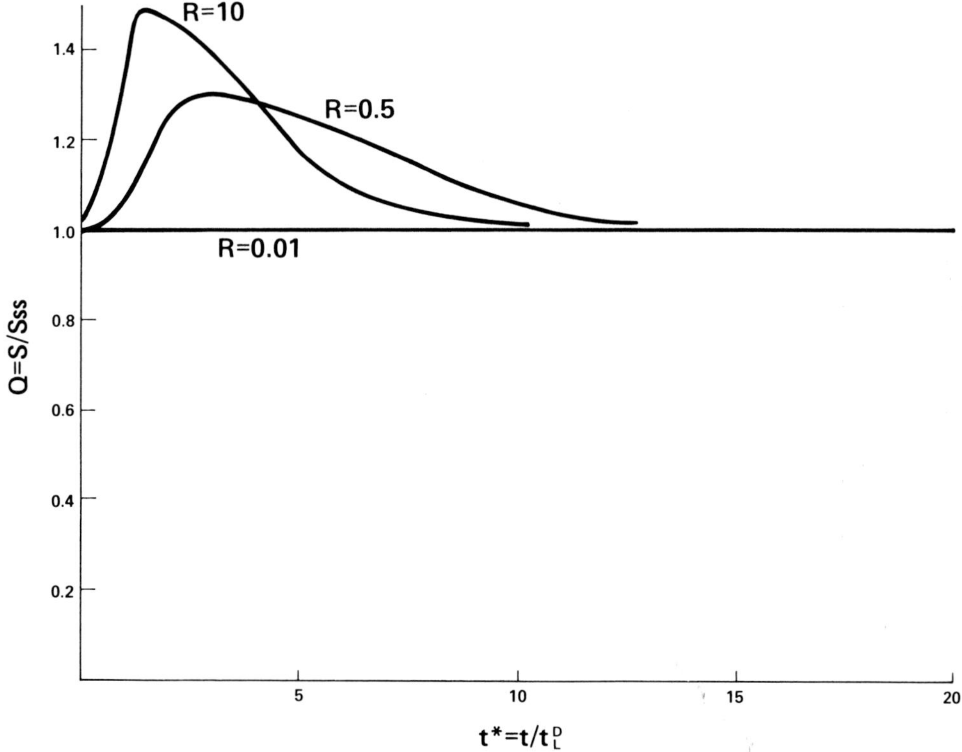

FIGURE 8. Dimensionless plasma levels and time after reapplication of a fresh transdermal device. Note the blood levels do not deviate far from the steady-state value of unity.

to zero or might rise to twice the steady-state blood level. We now demonstrate that even with rotating the site of patch application, transdermal delivery allows minimal deviation from steady-state plasma levels.[13]

This patch reapplication problem is modeled by the application of patch 1 at the first skin site for $t > t_L$ and then by the simultaneous removal of depleted patch 1 and application of fresh patch 2 to the second skin site. Identical assumptions are made for both sites and patches and these assumptions are the same as those made in the patch removal problem. One studies the plasma concentration of drug, under the influence of three processes, (1) depletion of the drug reservoir in the skin at the first site by diffusion into the blood, (2) diffusion of the drug from the patch through the stratum corneum at the second site into the blood, and (3) pharmacokinetic elimination. We again utilize the dimensionless variables Q and R (Equation 16).

When a depleted device is removed and a fresh patch is applied to a different skin site, the plasma levels may be perturbed from their steady-state value of $Q = 1$. We study the variation of Q from unity. Surprisingly, for all $R = kt_L^D$, Q is between 1 and 1.5 and consequently, transdermal delivery is always close to zero order.

The behavior of Q vs. t for several R is summarized in Figure 8. When $R << 0.4$ (pharmacokinetic elimination and not skin diffusion is rate-limiting), the plasma levels do not deviate from their steady-state levels throughout the entire patch reapplication process; that is

$$Q \approx 1 \tag{21}$$

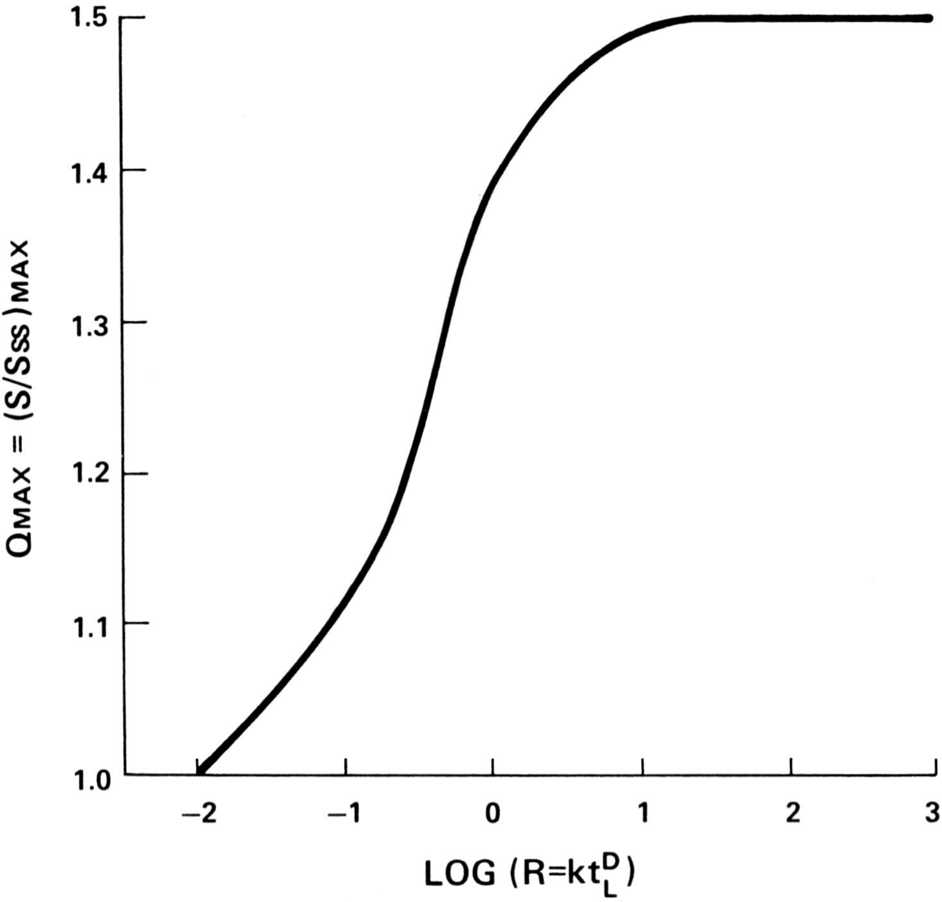

FIGURE 9. Q_{max}, the maximum deviation from steady-state plasma levels after reapplication of a fresh transdermal device vs. ln (R).

In the limit where skin diffusion is the rate-controlling process ($R >> 1.6$), $Q_{max} \approx 1.5$ (Figure 8). Even for intermediate cases of R, Q is close to one. For example, when $R = 0.5$, $Q_{max} \approx 1.3$. Thus, for any R, Q never exceeds between 1 and 1.5 (Figure 9), a remarkably narrow range of blood levels.

Multiple dose studies for the transdermal delivery of clonidine and scopolamine have been performed.[10,15] For both the clonidine and scopolamine examples, the patch membrane may, at least in part, control release; in contrast, this theory is for the skin-controlled limit. A comparison of these two limits for multiple dosing provides surprising results. To understand the patch-controlled limit, it is useful to recall Equation 11 for t_L. Depending on the extent of the "burst effect", t_L for the patch controlled limit can be shorter or longer than for the corresponding skin-controlled case for the same drug. For the patch-controlled case, Q may have a minimum rather than a maximum. This minimum has been observed for scopolamine[10] where $Q_{min} \approx 0.4$. By coincidence for clonidine ($k = 0.09$/hr and $t_L^D = 7$ hr or $R = 0.6$), $Q_{max} \approx 1.4$,[15] which is the predicted value of Q_{max} for $R = 0.6$ in Figure 3. While an experimental verification of the multiple dosing theory for the skin-controlled limit is lacking, one must admit the surprising possibility that in a multiple dosing regimen, a patch-controlled system may not be as good an approximation to zero-order delivery as a skin-controlled system.

In addition to aiding in the evaluation of the advantages of transdermal delivery, the combination of pharmacokinetics experiments involving patch removal and reapplication may provide a convenient approach to obtain pharmacokinetic information. By determining Q_{max} for a reapplied patch, one may observe the R regime ($R << 0.4$ or $R >> 1.6$) directly from Figure 9. Then from the slope of the ln Q vs. time plot after removing a patch (without applying a new patch), either k or t_L^D may be determined.

VII. THE LIMITATIONS OF THE MODEL

We have developed a simple pharmacokinetic and diffusion model and studied the effects of infinite vs. finite dose, urinary excretion vs. blood levels, patch removal, and multiple dosing.

There are, however, a number of limitations of the pharmacokinetic model which may be important in experimental design and interpretations. The following is a discussion of some of the underlying assumptions in the pharmacokinetic model:

1. A linear, single compartment pharmacokinetic model is assumed. Nonlinear or multicompartment models may be more appropriate. The inappropriateness of the model is suggested (a) by experiment differences observed in the concentration of nitroglycerin in the blood when the patch application site or the blood sampling site is varied[9] and (b) by the localized accumulations and different physiological distributions of certain drugs when delivered transdermally as compared to intravenously.[16]
2. Good patch-skin contact is assumed. When this contact is poor, there may be a lower steady-state flux than predicted from in vitro data. The poor patch contact may lead to an anomalously long time lag. That is, skin areas with poor patch contact may collect water under the occluded patch. The water soluble drug may dissolve in these wet areas, and eventually one obtains "good contact".
3. The ideality of diffusion in the stratum corneum is assumed. When penetration enhancers are used, skin diffusion is certainly not ideal.
4. For the penetration of highly lipophilic drugs, the stratum corneum may not be the rate-limiting barrier. For such drugs, there is currently no in vitro model to predict in vivo pharmacokinetics.

VIII. SUMMARY

1. To obtain useful skin permeation data, it is simplest to interpret the cumulative urinary excretion of drug and/or metabolite. An infinite dose of drug simplifies the interpretation and allows data to be extracted from the slope and pharmacokinetic time lag of the linear asymptote. When urinary data are not available, integrated plasma levels may be utilized, but are more difficult to interpret. The slope of the linear asymptote may be related to skin permeability and the pharmacokinetic time lag may be related to the patch "burst effect", the skin, and pharmacokinetic elimination.
2. The useful device lifetime is the sum of the pharmacokinetic time lag and the decay time for the device, which is related to the time lag for diffusion through the stratum corneum, the size of the dose, and the useful therapeutic range.
3. Finite dose percutaneous absorption experiments are only related to the skin permeability under sufficiently large dosing conditions. In principle, for $R < 15$ study of the dose dependence may give information about both skin permeation and the pharmacokinetics. Caution should be exercised in interpreting finite dose experiments.
4. Transdermal delivery can be terminated rapidly compared to other dosage forms. However, when $R >> 0.4$ and t_L^D is long, it may take longer to terminate transdermal delivery than other forms.
5. In the period after a depleted patch is replaced with a fresh transdermal patch, the plasma levels remain surprisingly close to their steady-state value.

REFERENCES

1. **Gibaldi, M. and Perrier, D.,** *Pharmacokinetics,* 2nd ed., Marcel Dekker, New York, 1982.
2. **Cooper, E. R.,** Pharmacokinetics of skin penetration, *J. Pharm. Sci.,* 65, 1396, 1976.
3. **Scheuplein, R. J. and Blank, I. H.,** Permeability of the skin, *Physiol. Rev.,* 51, 702, 1971.
4. **Crank, J.,** *The Mathematics of Diffusion,* Oxford University Press, London, 1975.
5. **Berner, B.,** Pharmacokinetics of transdermal drug delivery, *J. Pharm. Sci.,* 74, 718, 1985.
6. **Ash, R., Barrer, R. M., and Palmer, D. G.,** Diffusion in multiple laminates, *Br. J. Appl. Phys.,* 16, 873, 1965.
7. **Chien, Y. W., Keshary, P. R., Huang, Y. C., and Sarpotdar, P. P.,** Comparative controlled skin permeation of nitroglycerin from marketed transdermal delivery systems, *J. Pharm. Sci.,* 72, 968, 1983.
8. **McNiff, E. F., Yacobi, A., Young-Chang, F. M., Golden, L. H., Goldfarb, A., and Fung, H. L.,** Nitroglycerin pharmacokinetics after intravenous infusion in normal subjects, *J. Pharm. Sci.,* 70, 1054, 1981.
9. **Karim, A.,** Transdermal absorption of nitroglycerin from microseal drug delivery (MDD) system, *Angiology,* 34, 11, 1983.
10. **Chandrasekaran, S. K., Bayne, W., and Shaw, J. E.,** Pharmacokinetics of drug permeation through human skin, *J. Pharm. Sci.,* 67, 1730, 1978.
11. **Cooper, E. R. and Berner, B.,** Finite dose pharmacokinetics of skin penetration, *J. Pharm. Sci.,* 74, 1100, 1985.
12. **Carslaw, H. S. and Jaeger, J. C.,** *Conduction of Heat in Solids,* 2nd Edition, Oxford University Press, London, 1959, 100.
13. **Berner, B.,** The pharmacokinetics of the removal and re-application of transdermal patches, *J. Controlled Release,* 1, 127, 1984.
14. **Bochner, F., Carruthers, G., Kampmann, J., and Steiner, J.,** *Handbook of Clinical Pharmacology,* 2nd ed., Little Brown and Co., Boston, 1983, 111, 151.
15. **Arndts, D. and Arndts, K.,** Pharmacokinetics and Pharmacodynamics of Transdermally Administered Clonidine, *Eur. J. Clin. Pharmacol.,* 26, 79, 1984.
16. **Guy, R. H. and Maibach, H. I.,** Drug delivery to local subcutaneous structures following topical administration, *J. Pharm. Sci.,* 72, 1375, 1983.

Index

INDEX

E

F

G

H

I

K

L

M

T

V

W